MONOLOGUES
FOR CALCULATING
THE DENSITY OF BLACK HOLES

by ANDERS NILSEN

PREFACE

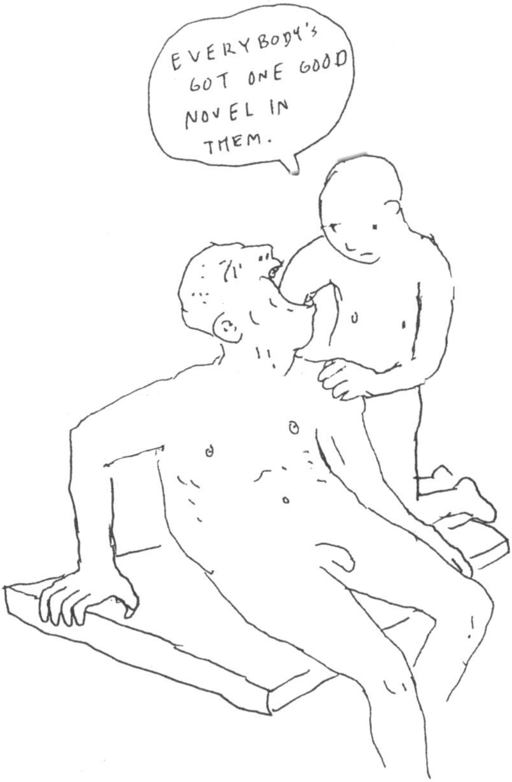
EVERYBODY'S GOT ONE GOOD NOVEL IN THEM.

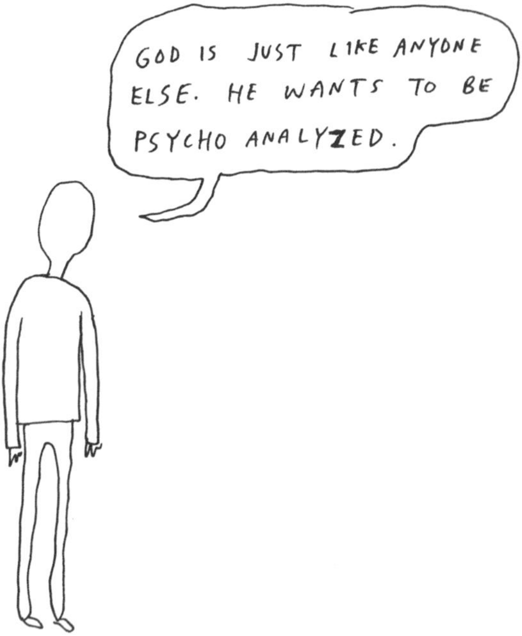
GOD IS JUST LIKE ANYONE ELSE. HE WANTS TO BE PSYCHO ANALYZED.

PART 1

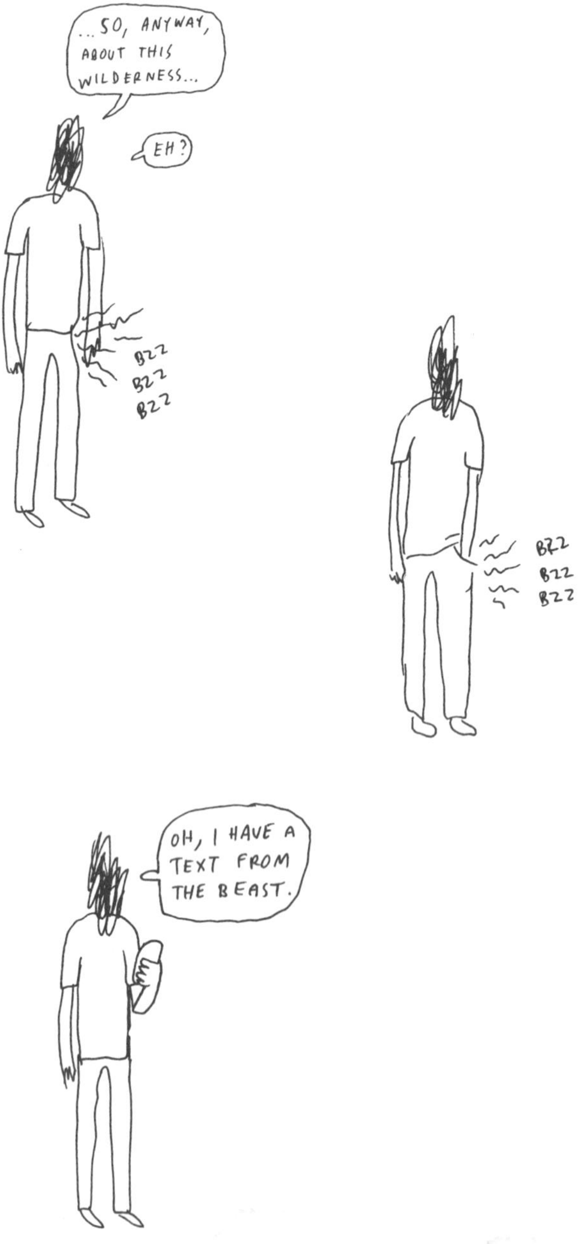
...SO, ANYWAY, ABOUT THIS WILDERNESS...
EH?
BZZ BZZ BZZ
BZZ BZZ BZZ
OH, I HAVE A TEXT FROM THE BEAST.

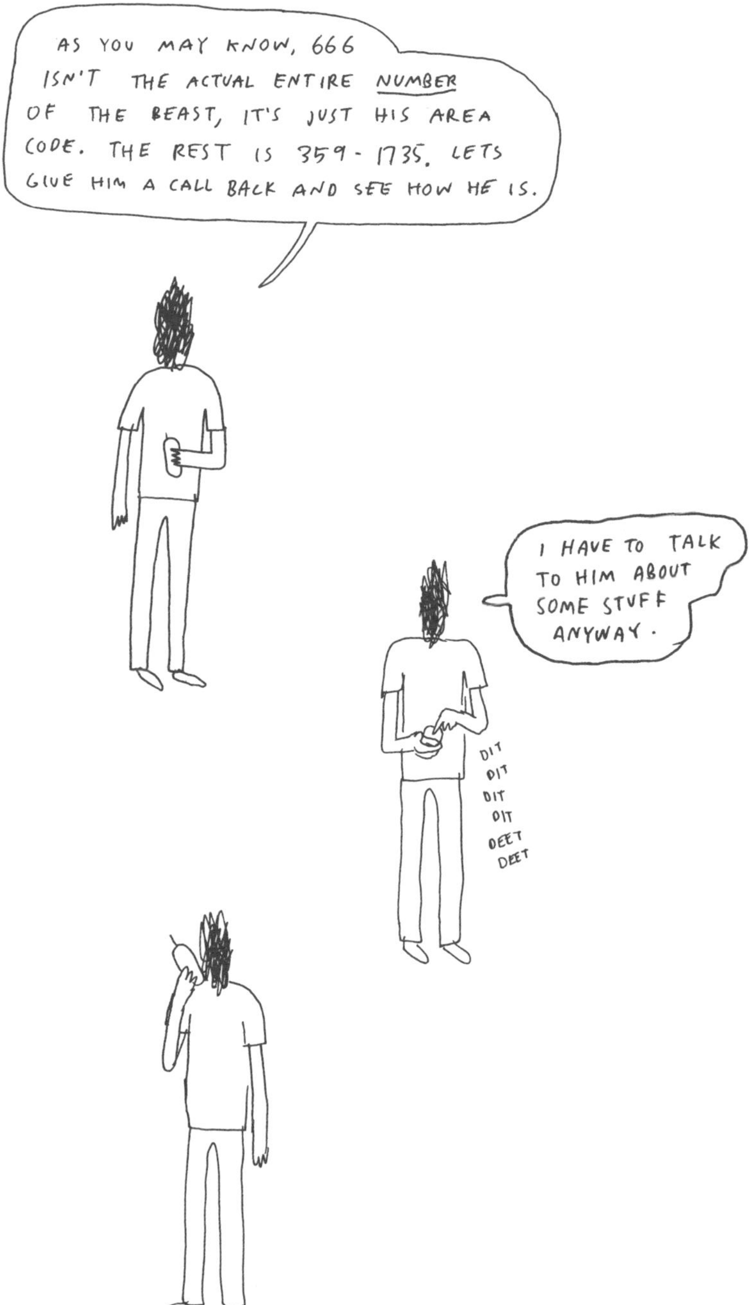
AS YOU MAY KNOW, 666 ISN'T THE ACTUAL ENTIRE NUMBER OF THE BEAST, IT'S JUST HIS AREA CODE. THE REST IS 359-1735. LETS GIVE HIM A CALL BACK AND SEE HOW HE IS.
I HAVE TO TALK TO HIM ABOUT SOME STUFF ANYWAY.
DIT DIT DIT DIT DEET DEET

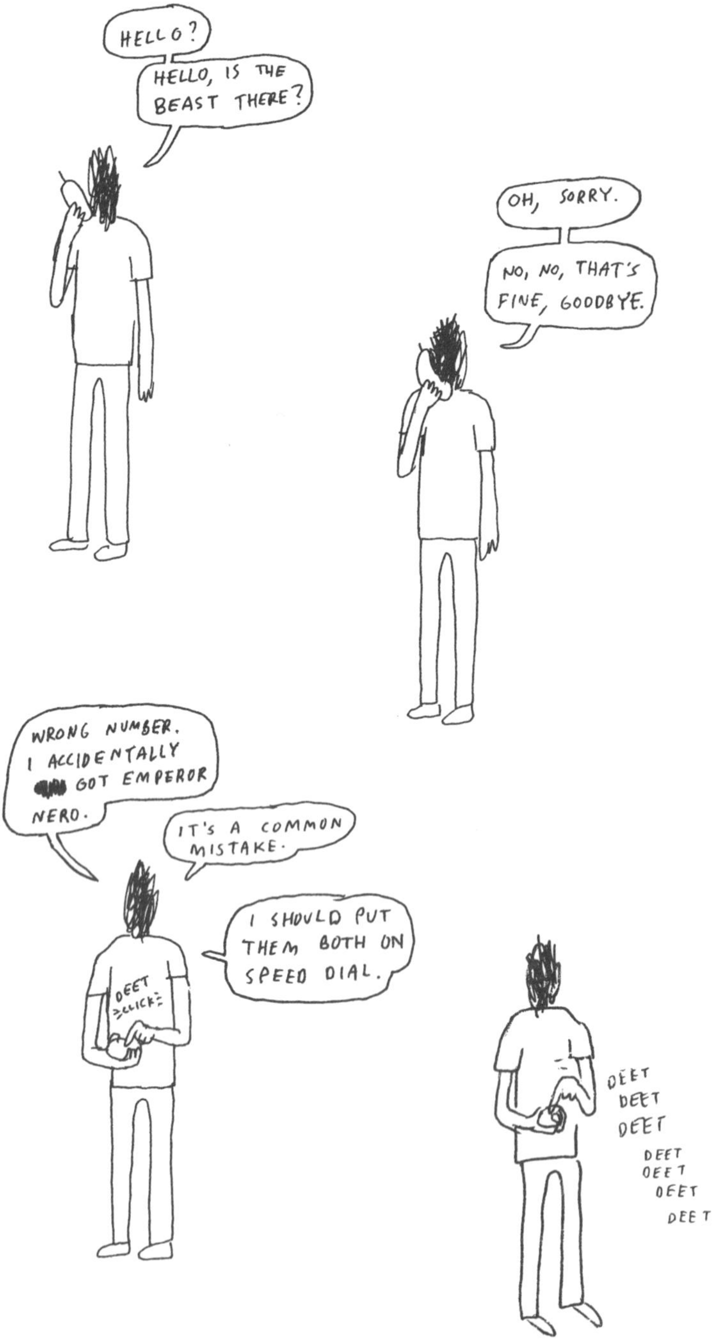
HELLO?
HELLO, IS THE BEAST THERE?
OH, SORRY.
NO, NO, THAT'S FINE, GOODBYE.
WRONG NUMBER. I ACCIDENTALLY [redacted] GOT EMPEROR NERO.
IT'S A COMMON MISTAKE.
DEET
CLICK
I SHOULD PUT THEM BOTH ON SPEED DIAL.
DEET DEET DEET DEET DEET DEET DEET

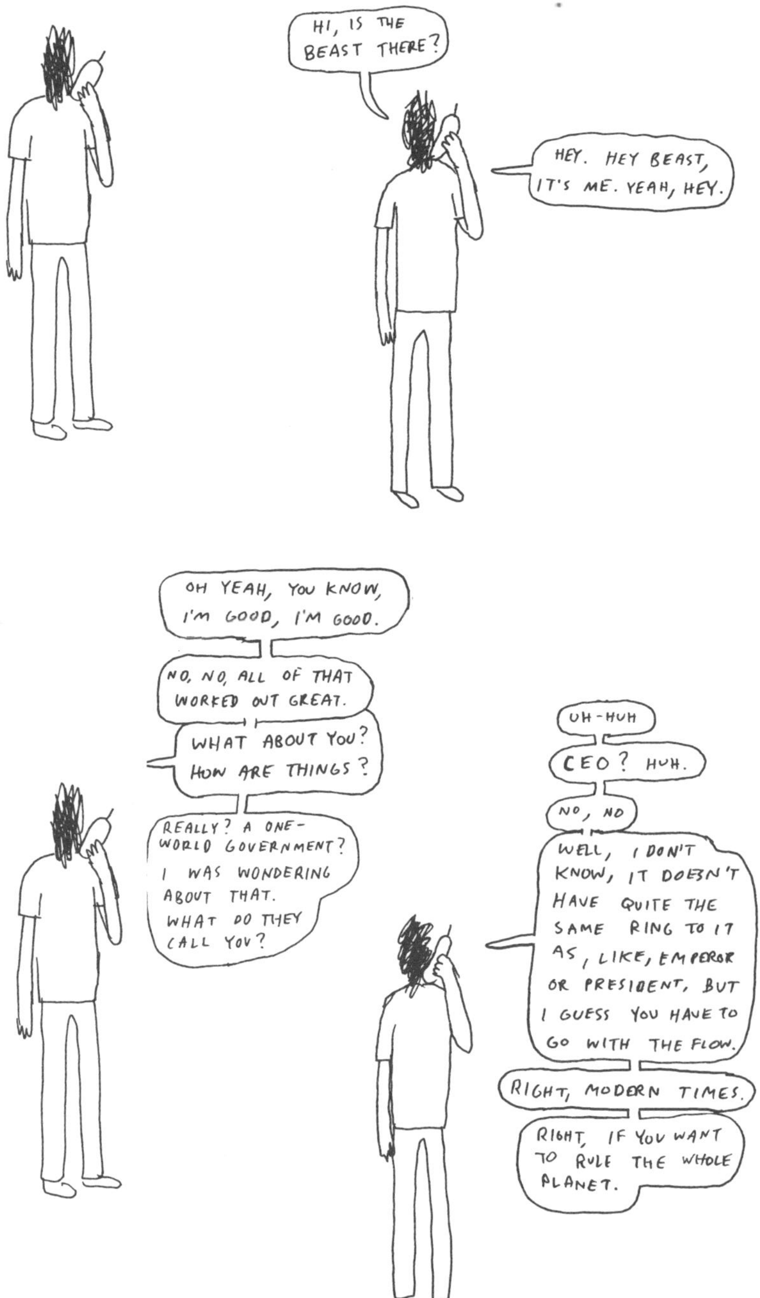
HI, IS THE BEAST THERE?
HEY. HEY BEAST, IT'S ME. YEAH, HEY.
OH YEAH, YOU KNOW, I'M GOOD, I'M GOOD.
NO, NO, ALL OF THAT WORKED OUT GREAT.
WHAT ABOUT YOU? HOW ARE THINGS?
REALLY? A ONE-WORLD GOVERNMENT? I WAS WONDERING ABOUT THAT. WHAT DO THEY CALL YOU?
UH-HUH
CEO? HUH.
NO, NO
WELL, I DON'T KNOW, IT DOESN'T HAVE QUITE THE SAME RING TO IT AS, LIKE, EMPEROR OR PRESIDENT, BUT I GUESS YOU HAVE TO GO WITH THE FLOW.
RIGHT, MODERN TIMES.
RIGHT, IF YOU WANT TO RULE THE WHOLE PLANET.

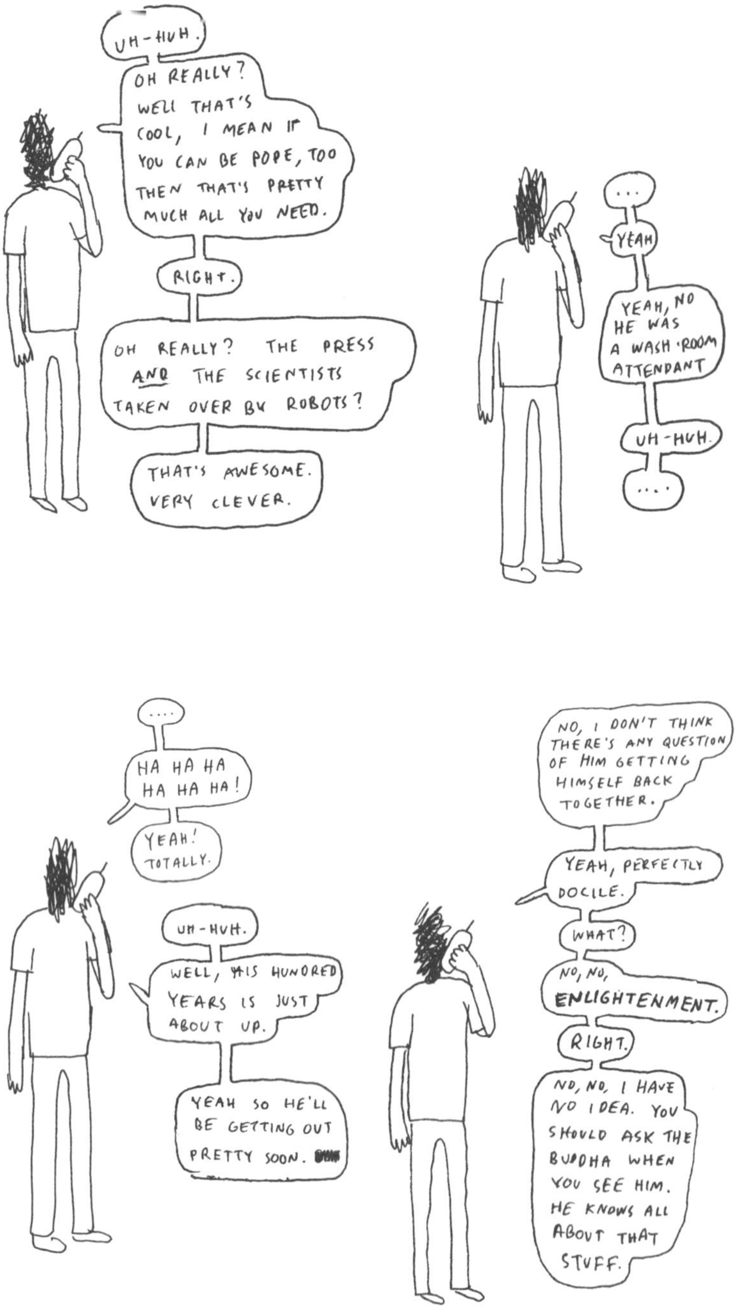
UH-HUH.
OH REALLY? WELL THAT'S COOL, I MEAN IF YOU CAN BE POPE, TOO THEN THAT'S PRETTY MUCH ALL YOU NEED.
RIGHT.
OH REALLY? THE PRESS AND THE SCIENTISTS TAKEN OVER BY ROBOTS?
THAT'S AWESOME. VERY CLEVER.
...
YEAH
YEAH, NO HE WAS A WASH-ROOM ATTENDANT
UH-HUH.
...
....
HA HA HA HA HA HA!
YEAH! TOTALLY.
UH-HUH.
WELL, THIS HUNDRED YEARS IS JUST ABOUT UP.
YEAH SO HE'LL BE GETTING OUT PRETTY SOON. [redacted]
NO, I DON'T THINK THERE'S ANY QUESTION OF HIM GETTING HIMSELF BACK TOGETHER.
YEAH, PERFECTLY DOCILE.
WHAT?
NO, NO, ENLIGHTENMENT.
RIGHT.
NO, NO, I HAVE NO IDEA. YOU SHOULD ASK THE BUDDHA WHEN YOU SEE HIM. HE KNOWS ALL ABOUT THAT STUFF.

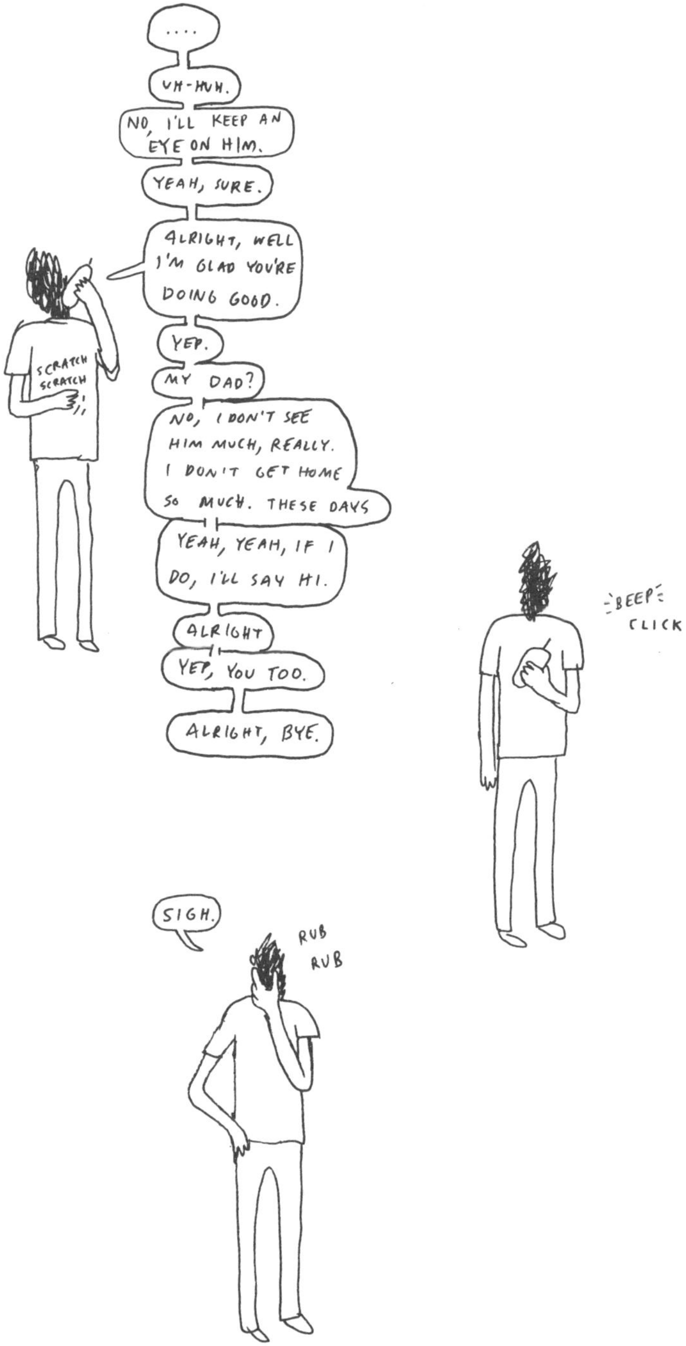
....
UH-HUH.
NO, I'LL KEEP AN EYE ON HIM.
YEAH, SURE.
ALRIGHT, WELL I'M GLAD YOU'RE DOING GOOD.
YEP.
MY DAD?
NO, I DON'T SEE HIM MUCH, REALLY. I DON'T GET HOME SO MUCH. THESE DAYS
YEAH, YEAH, IF I DO, I'LL SAY HI.
ALRIGHT
YEP, YOU TOO.
ALRIGHT, BYE.
SCRATCH SCRATCH
BEEP
CLICK
SIGH.
RUB RUB

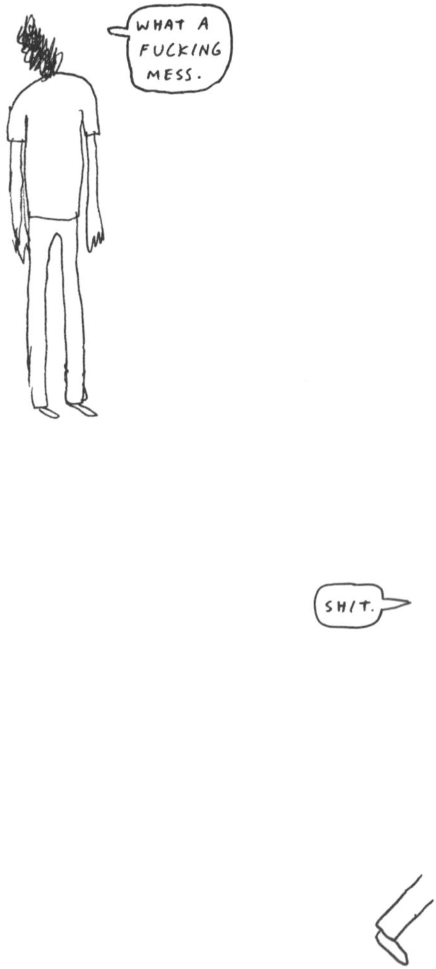
WHAT A FUCKING MESS.
SHIT.

PART II

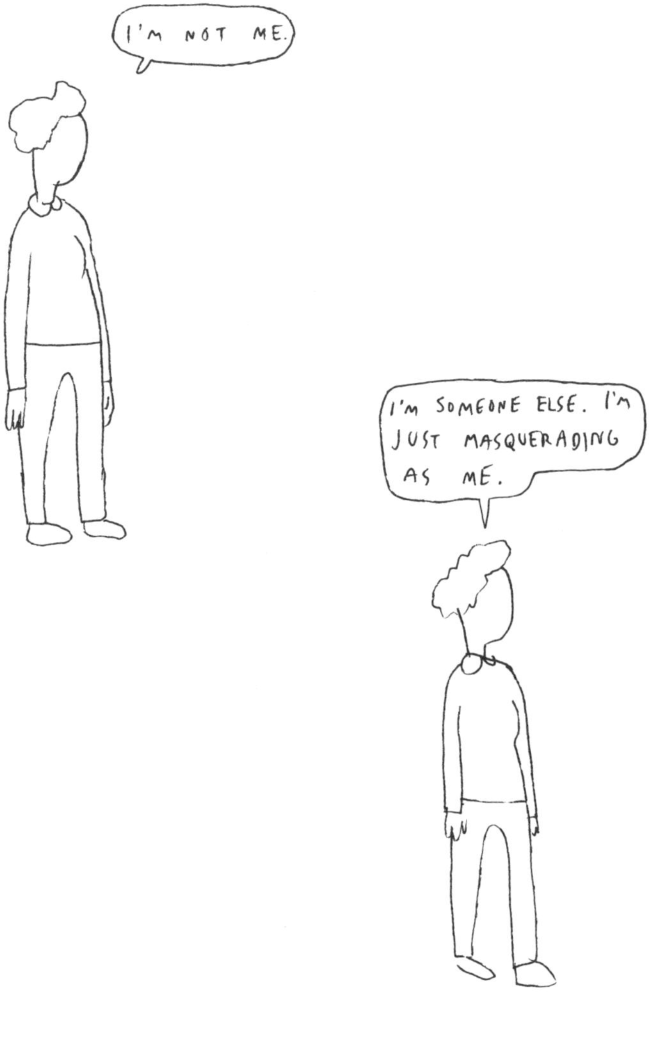
I'M NOT ME.
I'M SOMEONE ELSE. I'M JUST MASQUERADING AS ME.

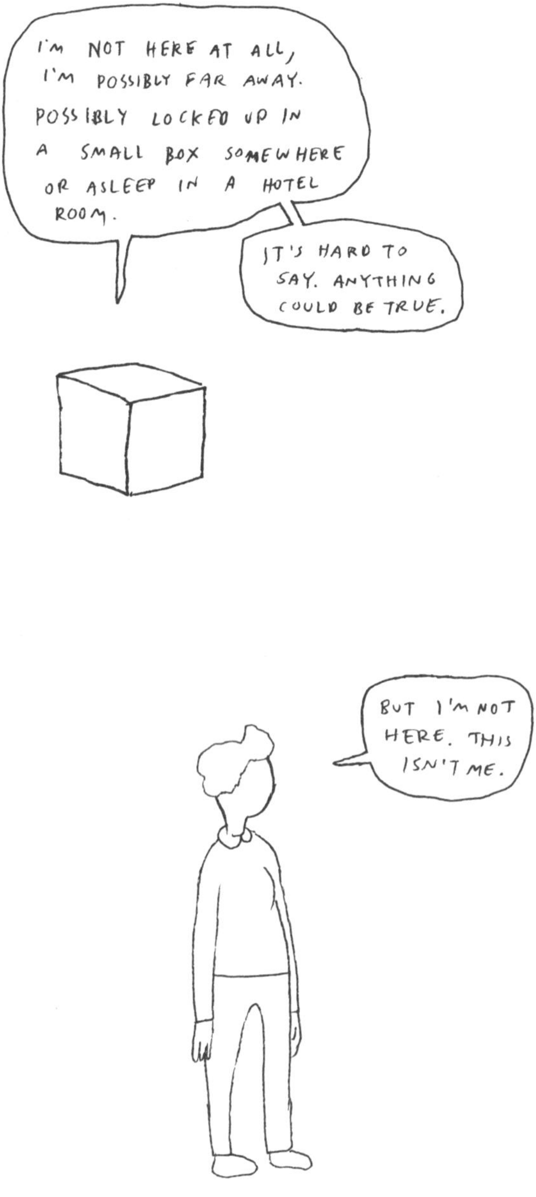
I'M NOT HERE AT ALL, I'M POSSIBLY FAR AWAY. POSSIBLY LOCKED UP IN A SMALL BOX SOMEWHERE OR ASLEEP IN A HOTEL ROOM.
IT'S HARD TO SAY. ANYTHING COULD BE TRUE.
BUT I'M NOT HERE. THIS ISN'T ME.

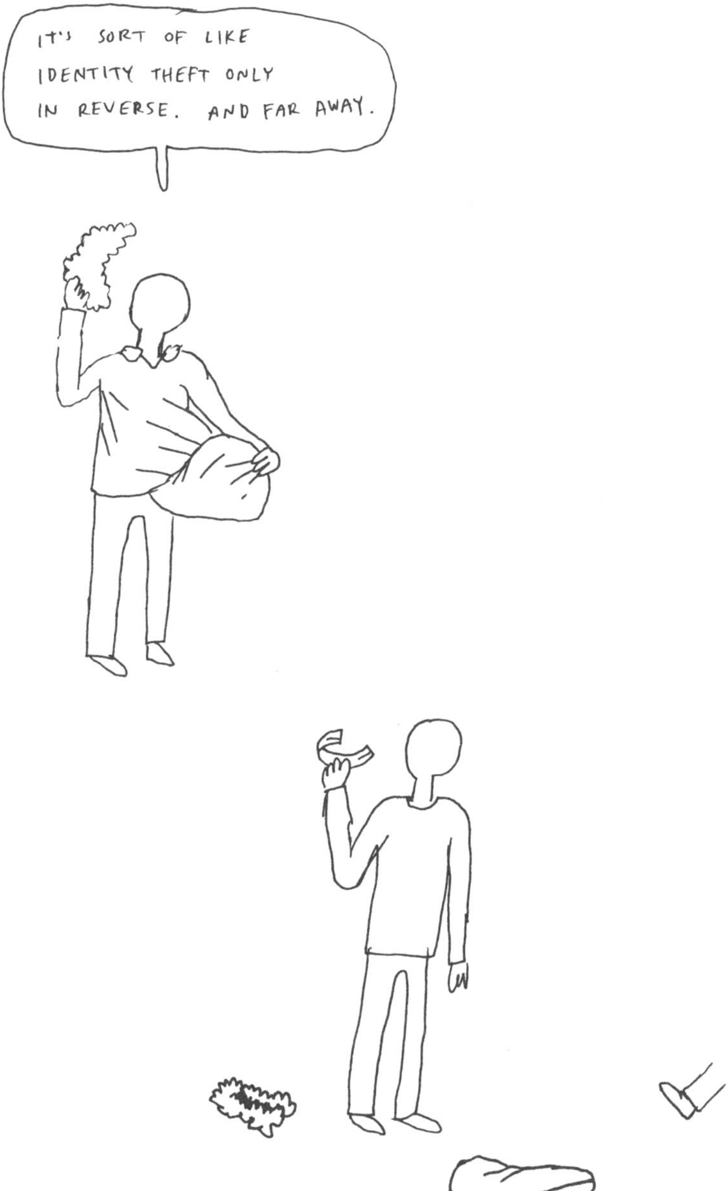
IT'S SORT OF LIKE IDENTITY THEFT ONLY IN REVERSE. AND FAR AWAY.

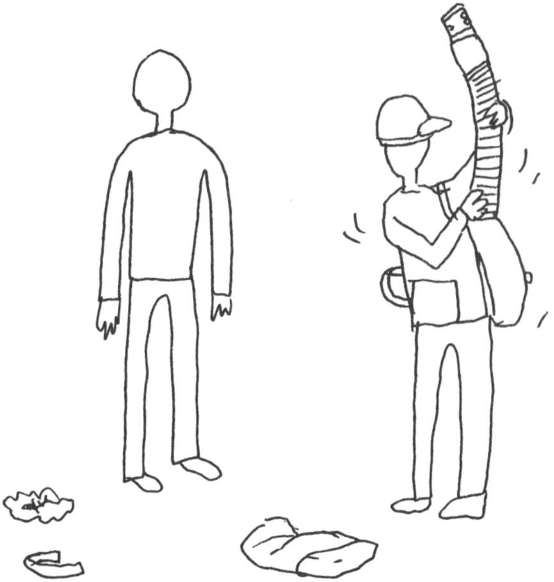

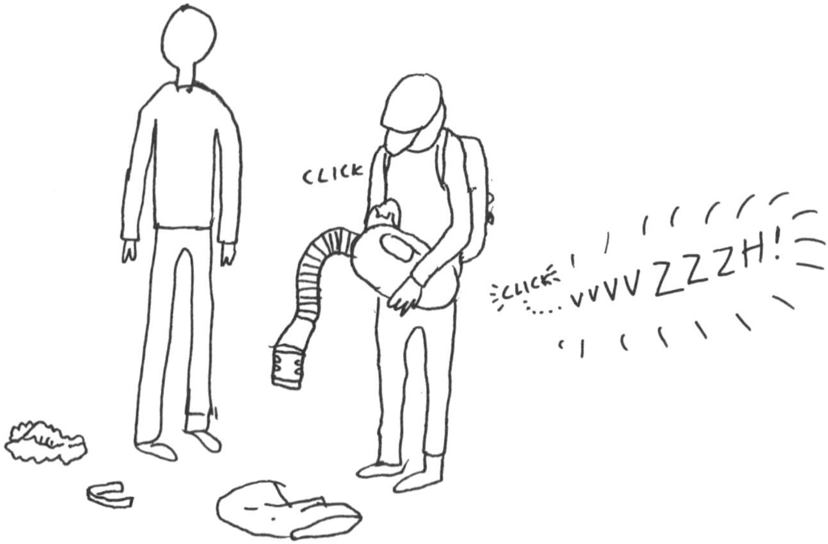
CLICK
CLICK
VVVVZZZZH!

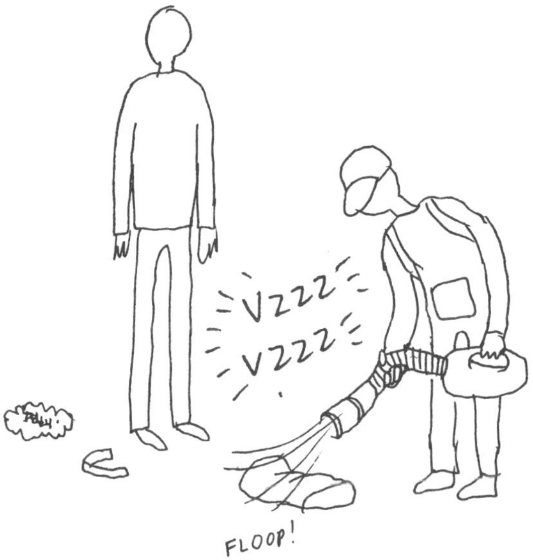

VZZZ
VZZZ
FLOOP!

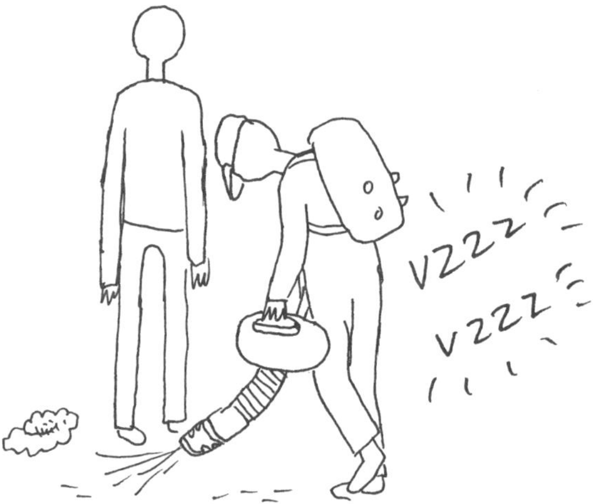

VZZZ
VZZZ
FLOOP!

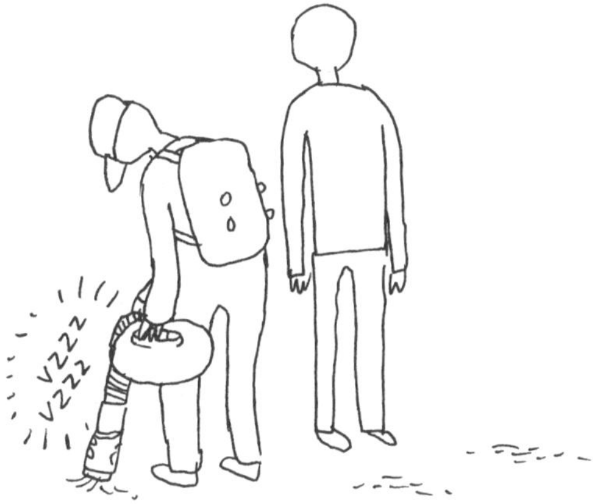
VZZZ
VZZZ

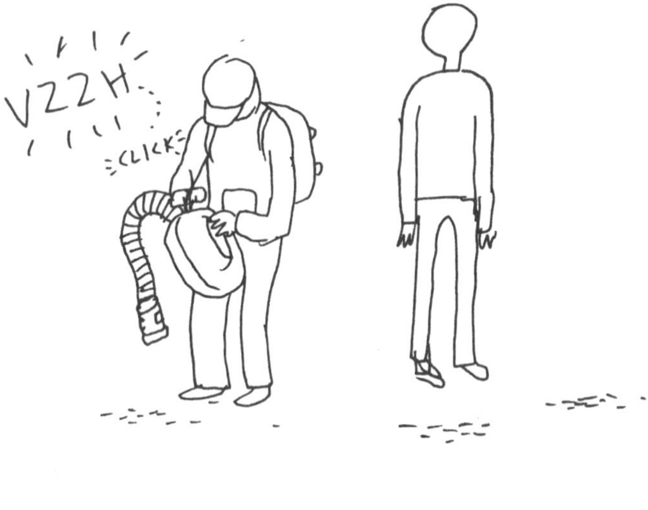
VZZH
CLICK

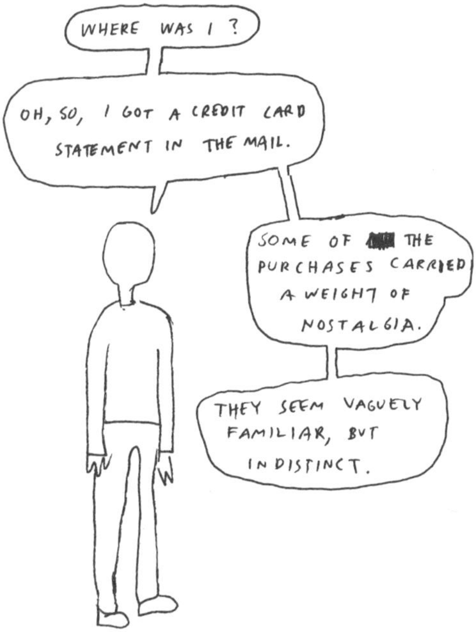
WHERE WAS I ?
OH, SO, I GOT A CREDIT CARD STATEMENT IN THE MAIL.
SOME OF [redacted] THE PURCHASES CARRIED A WEIGHT OF NOSTALGIA.
THEY SEEM VAGUELY FAMILIAR, BUT INDISTINCT.

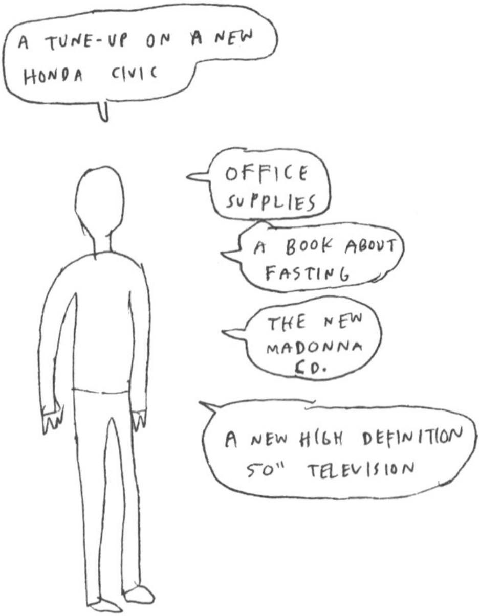
A TUNE-UP ON A NEW HONDA CIVIC
OFFICE SUPPLIES
A BOOK ABOUT FASTING
THE NEW MADONNA CD.
A NEW HIGH DEFINITION 50" TELEVISION

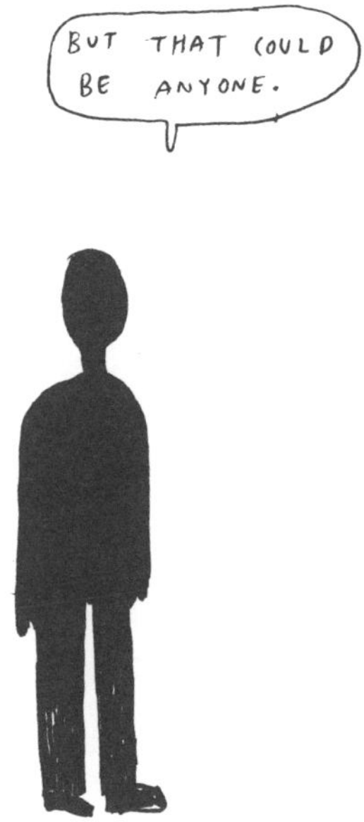
BUT THAT COULD BE ANYONE.

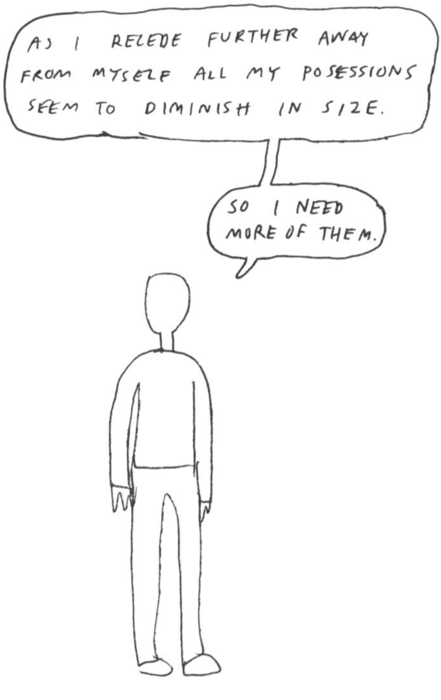
AS I RECEDE FURTHER AWAY FROM MYSELF ALL MY POSESSIONS SEEM TO DIMINISH IN SIZE.
SO I NEED MORE OF THEM.

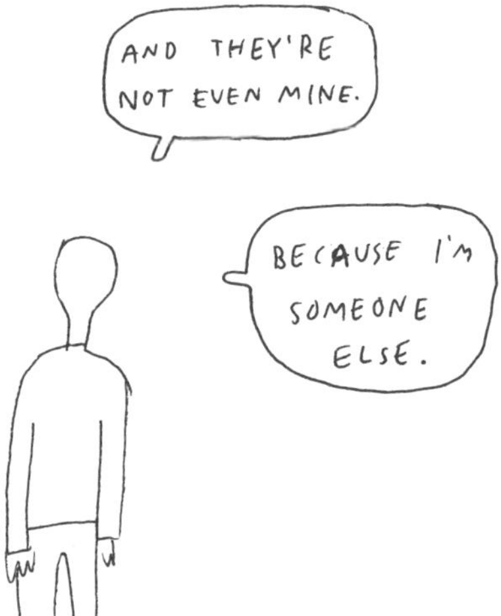
AND THEY'RE NOT EVEN MINE.
BECAUSE I'M SOMEONE ELSE.

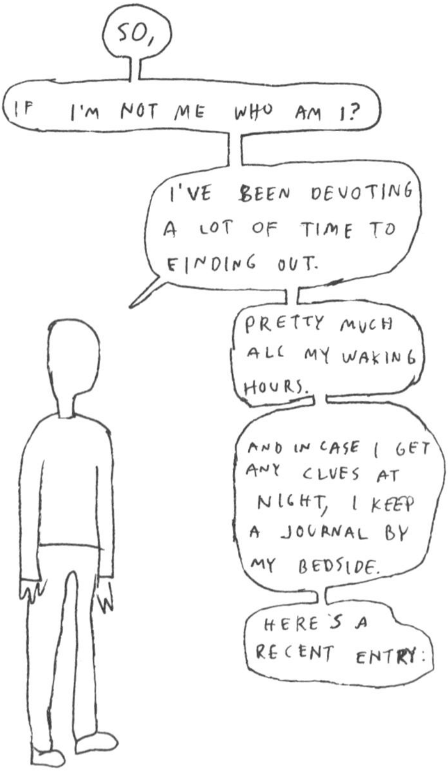
SO,
IF I'M NOT ME WHO AM I?
I'VE BEEN DEVOTING A LOT OF TIME TO FINDING OUT.
PRETTY MUCH ALL MY WAKING HOURS.
AND IN CASE I GET ANY CLUES AT NIGHT, I KEEP A JOURNAL BY MY BEDSIDE.
HERE'S A RECENT ENTRY:

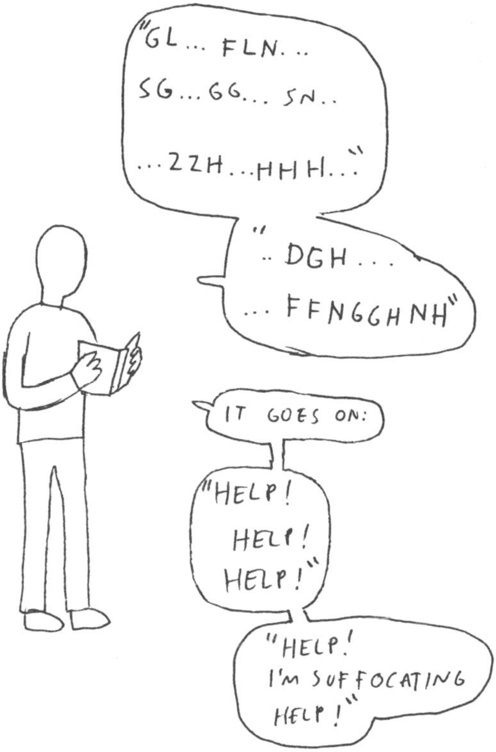
"GL... FLN..
SG...GG... SN..
...ZZH...HHH..."
"..DGH...
...FFNGGHNH"
IT GOES ON:
"HELP!
HELP!
HELP!"
"HELP!
I'M SUFFOCATING
HELP!"

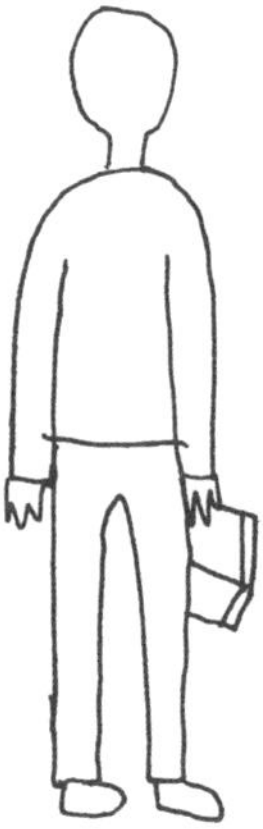

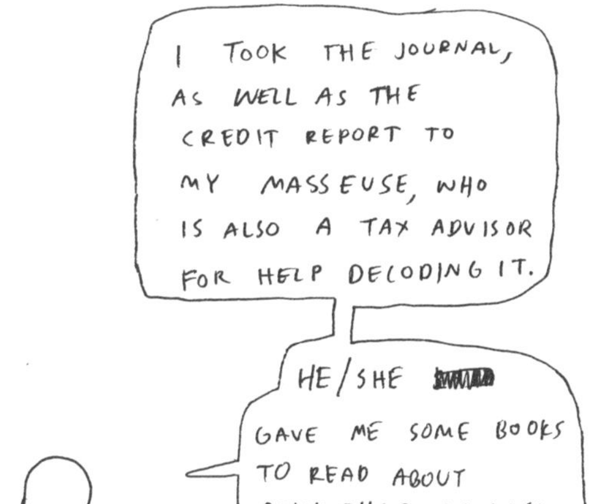

I TOOK THE JOURNAL, AS WELL AS THE CREDIT REPORT TO MY MASSEUSE, WHO IS ALSO A TAX ADVISOR FOR HELP DECODING IT.

HE/SHE ~~SHITTED~~ GAVE ME SOME BOOKS TO READ ABOUT PSYCHOPHARMACOLOGY. I READ THEM AND DECIDED I COULD BENEFIT FROM MEDICATION, BUT ~~when you get medical~~ WHEN I WENT BACK TO MY MASSEUSE HE/SHE SAID I HAD MISSED THE POINT AND THREW ME OUT OF HER OFFICE.

THAT'S WHEN I REALIZED
SHE HAD KEPT THE CREDIT
REPORT.

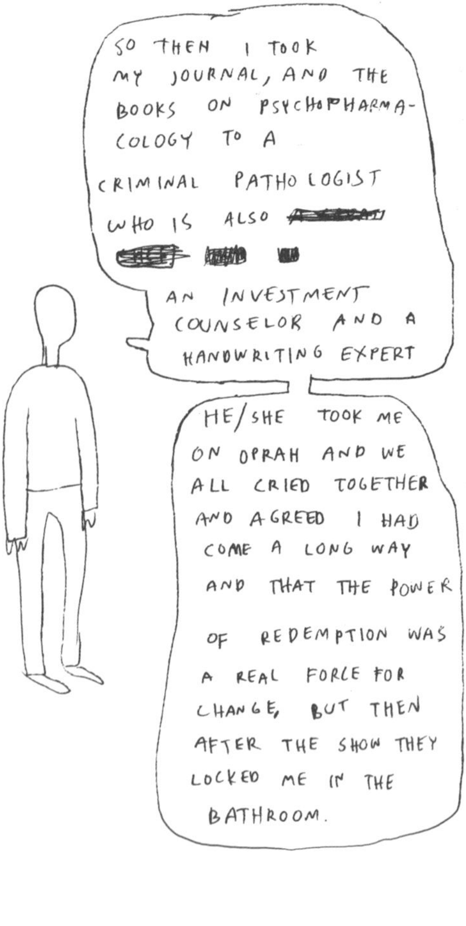

SO THEN I TOOK
MY JOURNAL, AND THE
BOOKS ON PSYCHOPHARMA-
COLOGY TO A
CRIMINAL PATHOLOGIST
WHO IS ALSO ~~[scribbled out]~~
~~[scribbled out]~~ ~~[scribbled out]~~ ~~[scribbled out]~~
AN INVESTMENT
COUNSELOR AND A
HANDWRITING EXPERT

HE/SHE TOOK ME
ON OPRAH AND WE
ALL CRIED TOGETHER
AND AGREED I HAD
COME A LONG WAY
AND THAT THE POWER
OF REDEMPTION WAS
A REAL FORCE FOR
CHANGE, BUT THEN
AFTER THE SHOW THEY
LOCKED ME IN THE
BATHROOM.

THEY SAID THEY WOULDN'T LET ME OUT UNTIL I STOPPED CRYING.

I ESCAPED OUT THE WINDOW, BUT LATER REALIZED I HAD LEFT MY JOURNAL IN THE STUDIO AND THE BOOK ON PSYCHO-PHARMACOLOGY IN THE BATHROOM.

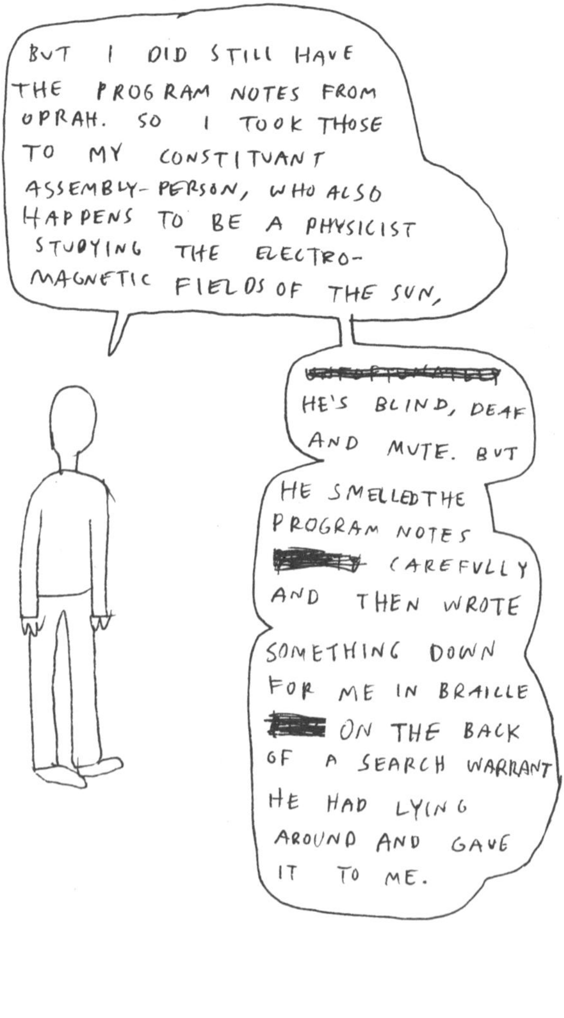
BUT I DID STILL HAVE THE PROGRAM NOTES FROM OPRAH. SO I TOOK THOSE TO MY CONSTITUANT ASSEMBLY-PERSON, WHO ALSO HAPPENS TO BE A PHYSICIST STUDYING THE ELECTRO-MAGNETIC FIELDS OF THE SUN,
[redacted] HE'S BLIND, DEAF AND MUTE. BUT HE SMELLED THE PROGRAM NOTES [redacted] CAREFULLY AND THEN WROTE SOMETHING DOWN FOR ME IN BRAILLE [redacted] ON THE BACK OF A SEARCH WARRANT HE HAD LYING AROUND AND GAVE IT TO ME.

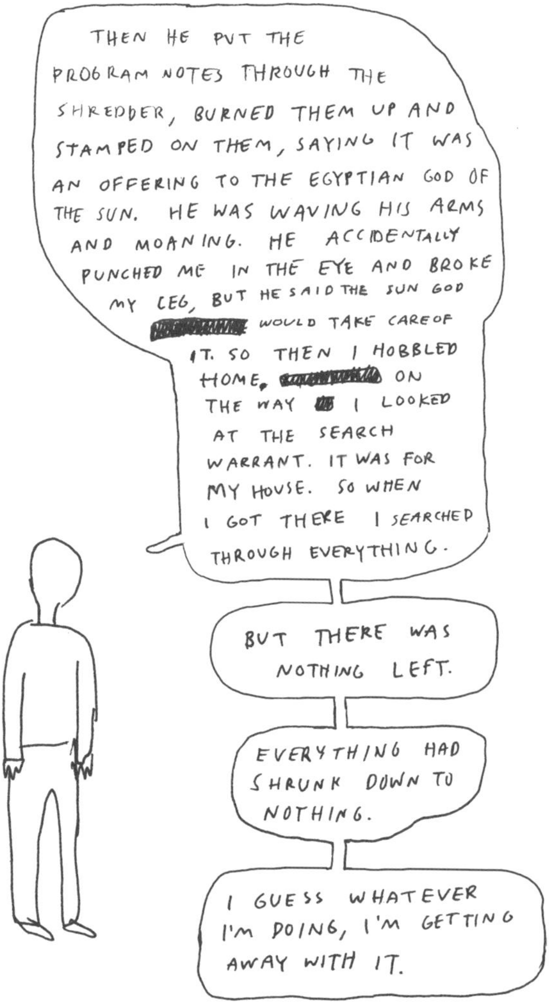

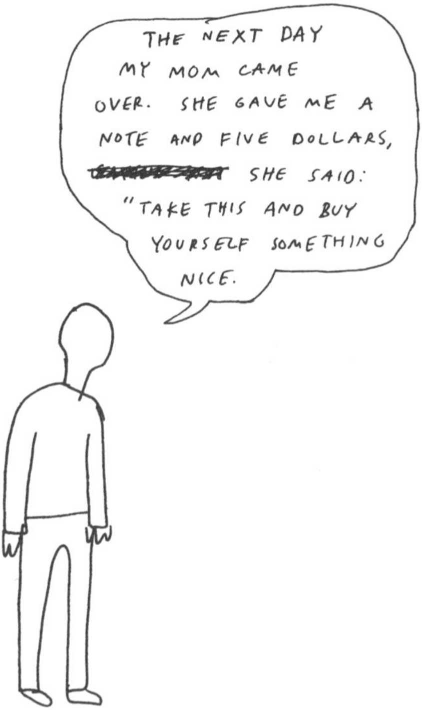
THE NEXT DAY MY MOM CAME OVER. SHE GAVE ME A NOTE AND FIVE DOLLARS, SHE SAID: "TAKE THIS AND BUY YOURSELF SOMETHING NICE.

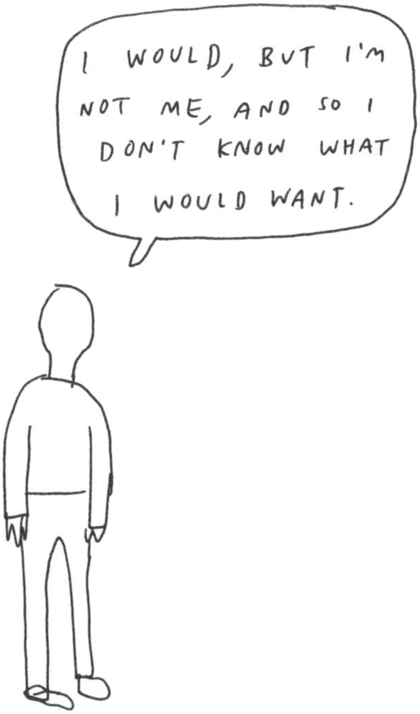
I WOULD, BUT I'M NOT ME, AND SO I DON'T KNOW WHAT I WOULD WANT.

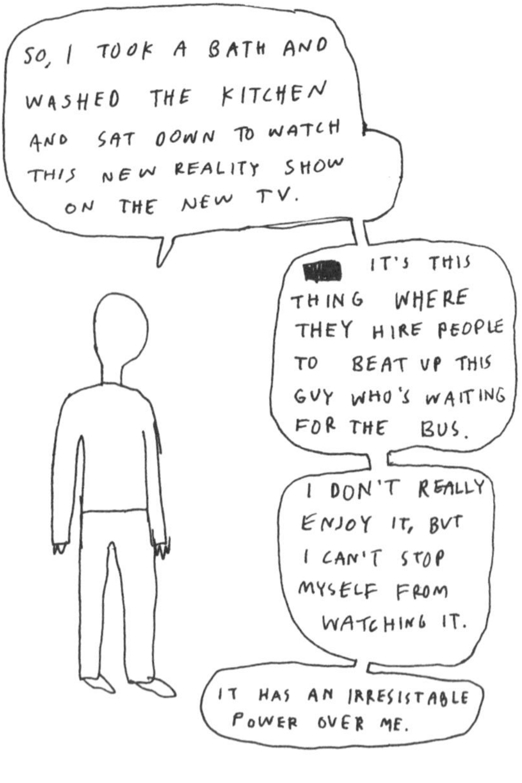
SO, I TOOK A BATH AND WASHED THE KITCHEN AND SAT DOWN TO WATCH THIS NEW REALITY SHOW ON THE NEW TV.
[redacted] IT'S THIS THING WHERE THEY HIRE PEOPLE TO BEAT UP THIS GUY WHO'S WAITING FOR THE BUS.
I DON'T REALLY ENJOY IT, BUT I CAN'T STOP MYSELF FROM WATCHING IT.
IT HAS AN IRRESISTABLE POWER OVER ME.

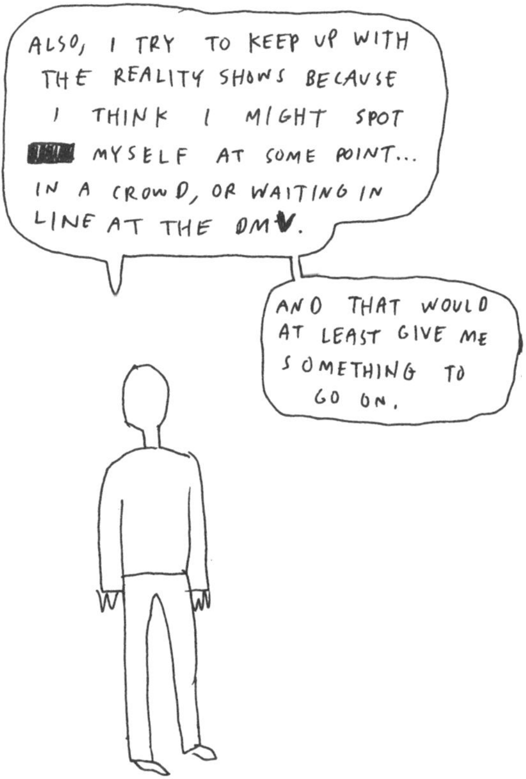
ALSO, I TRY TO KEEP UP WITH THE REALITY SHOWS BECAUSE I THINK I MIGHT SPOT [redacted] MYSELF AT SOME POINT... IN A CROWD, OR WAITING IN LINE AT THE DMV.
AND THAT WOULD AT LEAST GIVE ME SOMETHING TO GO ON.

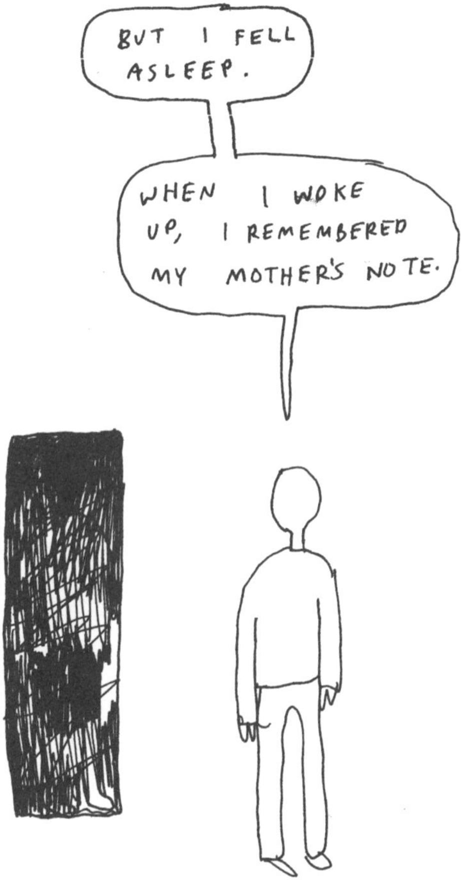
BUT I FELL ASLEEP.
WHEN I WOKE UP, I REMEMBERED MY MOTHER'S NOTE.

BUT THEN THE PHONE RANG. IT WAS MY BOSS. HE SAID I HADN'T SHOWN UP FOR WORK FOR OVER THREE MONTHS. AND THAT HE WAS GOING TO HAVE TO FIRE ME.

AT FIRST I SAID I WAS SORRY. I HAD FORGOTTEN.

BUT THEN I THOUGHT I SHOULD BE HONEST. SO I TRIED TO EXPLAIN THAT I'M NOT ME AND IT'S REALLY NOT MY JOB.

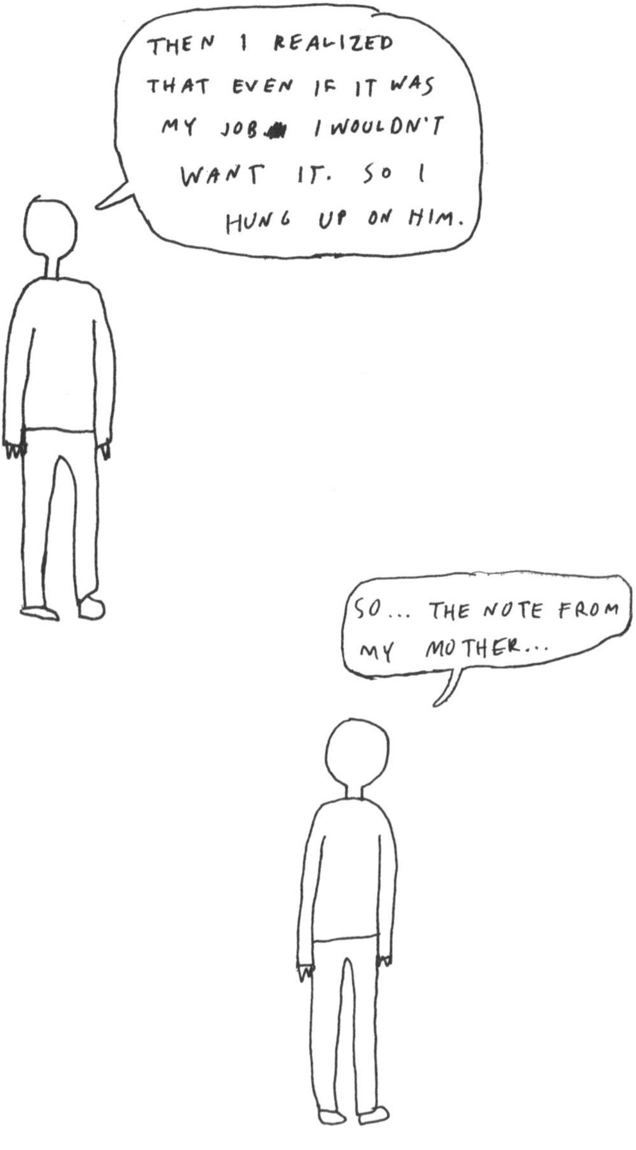
THEN I REALIZED THAT EVEN IF IT WAS MY JOB I WOULDN'T WANT IT. SO I HUNG UP ON HIM.
SO... THE NOTE FROM MY MOTHER...

OH. BEFORE I GOT BACK TO IT I LOOKED UP, AND THERE, AT MY WINDOW WERE THREE SECRET SERVICE AGENTS. THEY WERE TIED UP AND GAGGED.

I LET THEM IN, LET THEM TAKE A SHOWER AND MADE THEM SOME TOAST.

WE EXCHANGED STORIES OVER ROOT BEER AND I DECIDED TO SHOW THEM MY MOTHER'S NOTE.

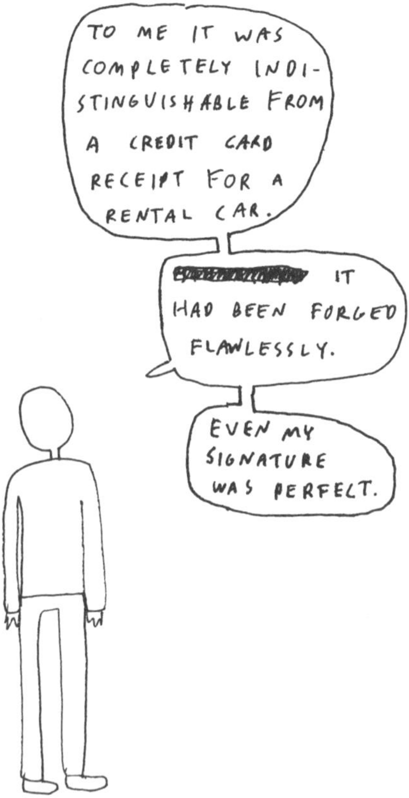
TO ME IT WAS COMPLETELY INDI-STINGUISHABLE FROM A CREDIT CARD RECEIPT FOR A RENTAL CAR.
[redacted] IT HAD BEEN FORGED FLAWLESSLY.
EVEN MY SIGNATURE WAS PERFECT.

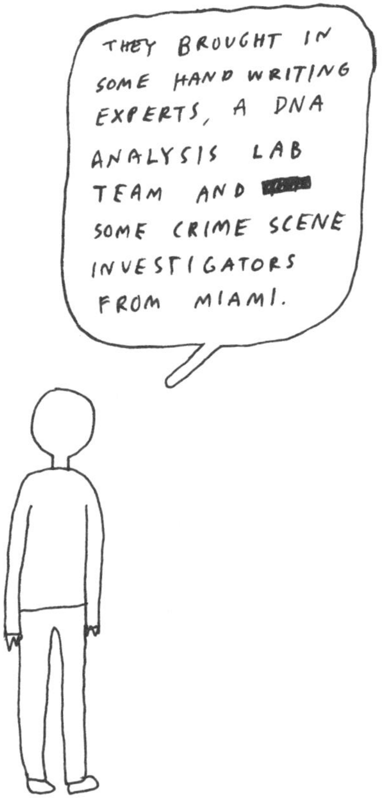
THEY BROUGHT IN SOME HAND WRITING EXPERTS, A DNA ANALYSIS LAB TEAM AND [redacted] SOME CRIME SCENE INVESTIGATORS FROM MIAMI.

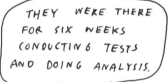

THEY WERE THERE FOR SIX WEEKS CONDUCTING TESTS AND DOING ANALYSIS.

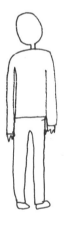

FOR A WHILE I WAS CONNECTED TO AN EKG FOR TWENTY FOUR HOURS A DAY, TIED DOWN TO THE TABLE, AND ALL MY THOUGHTS WERE PROJECTED ON A SCREEN IN A CONFERENCE ROOM AT THE PENTAGON.

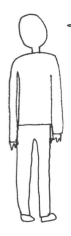

IT WAS REALLY NEAT ████ . BUT AFTER SIX WEEKS THEY FINISHED UP AND WENT HOME.

THAT SAME NIGHT THE ~~CIA~~ UNDERCOVER CIA AGENT CALLED TO SAY THE RESULTS WERE INCONCLUSIVE, BUT WOULD BE CLASSIFIED BECAUSE OF NATIONAL SECURITY.

SHE ALSO THANKED ME FOR THE ROOT BEER AND TOAST.

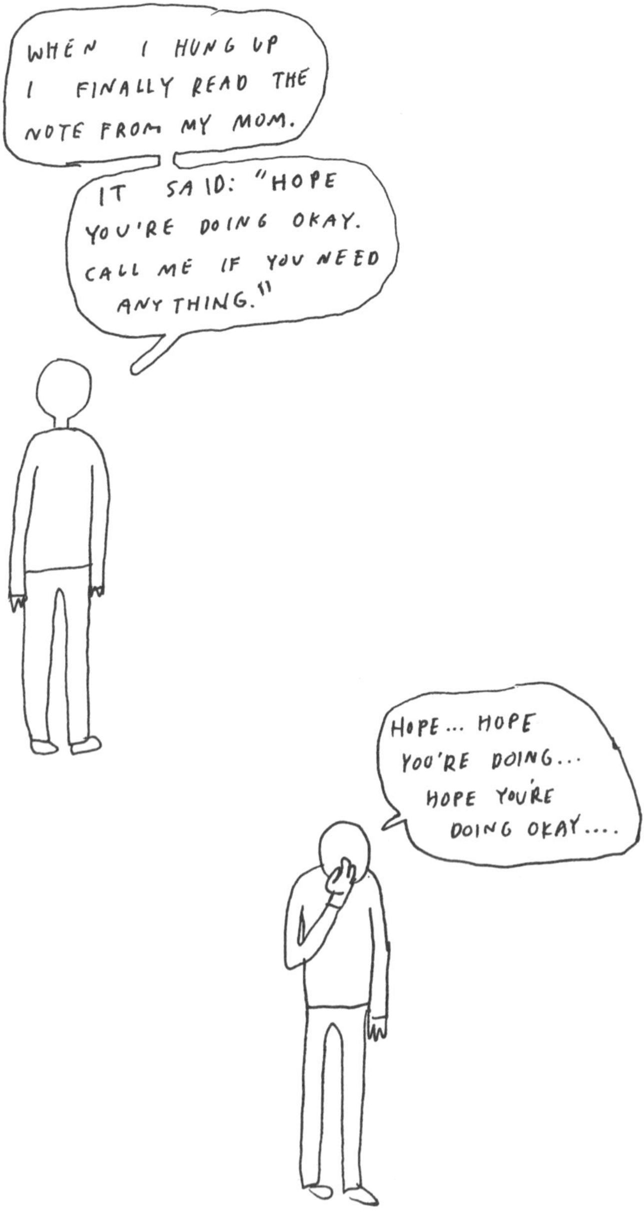
WHEN I HUNG UP I FINALLY READ THE NOTE FROM MY MOM.
IT SAID: "HOPE YOU'RE DOING OKAY. CALL ME IF YOU NEED ANYTHING."
HOPE... HOPE YOU'RE DOING... HOPE YOU'RE DOING OKAY....

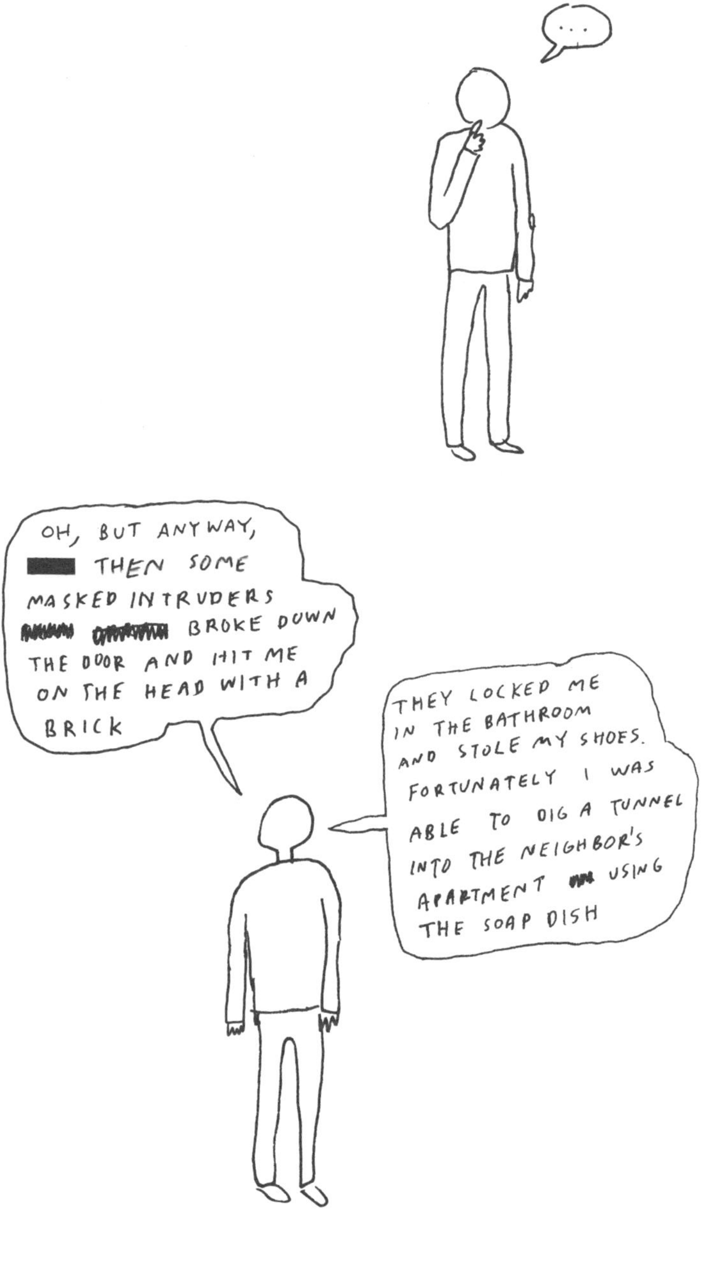
. . .
OH, BUT ANYWAY, [redacted] THEN SOME MASKED INTRUDERS [redacted] BROKE DOWN THE DOOR AND HIT ME ON THE HEAD WITH A BRICK
THEY LOCKED ME IN THE BATHROOM AND STOLE MY SHOES. FORTUNATELY I WAS ABLE TO DIG A TUNNEL INTO THE NEIGHBOR'S APARTMENT [redacted] USING THE SOAP DISH

OH! THE NOTE FROM MY MOM! I ALMOST FORGOT, HERE, I'LL SHOW YOU...

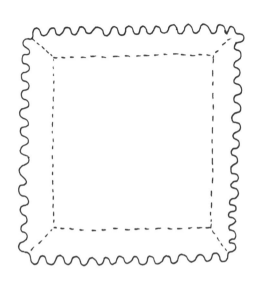

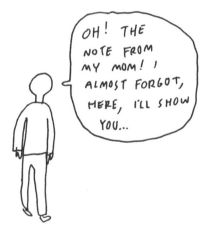

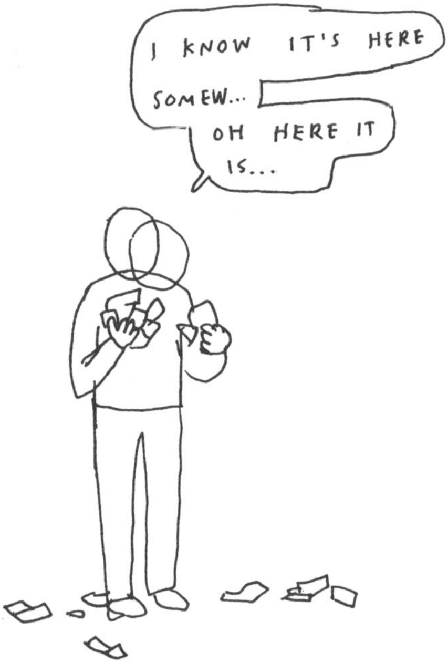
I KNOW IT'S HERE SOMEW...
OH HERE IT IS...

[redacted]

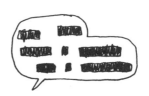

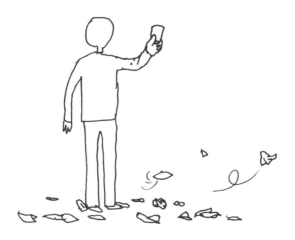

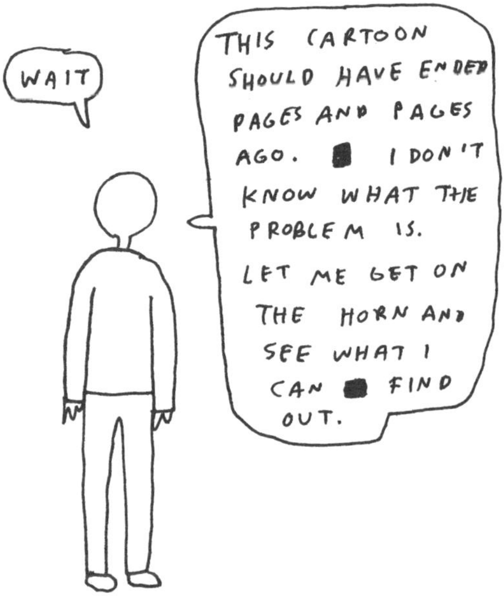
WAIT
THIS CARTOON SHOULD HAVE ENDED PAGES AND PAGES AGO. [redacted] I DON'T KNOW WHAT THE PROBLEM IS. LET ME GET ON THE HORN AND SEE WHAT I CAN [redacted] FIND OUT.

DEET
DEET
DEET
AH, IT'S RINGING.

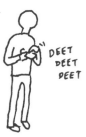

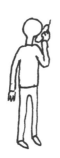

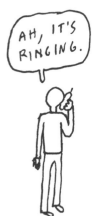

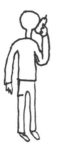

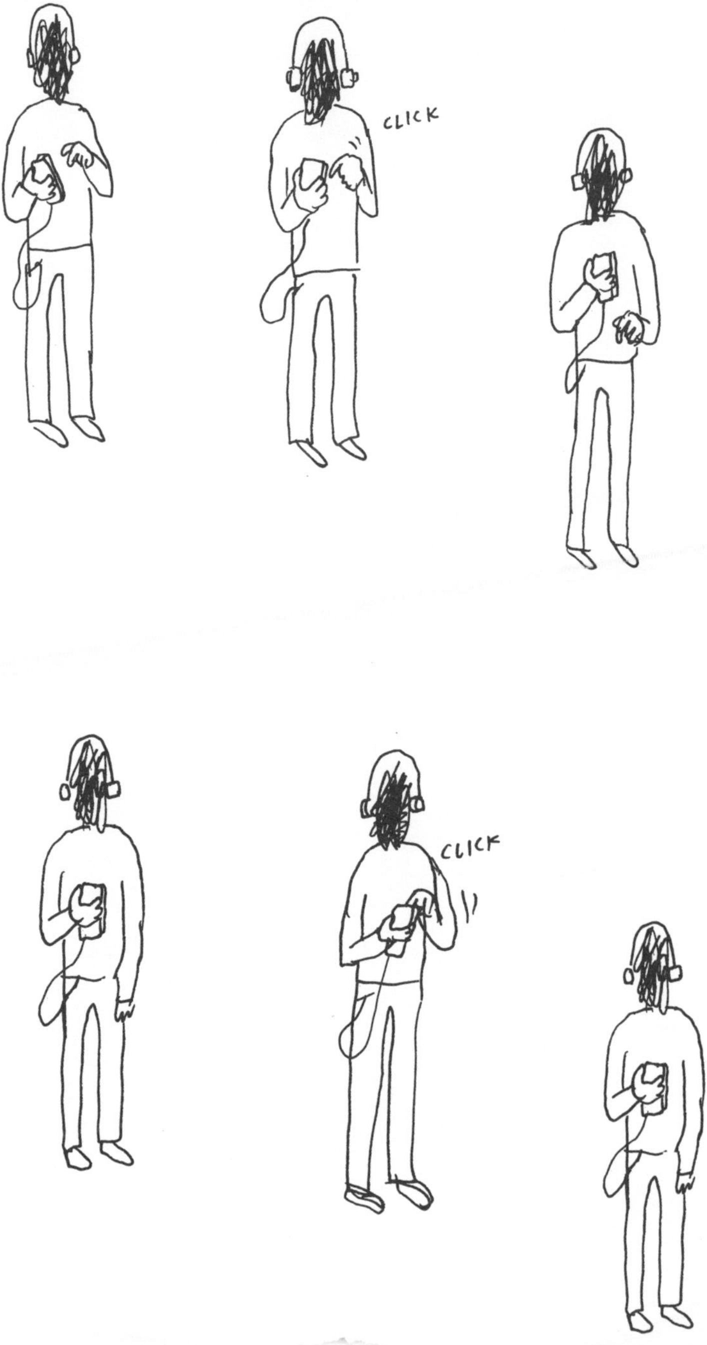
CLICK
CLICK

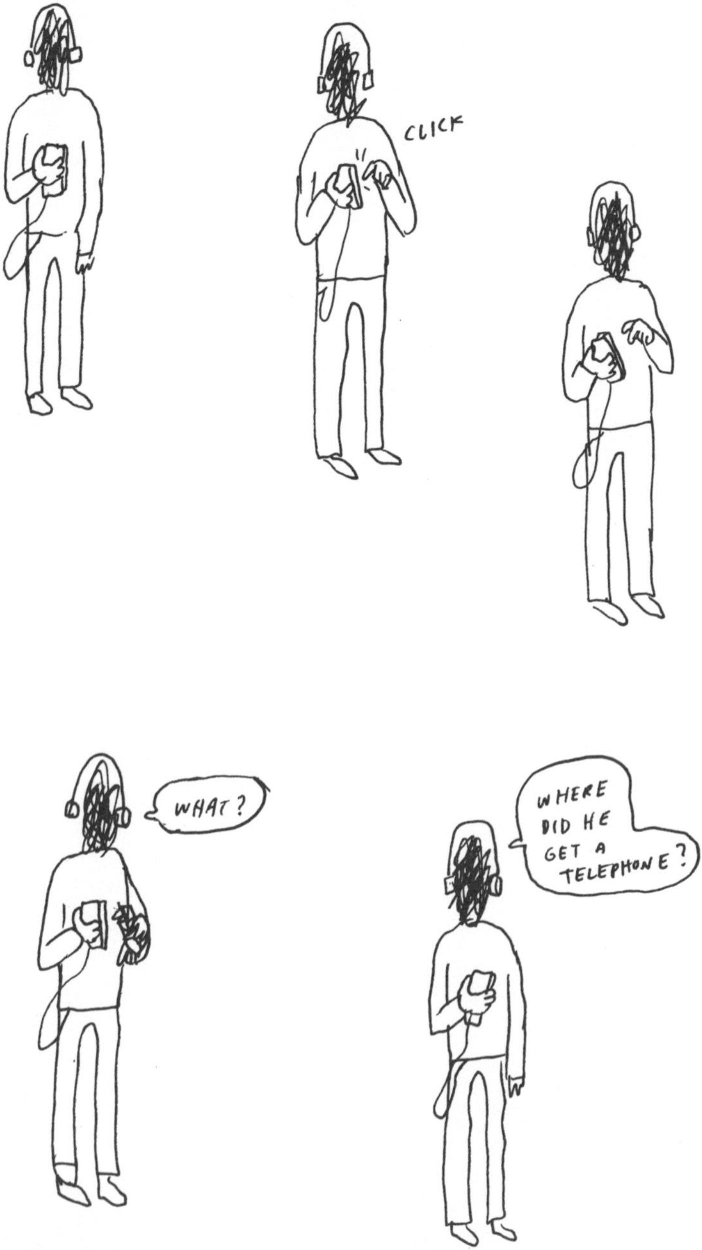
CLICK
WHAT?
WHERE DID HE GET A TELEPHONE?

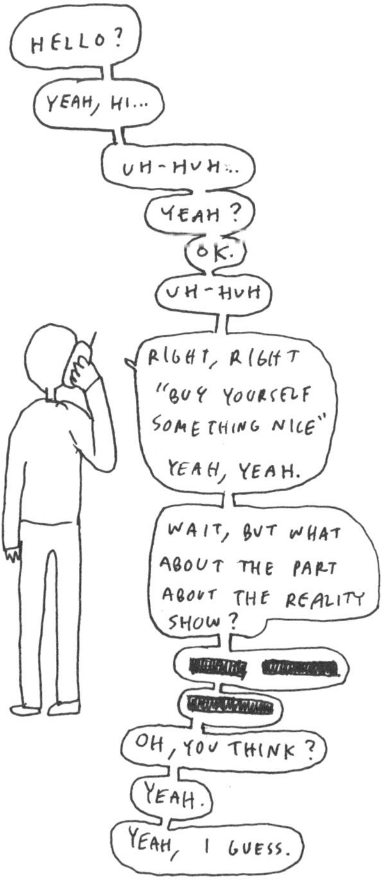
HELLO?
YEAH, HI...
UH-HUH...
YEAH?
OK.
UH-HUH
RIGHT, RIGHT "BUY YOURSELF SOMETHING NICE" YEAH, YEAH.
WAIT, BUT WHAT ABOUT THE PART ABOUT THE REALITY SHOW?
[redacted]
[redacted]
OH, YOU THINK?
YEAH.
YEAH, I GUESS.

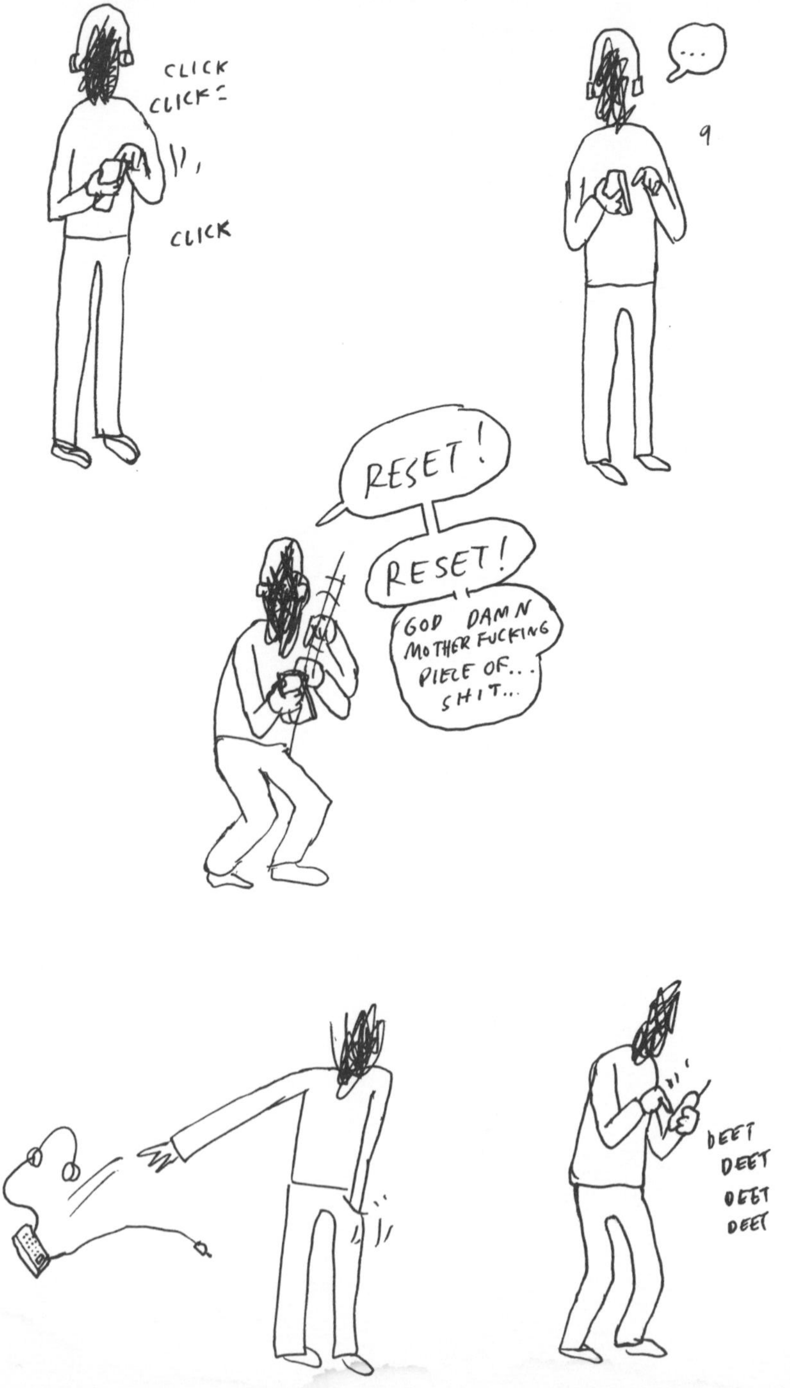
CLICK
CLICK
CLICK
...
RESET!
RESET!
GOD DAMN MOTHER FUCKING PIECE OF... SHIT...
DEET
DEET
DEET
DEET

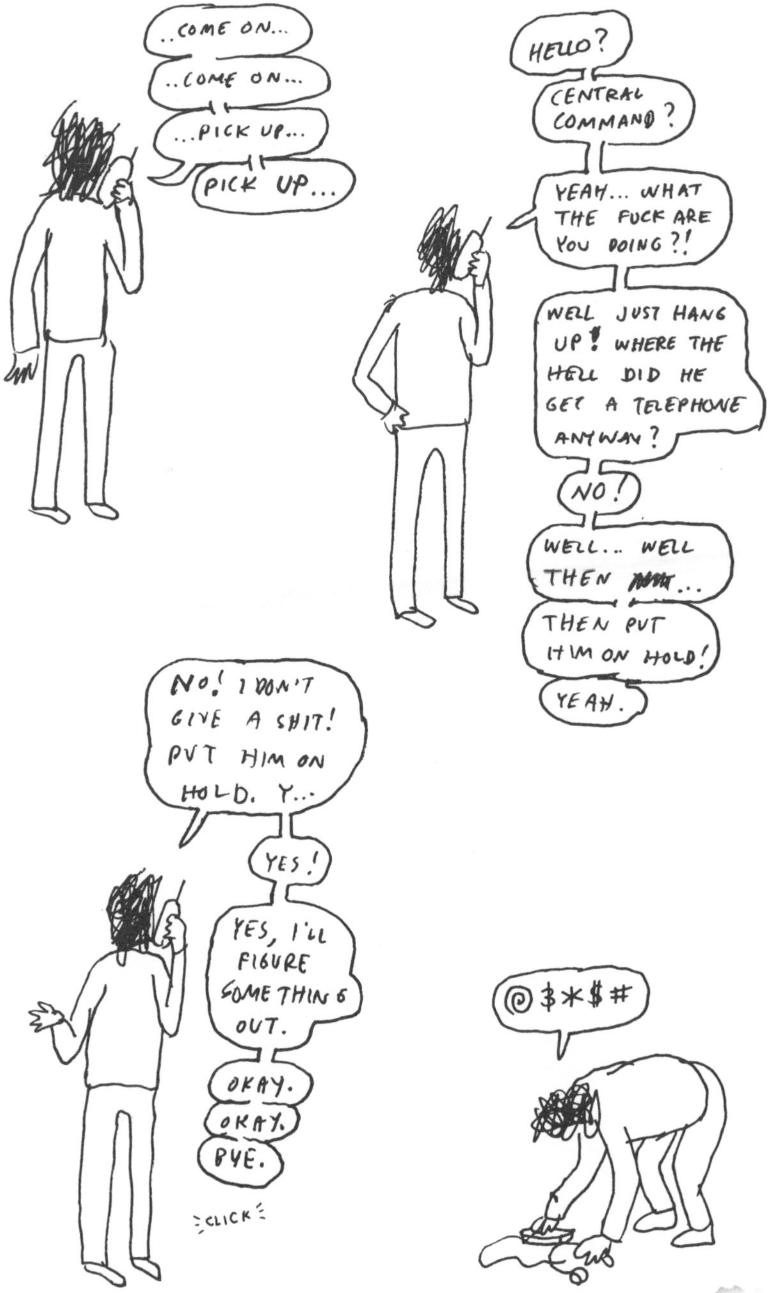
..COME ON...
..COME ON...
...PICK UP...
PICK UP...
HELLO?
CENTRAL COMMAND?
YEAH... WHAT THE FUCK ARE YOU DOING?!
WELL JUST HANG UP! WHERE THE HELL DID HE GET A TELEPHONE ANYWAY?
NO!
WELL... WELL THEN ...
THEN PUT HIM ON HOLD!
YEAH.
NO! I DON'T GIVE A SHIT! PUT HIM ON HOLD. Y...
YES!
YES, I'LL FIGURE SOMETHING OUT.
OKAY.
OKAY.
BYE.
CLICK
@$*$#

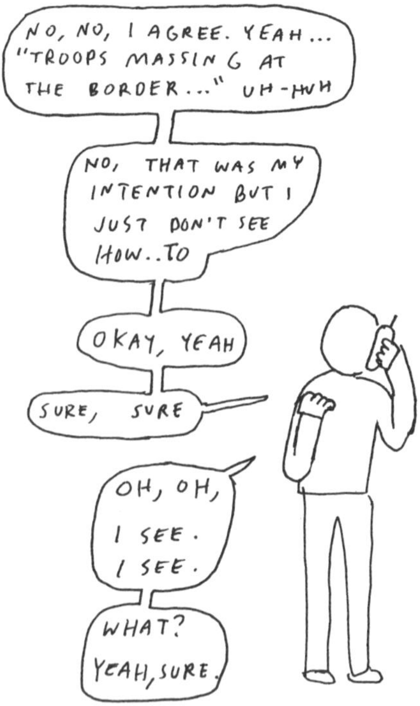
NO, NO, I AGREE. YEAH... "TROOPS MASSING AT THE BORDER..." UH-HUH
NO, THAT WAS MY INTENTION BUT I JUST DON'T SEE HOW..TO
OKAY, YEAH
SURE, SURE
OH, OH, I SEE. I SEE.
WHAT? YEAH, SURE.

SORRY.
IM ON HOLD.

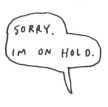

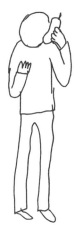

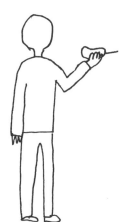

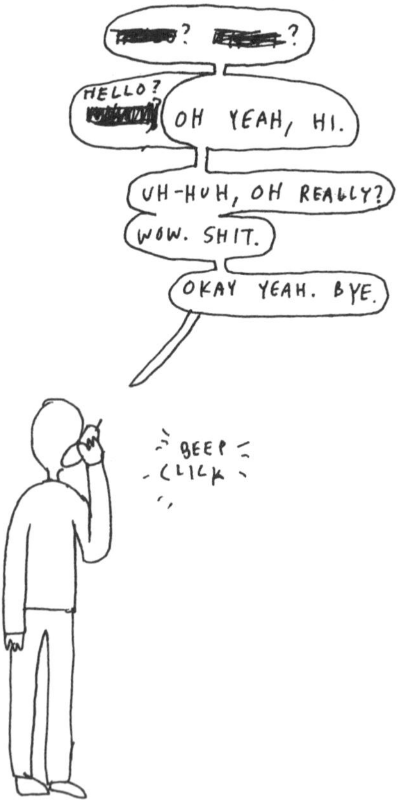
HELLO?
OH YEAH, HI.
UH-HUH, OH REALLY?
WOW. SHIT.
OKAY YEAH. BYE.
BEEP
CLICK

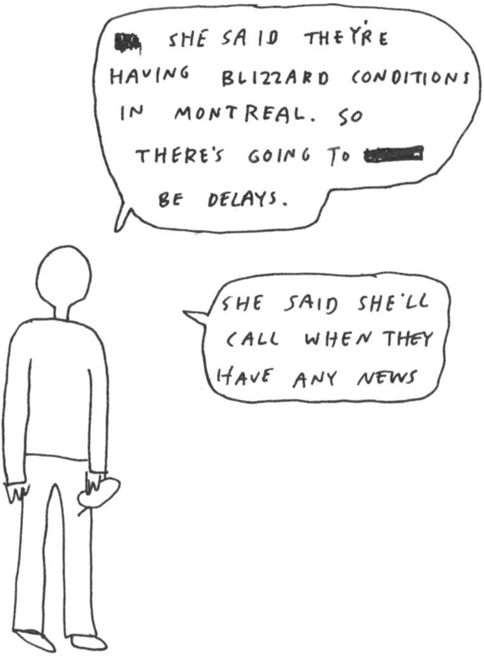
[redacted] SHE SAID THEY'RE HAVING BLIZZARD CONDITIONS IN MONTREAL. SO THERE'S GOING TO [redacted] BE DELAYS.
SHE SAID SHE'LL CALL WHEN THEY HAVE ANY NEWS

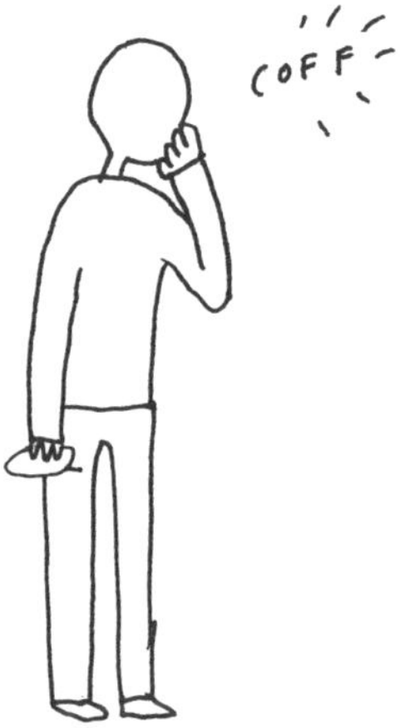
COFF

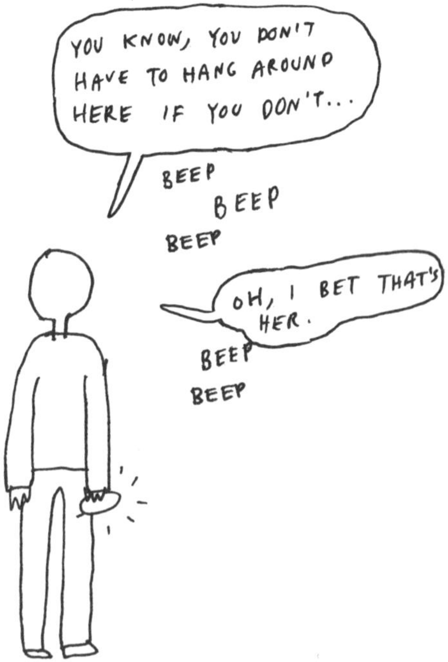
YOU KNOW, YOU DON'T HAVE TO HANG AROUND HERE IF YOU DON'T...
BEEP
BEEP
BEEP
OH, I BET THAT'S HER.
BEEP
BEEP

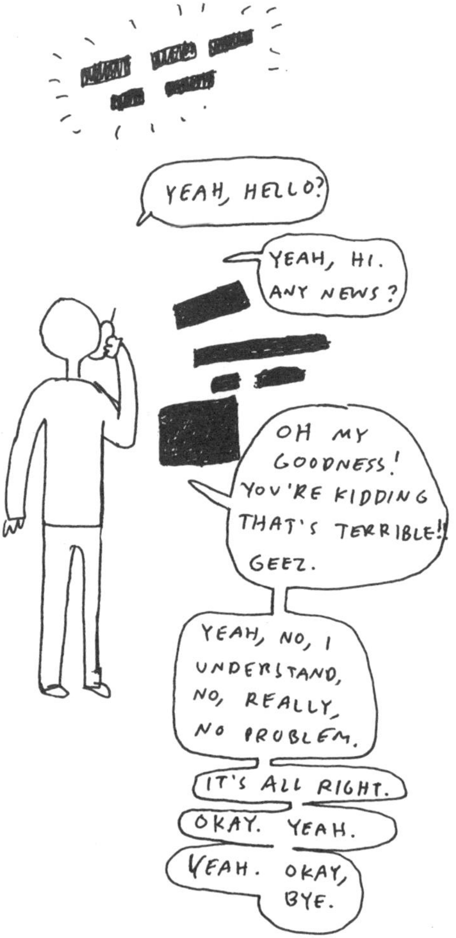
YEAH, HELLO?
YEAH, HI. ANY NEWS?
OH MY GOODNESS! YOU'RE KIDDING THAT'S TERRIBLE!! GEEZ.
YEAH, NO, I UNDERSTAND, NO, REALLY, NO PROBLEM.
IT'S ALL RIGHT.
OKAY. YEAH.
YEAH. OKAY, BYE.

WOW.
CLICK

THE WHOLE EASTERN SEABOARD HAS BEEN SHUT DOWN, APPARENTLY A MOUSE CHEWED THROUGH SOME WIRES.
THOUSANDS OF PEOPLE HAVE BEEN DISPLACED ALL THE HIGH-RISES ARE BEING EVACUATED, THE INTERNET HAS BECOME UNRELIABLE.
SO WE JUST HAVE TO WAIT.

INTERMISSION

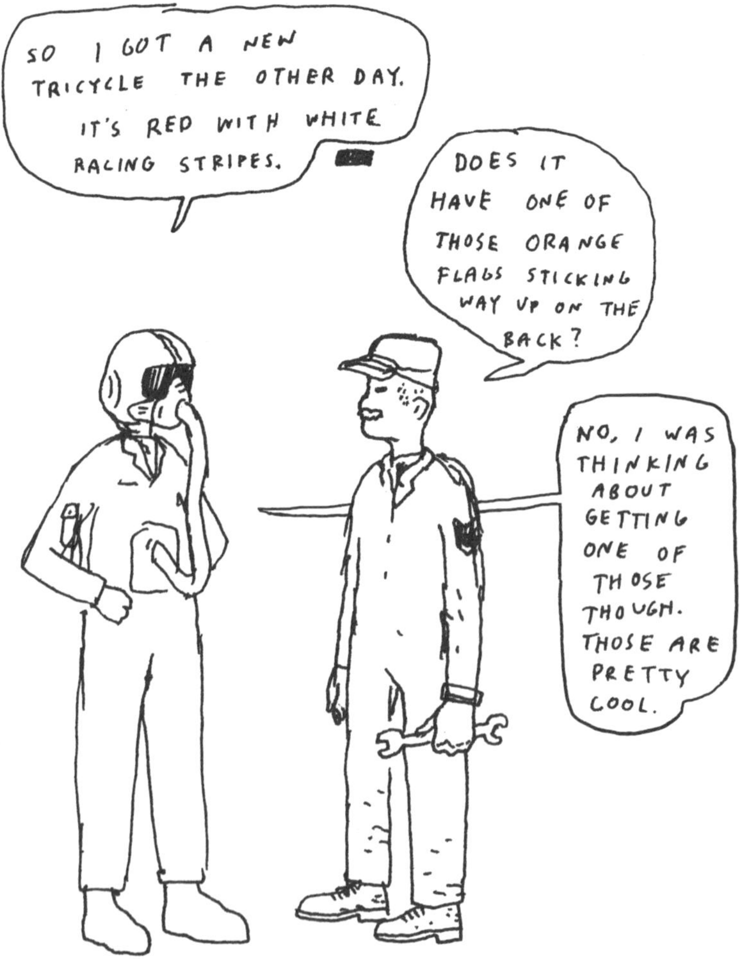
SO I GOT A NEW TRICYCLE THE OTHER DAY. IT'S RED WITH WHITE RACING STRIPES.
DOES IT HAVE ONE OF THOSE ORANGE FLAGS STICKING WAY UP ON THE BACK?
NO, I WAS THINKING ABOUT GETTING ONE OF THOSE THOUGH. THOSE ARE PRETTY COOL.

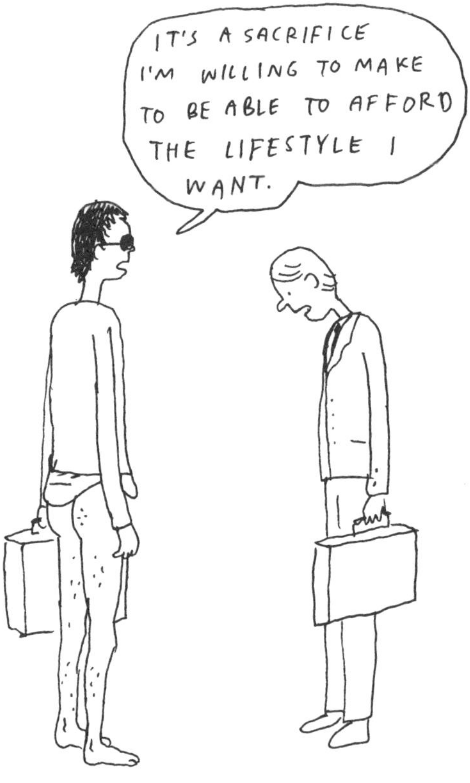
IT'S A SACRIFICE I'M WILLING TO MAKE TO BE ABLE TO AFFORD THE LIFESTYLE I WANT.

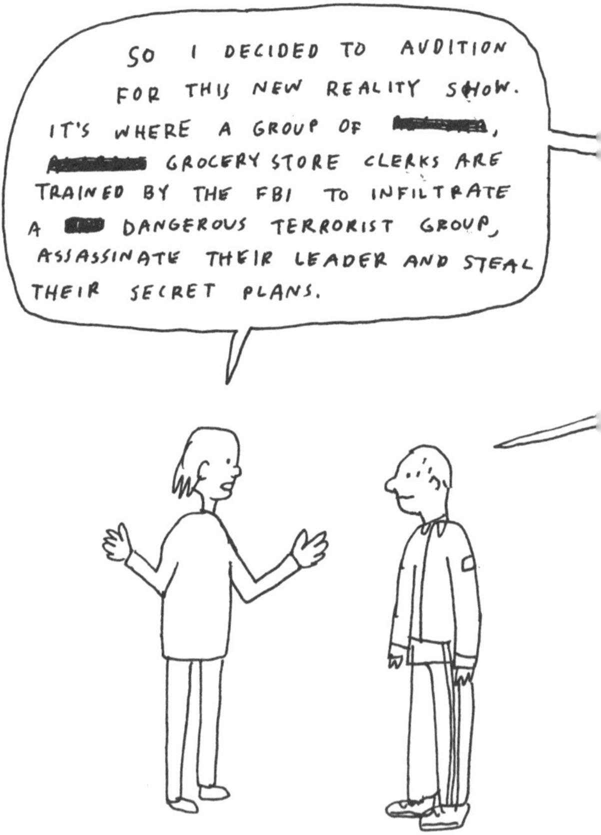
SO I DECIDED TO AUDITION FOR THIS NEW REALITY SHOW. IT'S WHERE A GROUP OF [redacted], [redacted] GROCERY STORE CLERKS ARE TRAINED BY THE FBI TO INFILTRATE A [redacted] DANGEROUS TERRORIST GROUP, ASSASSINATE THEIR LEADER AND STEAL THEIR SECRET PLANS.

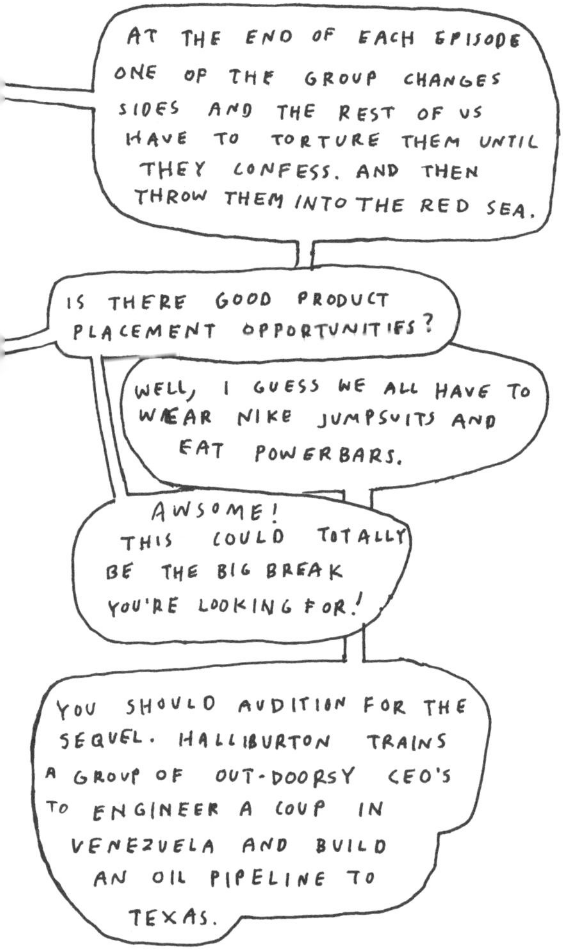
AT THE END OF EACH EPISODE ONE OF THE GROUP CHANGES SIDES AND THE REST OF US HAVE TO TORTURE THEM UNTIL THEY CONFESS. AND THEN THROW THEM INTO THE RED SEA.
IS THERE GOOD PRODUCT PLACEMENT OPPORTUNITIES?
WELL, I GUESS WE ALL HAVE TO WEAR NIKE JUMPSUITS AND EAT POWERBARS.
AWSOME! THIS COULD TOTALLY BE THE BIG BREAK YOU'RE LOOKING FOR!
YOU SHOULD AUDITION FOR THE SEQUEL. HALLIBURTON TRAINS A GROUP OF OUT-DOORSY CEO'S TO ENGINEER A COUP IN VENEZUELA AND BUILD AN OIL PIPELINE TO TEXAS.

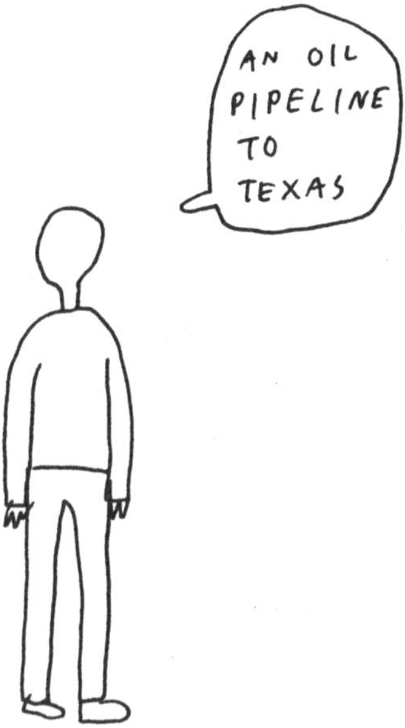
AN OIL
PIPELINE
TO
TEXAS

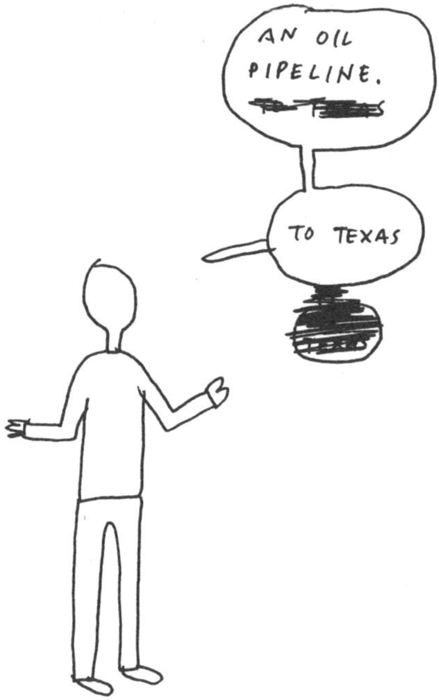
AN OIL PIPELINE.
TO TEXAS

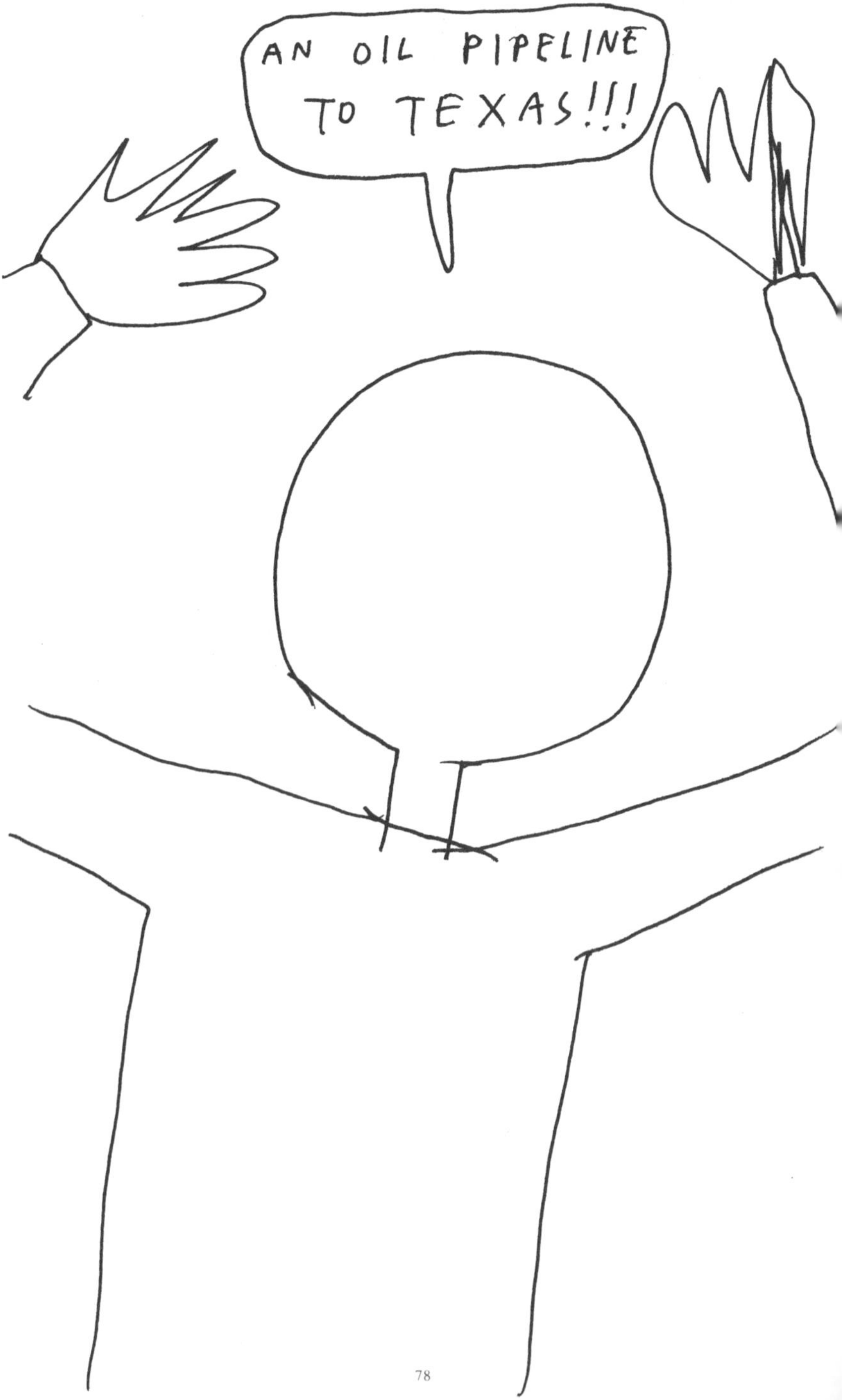
AN OIL PIPELINE TO TEXAS!!!

I MEAN...
CAN YOU BELIEVE THIS WEATHER WE'RE HAVING?

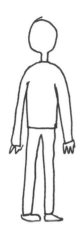

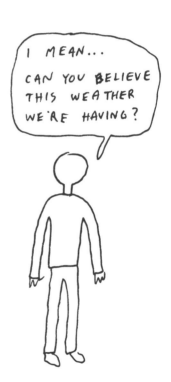

WHAT?
WHAT ARE YOU LOOKING AT? GO TO THE NEXT PAGE.

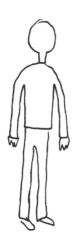

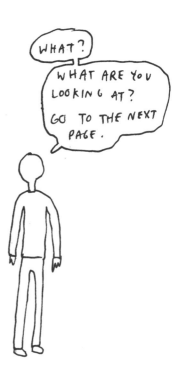

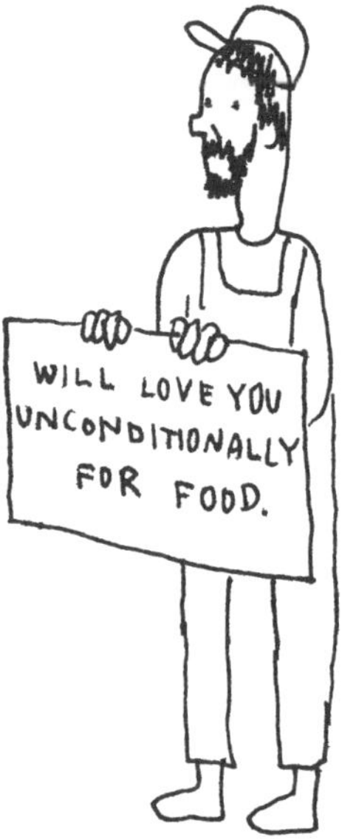
WILL LOVE YOU
UNCONDITIONALLY
FOR FOOD.

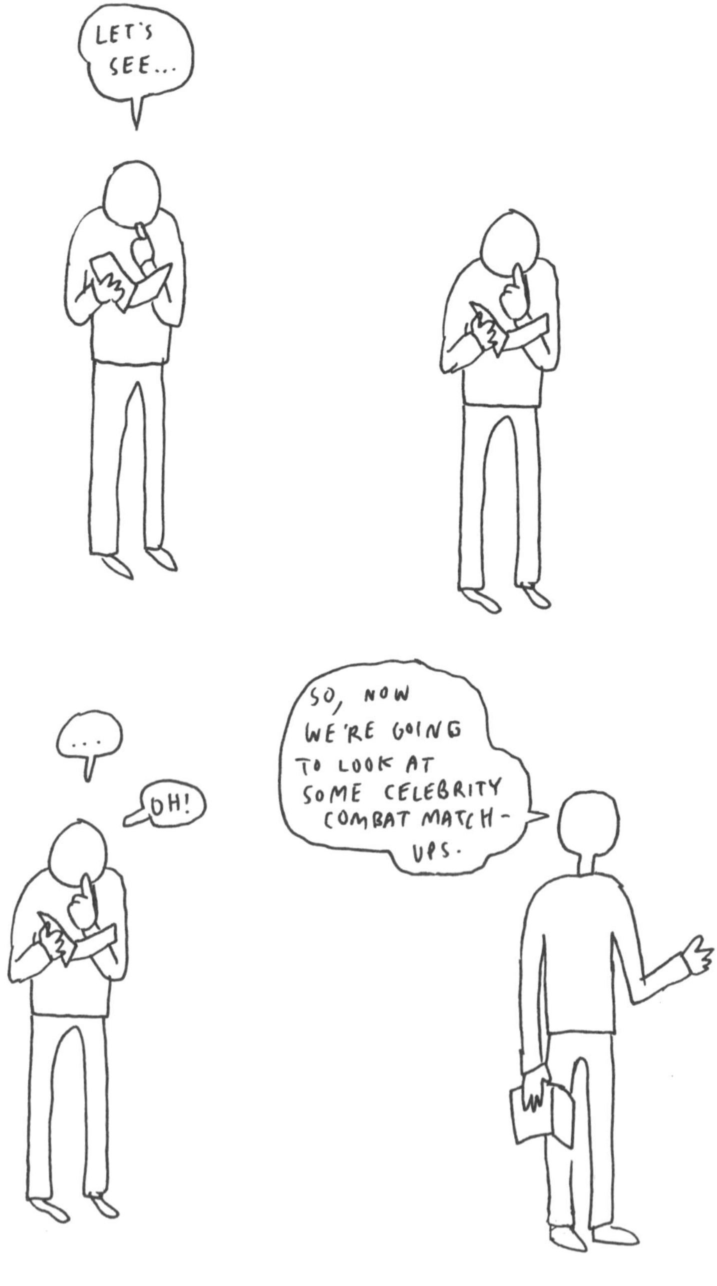
LET'S SEE...
...
OH!
SO, NOW WE'RE GOING TO LOOK AT SOME CELEBRITY COMBAT MATCH-UPS.

CELEBRITY COMBAT
MATCH-UPS

WHO DO YOU THINK
WOULD WIN IN A
BATTLE BETWEEN
JEAN PAUL SARTRE AND
MADONNA?

BRITNEY SPEARS

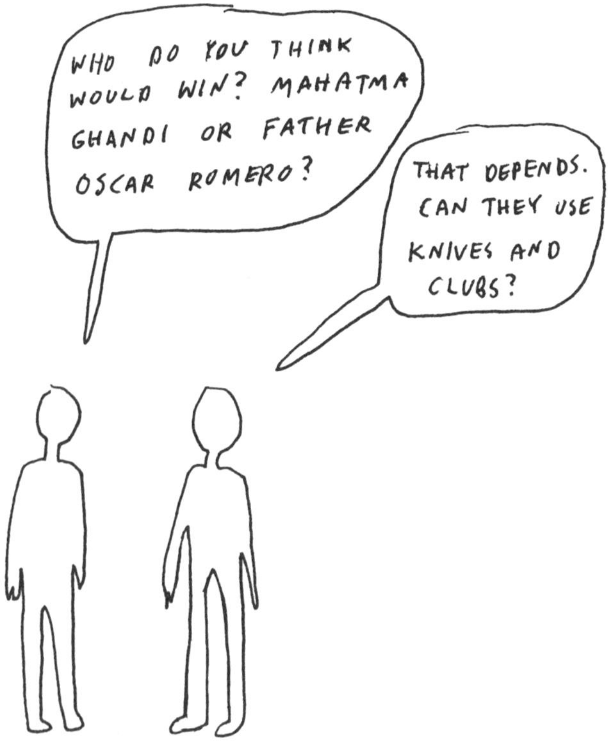
WHO DO YOU THINK WOULD WIN? MAHATMA GHANDI OR FATHER OSCAR ROMERO?
THAT DEPENDS. CAN THEY USE KNIVES AND CLUBS?

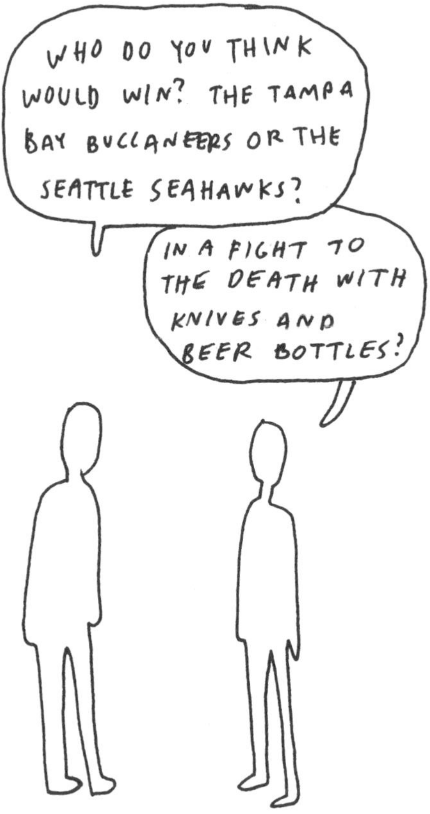
WHO DO YOU THINK WOULD WIN? THE TAMPA BAY BUCCANEERS OR THE SEATTLE SEAHAWKS?
IN A FIGHT TO THE DEATH WITH KNIVES AND BEER BOTTLES?

WHO DO YOU THINK WOULD WIN IN A BATTLE BETWEEN MARTHA STEWART AND LITTLE RICHARD... NO, WAIT... JAY-Z ?
WELL
GO OU

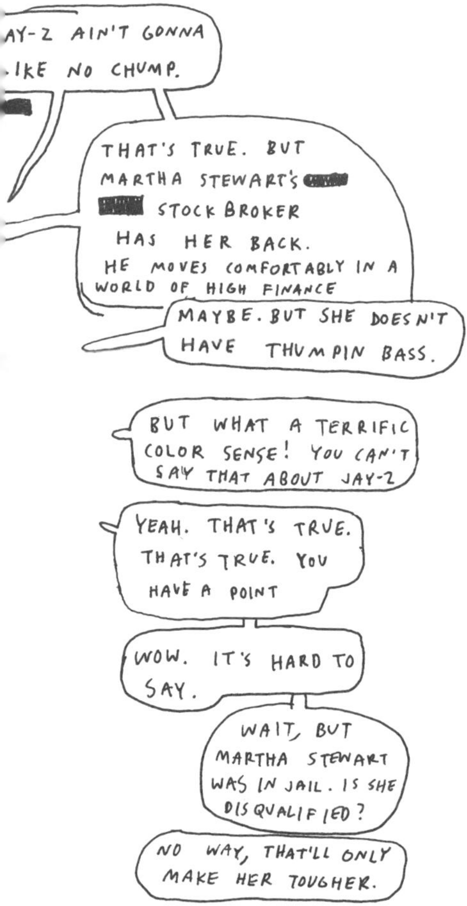

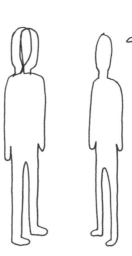

WHO WOULD WIN IN A BATTLE BETWEEN GODZILLA AND... RICHARD SIMMONS?

WELL THAT'S A TOUGH ONE. BECAUSE AT FIRST OF COURSE YOU THINK, "WELL, GODZILLA IS BIGGER AND MORE POWERFUL." BUT YOU HAVE TO RE-MEMBER ALL THE AEROBIC EXCERSIZE RICHARD SIMMONS DOES, SO HE PROBABLY HAS BETTER ENDURANCE.

ALSO, WHILE GODZILLA DOES HAVE FLAME BREATH, RICHARD SIMMONS HAS THAT HIGH, SQUEAKY, FRENETIC VOICE AND MANNER THAT CAN BE VERY DISTRACTING AND UNPREDICTABLE

I'D HAVE TO GO WITH SIMMONS.

YEAH, BUT GODZILLA CAN SURVIVE UNDER WATER.

HM. WELL, THAT'S TRUE. THAT'S TRUE.

MAYBE IT'S A TIE, AND IT GOES TO SUDDEN DEATH OVERTIME. IN WHICH CASE I'D HAVE TO GO WITH GODZILLA.

I HAVE TO AGREE.

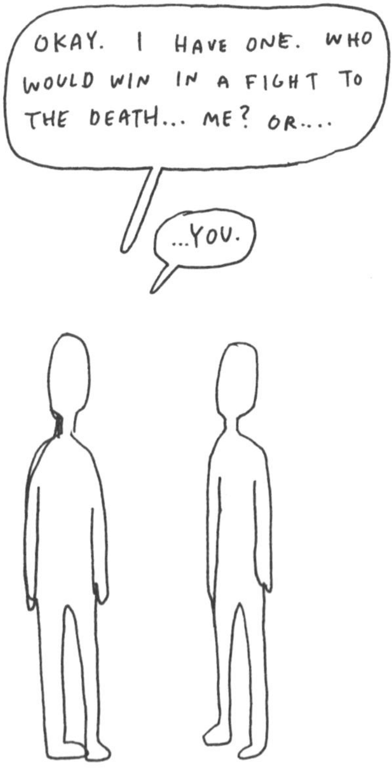
OKAY. I HAVE ONE. WHO WOULD WIN IN A FIGHT TO THE DEATH... ME? OR....
...YOU.

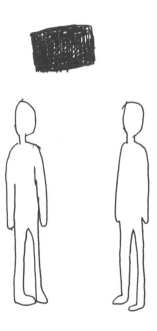

WHO DO YOU THINK WOULD WIN IN A FIGHT? GOD? OR SATAN?
[redacted] [redacted]

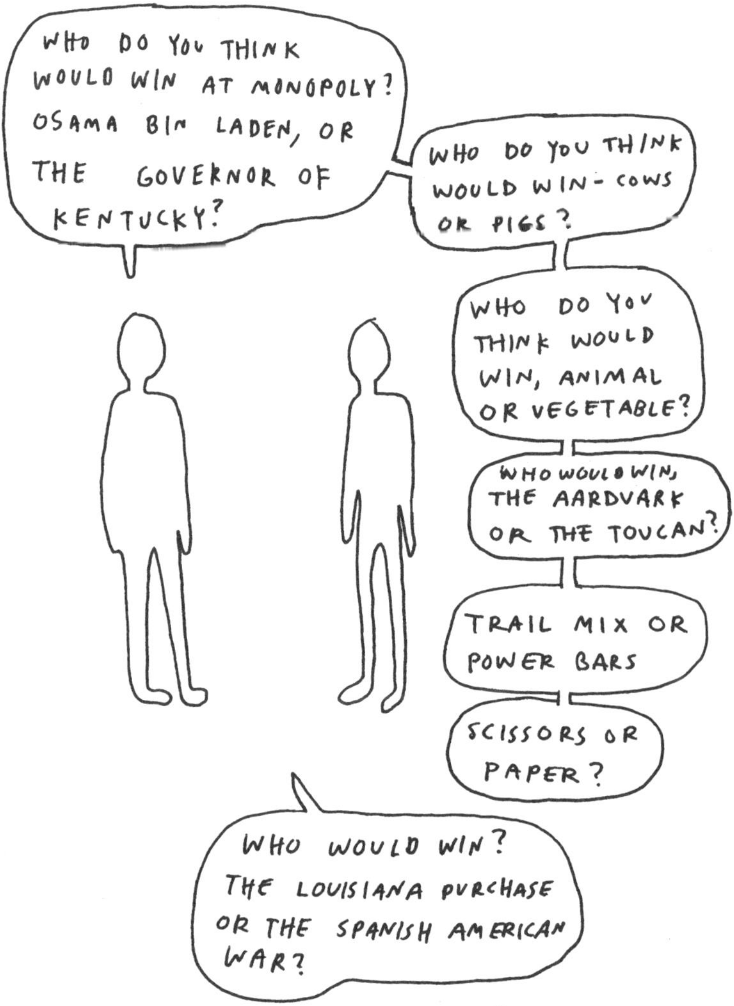
WHO DO YOU THINK WOULD WIN AT MONOPOLY? OSAMA BIN LADEN, OR THE GOVERNOR OF KENTUCKY?
WHO DO YOU THINK WOULD WIN - COWS OR PIGS?
WHO DO YOU THINK WOULD WIN, ANIMAL OR VEGETABLE?
WHO WOULD WIN, THE AARDVARK OR THE TOUCAN?
TRAIL MIX OR POWER BARS
SCISSORS OR PAPER?
WHO WOULD WIN? THE LOUISIANA PURCHASE OR THE SPANISH AMERICAN WAR?

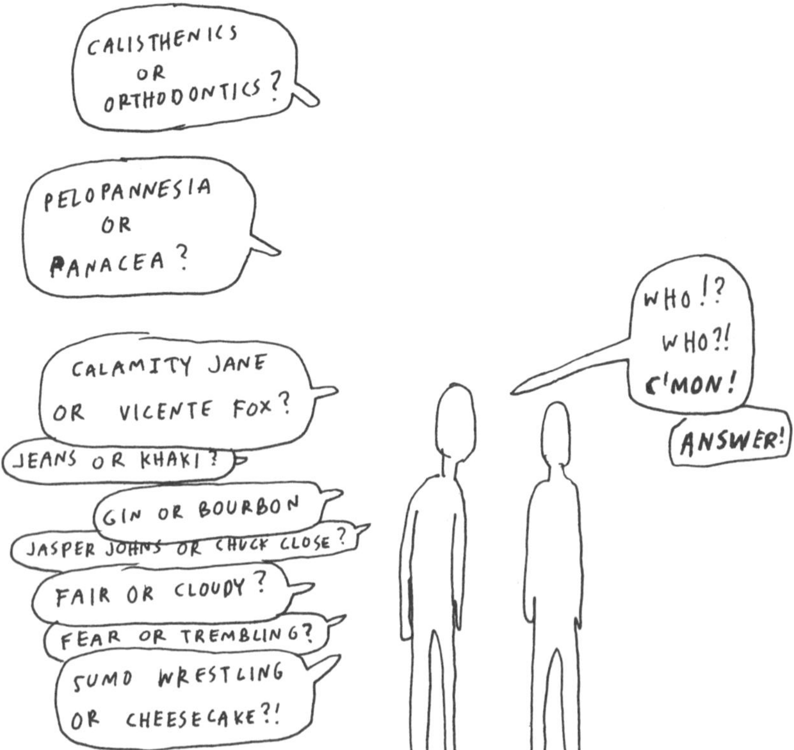
CALISTHENICS OR ORTHODONTICS?
PELOPANNESIA OR PANACEA?
CALAMITY JANE OR VICENTE FOX?
JEANS OR KHAKI?
GIN OR BOURBON
JASPER JOHNS OR CHUCK CLOSE?
FAIR OR CLOUDY?
FEAR OR TREMBLING?
SUMO WRESTLING OR CHEESECAKE?!
WHO!? WHO?! C'MON!
ANSWER!

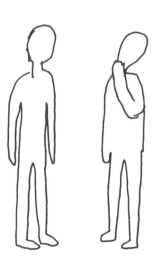

AHEM,
OK:
BUCCANEERS, BIN LADEN, PIGS, ANIMALS, AARDVARK POWER BARS, SCISSORS, SPANISH AMERICAN WAR CALISTHENICS, PANACEA CALAMITY JANE, JEANS, GIN, JOHNS, FAIR, FEAR, CHEESECAKE.

ALRIGHT.
ARE YOU WILLING TO PUT MONEY ON THAT?

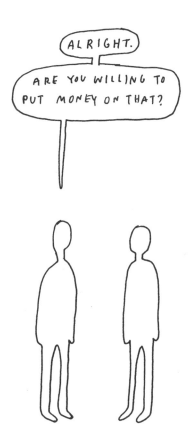

SHP
SHP
SHP
SHP
SHP

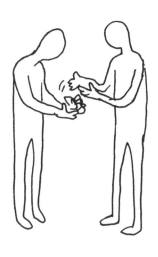

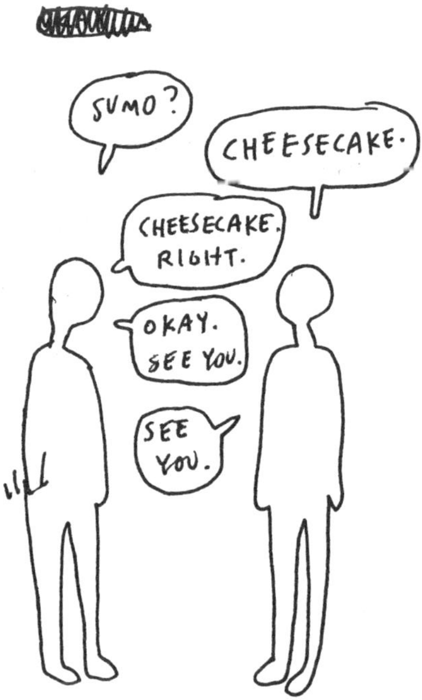
SUMO?
CHEESECAKE.
CHEESECAKE. RIGHT.
OKAY. SEE YOU.
SEE YOU.

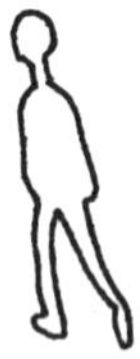

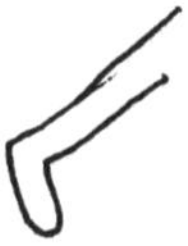

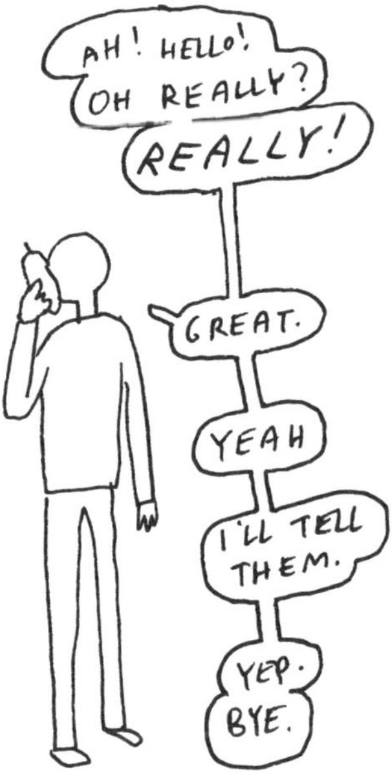
AH! HELLO!
OH REALLY?
REALLY!
GREAT.
YEAH
I'LL TELL THEM.
YEP.
BYE.

THEY FOUND THE MOUSE, SO APPARENTLY THE SITUATION OUT EAST IS GETTING RESOLVED AND WE CAN GET BACK TO THE STORY. FIRST, THOUGH WE'RE GOING TO RUN A COUPLE OF BLANK PAGES TO SORT OF, YOU KNOW, CLEANSE THE NARRATIVE PALATE OR WHATEVER.
READY? HERE WE GO.
CLICK, BEEP

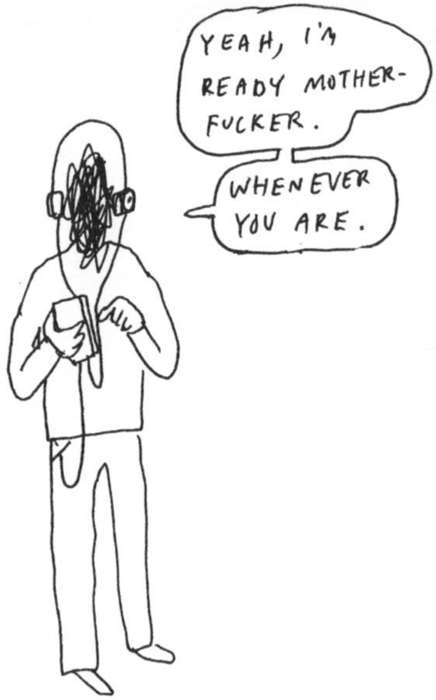
YEAH, I'M READY MOTHER-FUCKER.
WHENEVER YOU ARE.

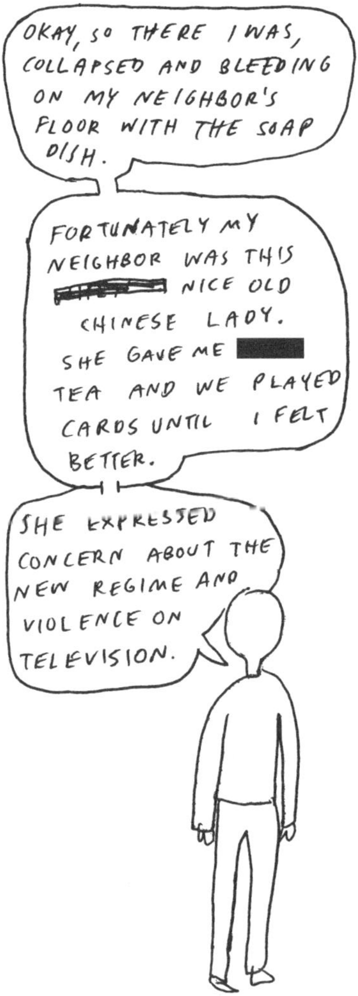

I WORKED FOR HER FOR A WHILE, TENDING HER GARDEN, MAKING HER BREAKFAST, TAKING DICTATION FOR LETTERS SHE'D WRITE TO HER GRANDCHILDREN.

SOMETIMES I WOULD DRIVE HER FRIENDS TO DOCTORS' APPOINTMENTS OR DO THEIR SHOPPING.

SHE PUT ME IN
HER WILL, I BECAME
VERY GOOD AT
BRIDGE. I WAS
VERY HAPPY.

FOR A WHILE I THOUGHT
MY SEARCH WAS OVER.

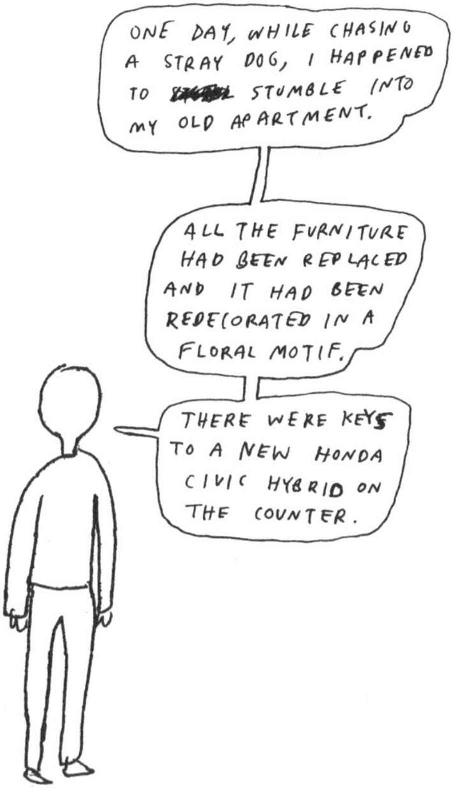
ONE DAY, WHILE CHASING A STRAY DOG, I HAPPENED TO STUMBLE INTO MY OLD APARTMENT.
ALL THE FURNITURE HAD BEEN REPLACED AND IT HAD BEEN REDECORATED IN A FLORAL MOTIF.
THERE WERE KEYS TO A NEW HONDA CIVIC HYBRID ON THE COUNTER.

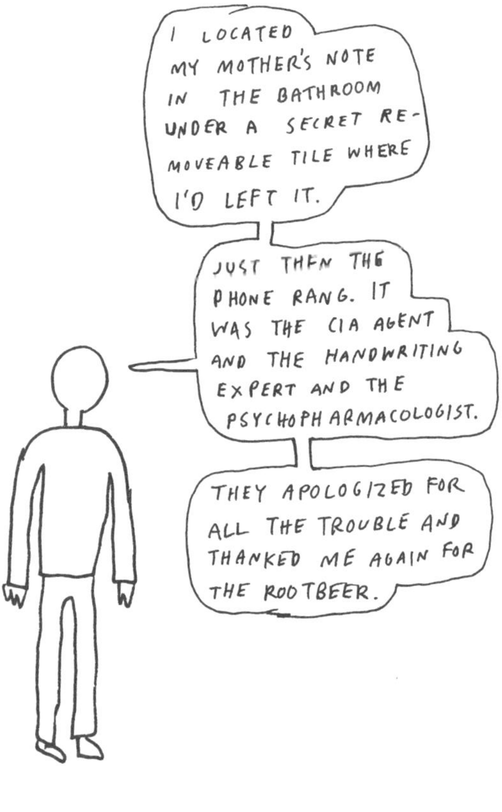
I LOCATED MY MOTHER'S NOTE IN THE BATHROOM UNDER A SECRET RE-MOVEABLE TILE WHERE I'D LEFT IT.
JUST THEN THE PHONE RANG. IT WAS THE CIA AGENT AND THE HANDWRITING EXPERT AND THE PSYCHOPHARMACOLOGIST.
THEY APOLOGIZED FOR ALL THE TROUBLE AND THANKED ME AGAIN FOR THE ROOTBEER.

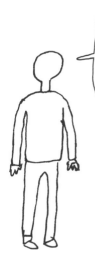

I DIDN'T REALLY UNDERSTAND WHAT THEY MEANT, BUT I WANTED TO BE POLITE, SO I ~~~~~~ WAS GOING TO SAY "HEY, NO PROBLEM" BUT JUST THEN THE ENTIRE BUILDING EXPLODED INTO FLAME AND I BLACKED OUT.

THE LAST THING I REMEMBER IS BEING STUFFED IN A SACK AND CHLOROPHORMED.

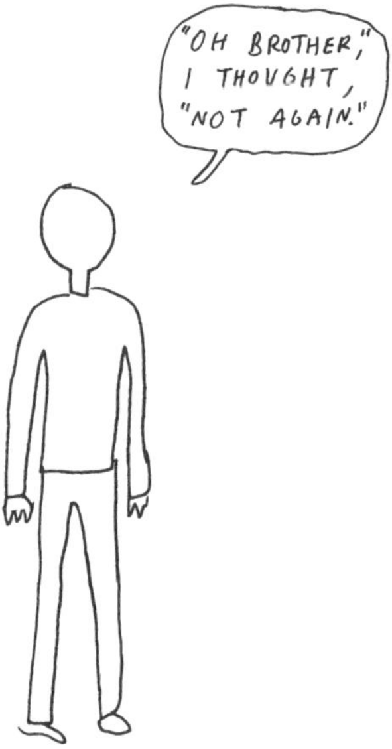
"OH BROTHER," I THOUGHT, "NOT AGAIN."

WHEN I WOKE UP I WAS LOCKED IN THE TRUNK OF A NEW HONDA CIVIC, BARRELLING DOWN STEEP MOUNTAIN ROADS AT HIGH SPEEDS. [redacted] I WAS FEELING AROUND FOR MY MOTHER'S NOTE WHEN THE CAR LOST CONTROL AND CAREENED OFF THE SIDE OF THE MOUNTAIN.

LUCKILY I WAS THROWN FREE AND LANDED IN A BUSH THAT WAS CLINGING TO THE SIDE OF A CLIFF. I SURVIVED THERE FOR THREE DAYS LIVING ON BUGS AND LEAVES.

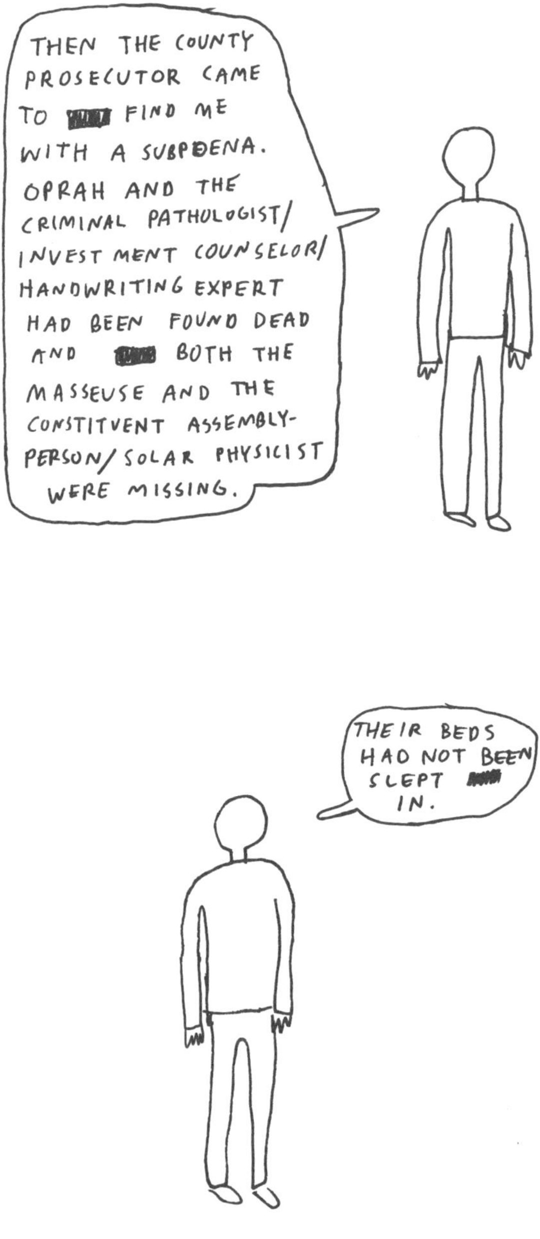
THEN THE COUNTY PROSECUTOR CAME TO [redacted] FIND ME WITH A SUBPOENA. OPRAH AND THE CRIMINAL PATHOLOGIST/ INVESTMENT COUNSELOR/ HANDWRITING EXPERT HAD BEEN FOUND DEAD AND [redacted] BOTH THE MASSEUSE AND THE CONSTITUENT ASSEMBLY-PERSON/ SOLAR PHYSICIST WERE MISSING.
THEIR BEDS HAD NOT BEEN SLEPT [redacted] IN.

THE PRESIDENT HAD BEEN KIDNAPPED, THE FIRST LADY HAD SEIZED CONTROL OF THE MILITARY, TEXAS HAD SECEDED.

ON THE WAY BACK TO THE CITY WE WERE ATTACKED BY GANGS OF MASKED CHRISTIAN FUNDAMENTALISTS.

WHEN WE GOT BACK THE PROSECUTER THREATENED ME WITH EXECUTION AND LARGE FINES, BUT SAID THAT IF I COOPERATED I COULD GO INTO THE WITNESS PROTECTION PROGRAM.

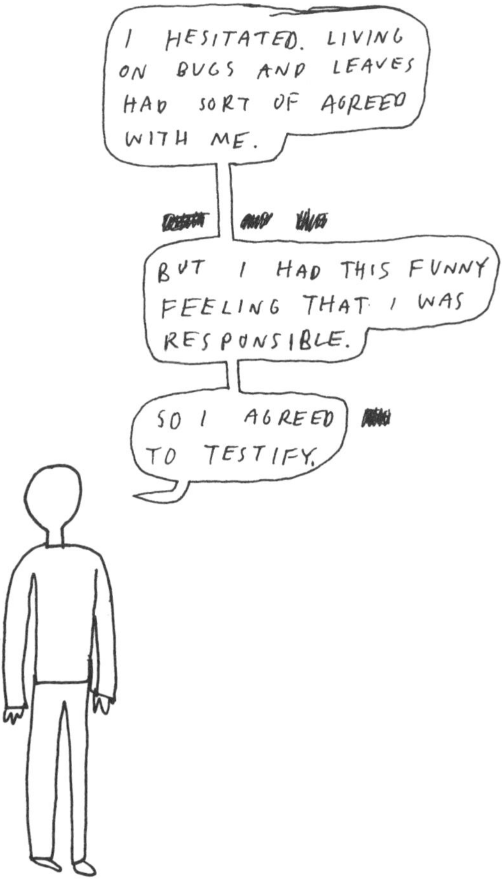
I HESITATED. LIVING ON BUGS AND LEAVES HAD SORT OF AGREED WITH ME.
BUT I HAD THIS FUNNY FEELING THAT I WAS RESPONSIBLE.
SO I AGREED TO TESTIFY.

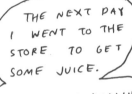

THE NEXT DAY I WENT TO THE STORE TO GET SOME JUICE.

BOMBS WERE FALLING. THE SKY WAS TURNING BLACK. BUILDINGS WERE BLOWING APART AND GETTING FLATTENED. HUGE CROWDS OF PEOPLE WERE RUNNING TO ESCAPE. THERE WERE HELICOPTERS EVERYWHERE.

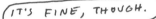

IT'S FINE, THOUGH.

THE WITNESS PROTECTION PROGRAM FEELS LIKE A GOOD FIT. I FEEL LIKE I'M GETTING A FRESH START. I'VE BEEN LOOKING THROUGH THEIR LIST OF NEW NAMES.

I'M OPTIMISTIC THAT I'LL FIND MYSELF SOON.

THE END.

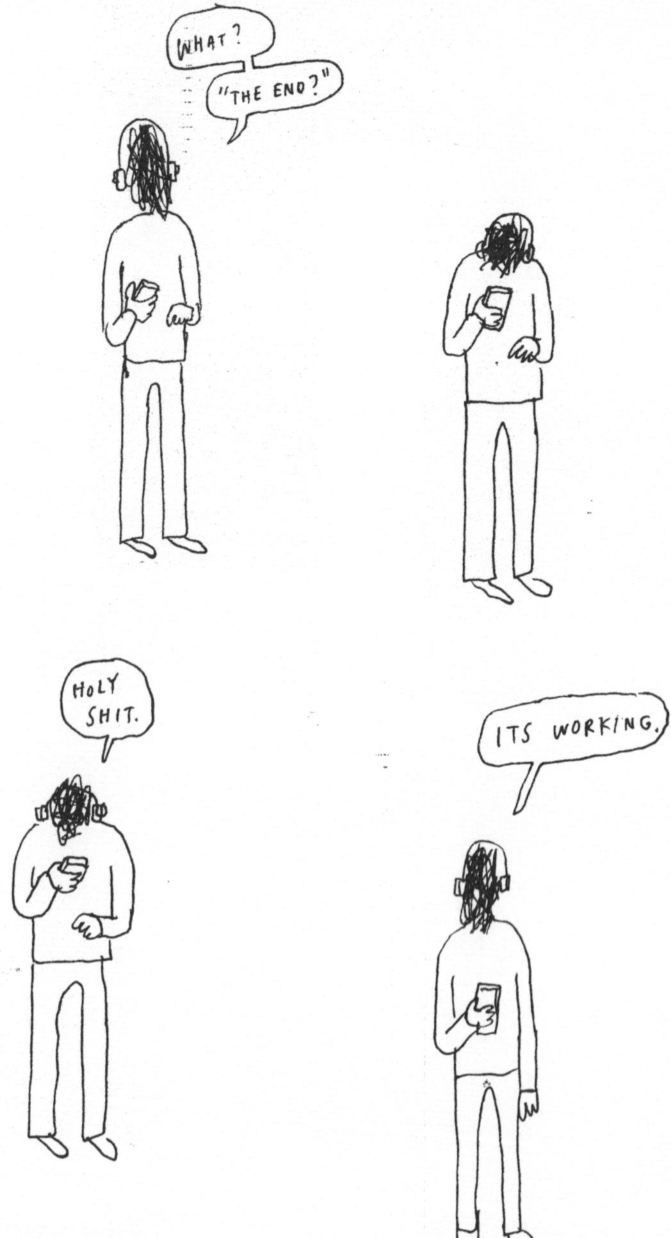
WHAT?
"THE END?"
HOLY SHIT.
ITS WORKING.

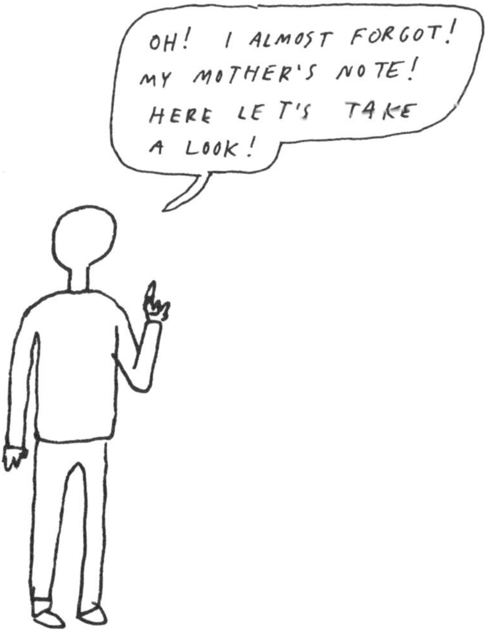
OH! I ALMOST FORGOT! MY MOTHER'S NOTE! HERE LET'S TAKE A LOOK!

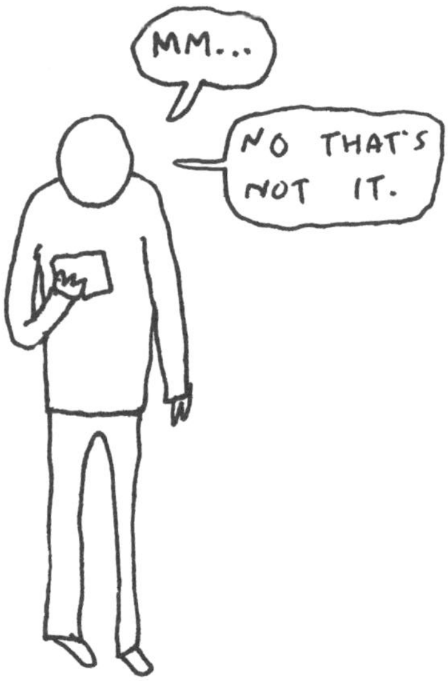
MM...
NO THAT'S NOT IT.

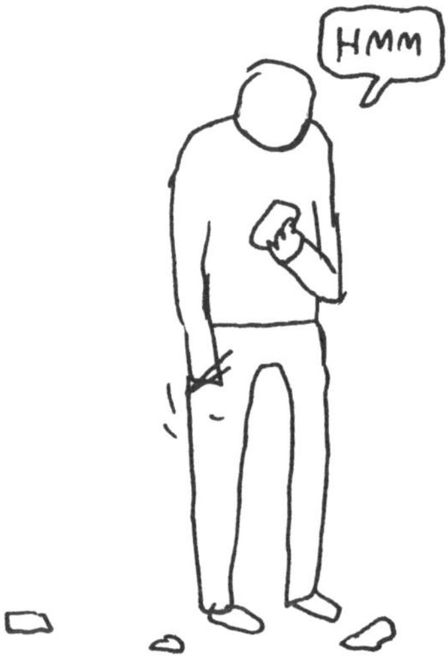
HMM

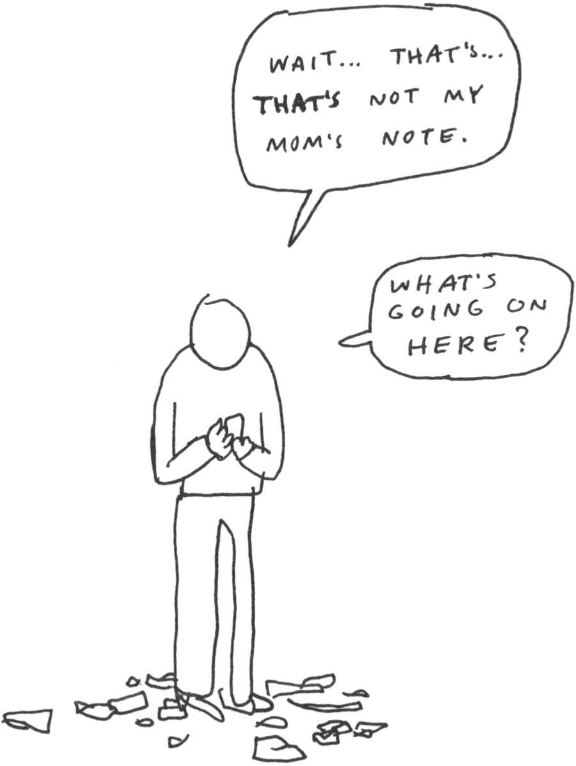
WAIT... THAT'S... THAT'S NOT MY MOM'S NOTE.
WHAT'S GOING ON HERE?

RUSTLE
RUSTLE

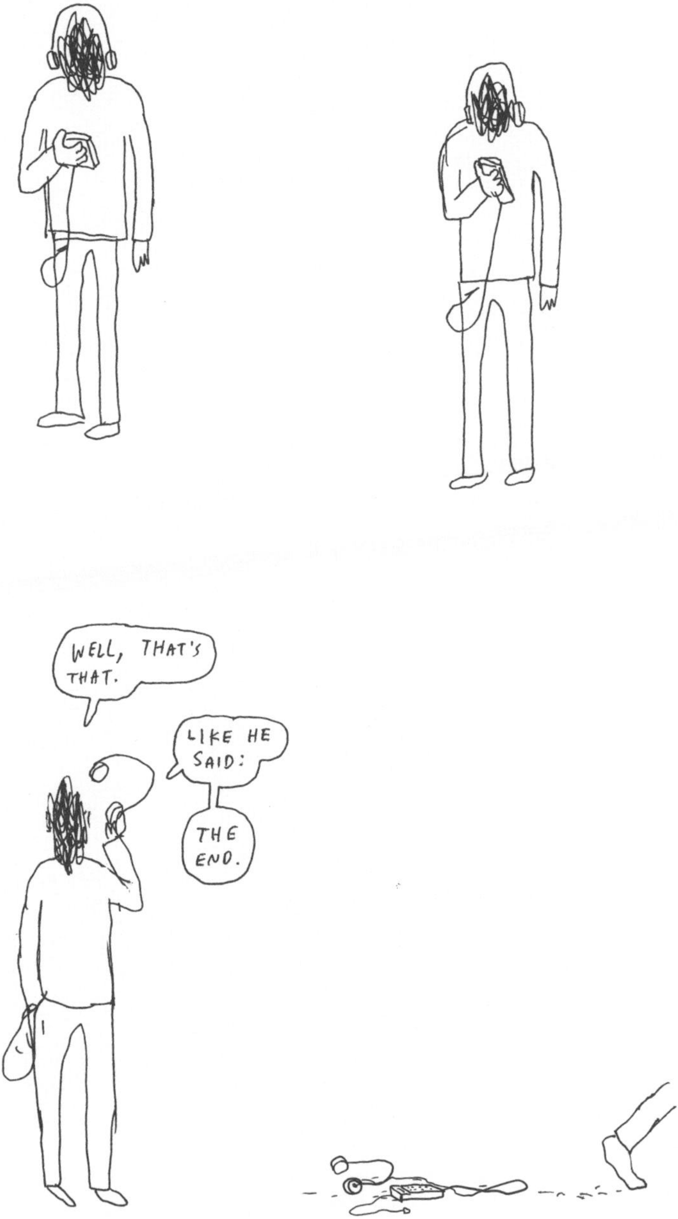
WELL, THAT'S THAT.
LIKE HE SAID:
THE END.

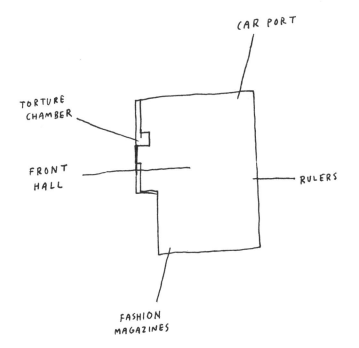

CAR PORT

TORTURE
CHAMBER

FRONT
HALL

RULERS

FASHION
MAGAZINES

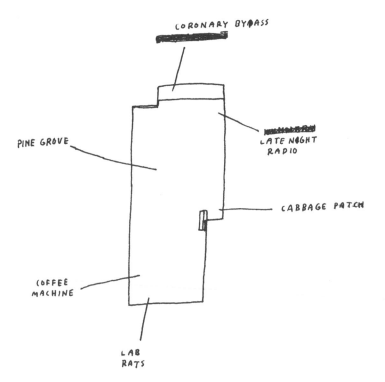

CORONARY BYPASS

LATE NIGHT
RADIO

PINE GROVE

CABBAGE PATCH

COFFEE
MACHINE

LAB
RATS

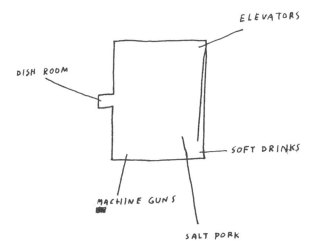

ELEVATORS

DISH ROOM

SOFT DRINKS

MACHINE GUNS

SALT PORK

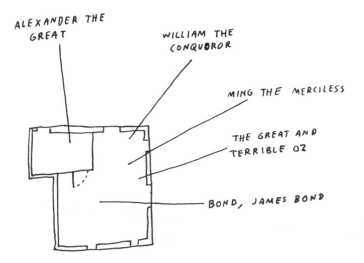

ALEXANDER THE
GREAT

WILLIAM THE
CONQUEROR

MING THE MERCILESS

THE GREAT AND
TERRIBLE OZ

BOND, JAMES BOND

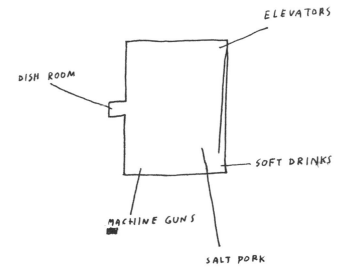

ELEVATORS

DISH ROOM

SOFT DRINKS

MACHINE GUNS

SALT PORK

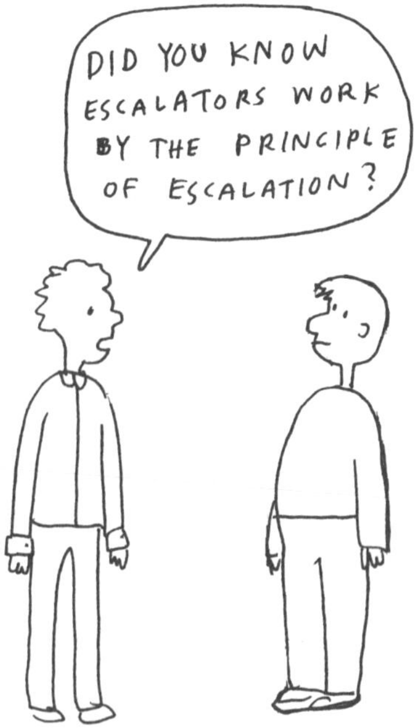
DID YOU KNOW ESCALATORS WORK BY THE PRINCIPLE OF ESCALATION?

ESCHATOLOGY ?
NO. ESCALATION
SCATALOGICAL ?
NO. ESCALATION
SCATTERGORIES ?
NO, ESCALATION
PATAGONIA ?
NO.....YES PATAGONIA.
REALLY? ESCALATORS ?

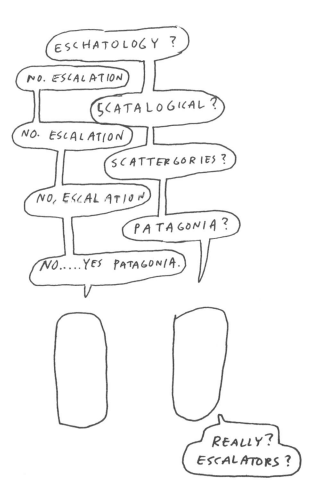

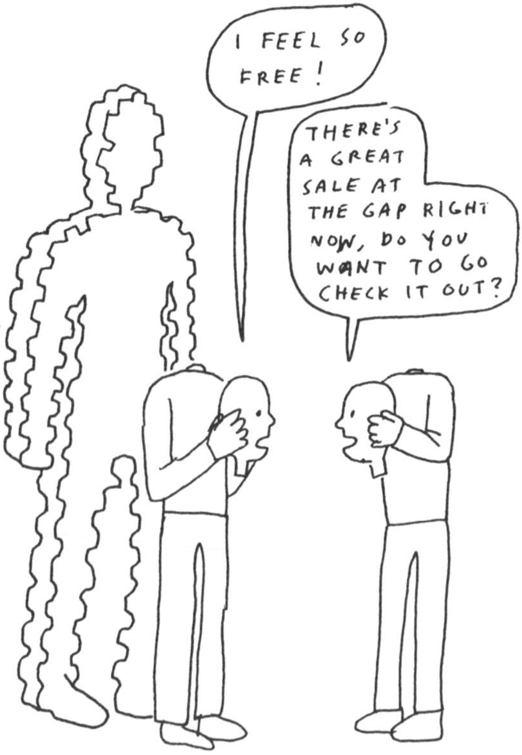
I FEEL SO FREE!
THERE'S A GREAT SALE AT THE GAP RIGHT NOW, DO YOU WANT TO GO CHECK IT OUT?

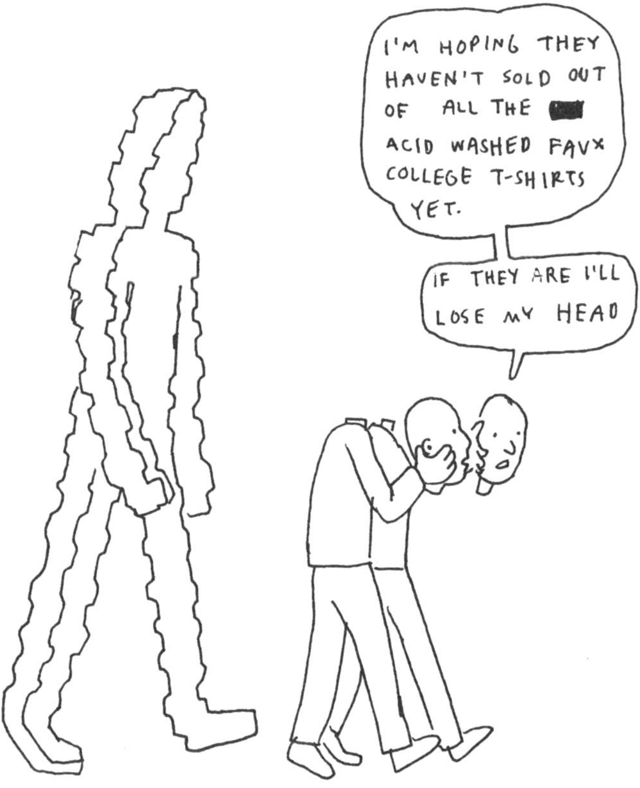
I'M HOPING THEY HAVEN'T SOLD OUT OF ALL THE [redacted] ACID WASHED FAUX COLLEGE T-SHIRTS YET.
IF THEY ARE I'LL LOSE MY HEAD

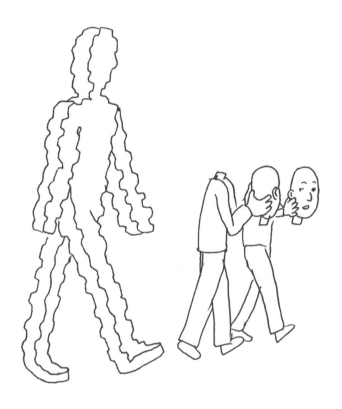

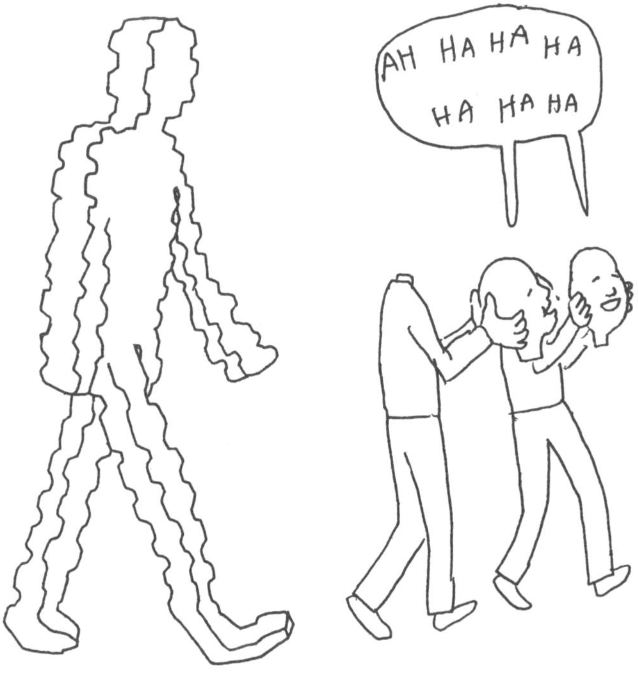
AH HA HA HA
HA HA HA

THE GA
DO YOU HAVE THIS IN A MEDIUM?
I'M GOING TO BUY ONE OF EVERYTHING AND JUST WAIT TIL IT BECOMES KITSCHY AND SELL IT ON E-BAY

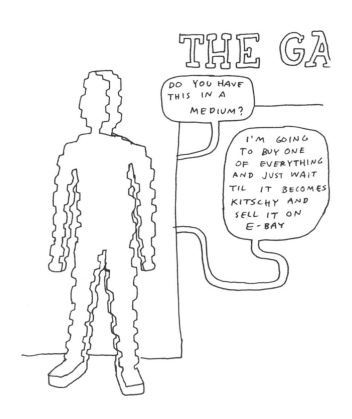

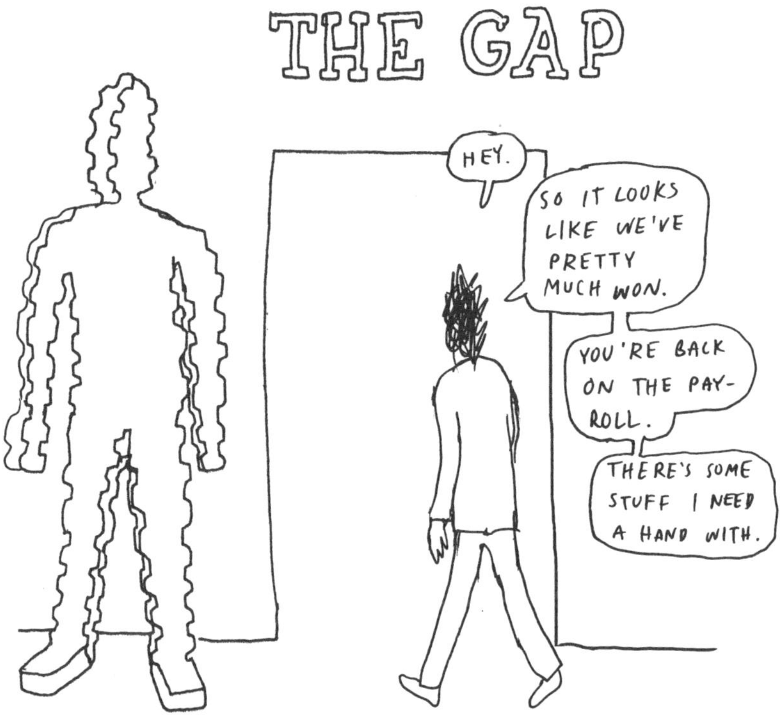
THE GAP
HEY.
SO IT LOOKS LIKE WE'VE PRETTY MUCH WON.
YOU'RE BACK ON THE PAY-ROLL.
THERE'S SOME STUFF I NEED A HAND WITH.

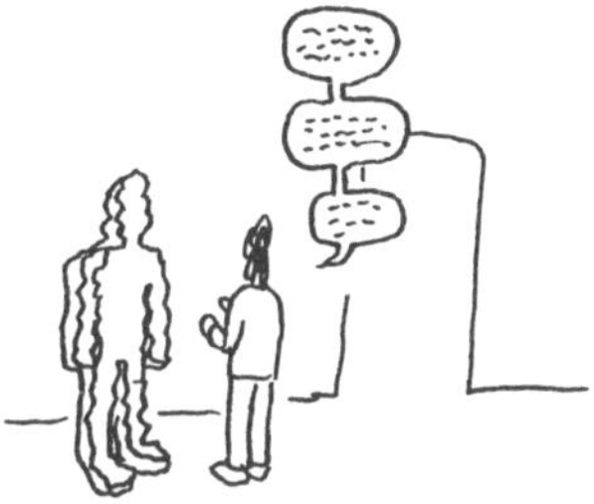

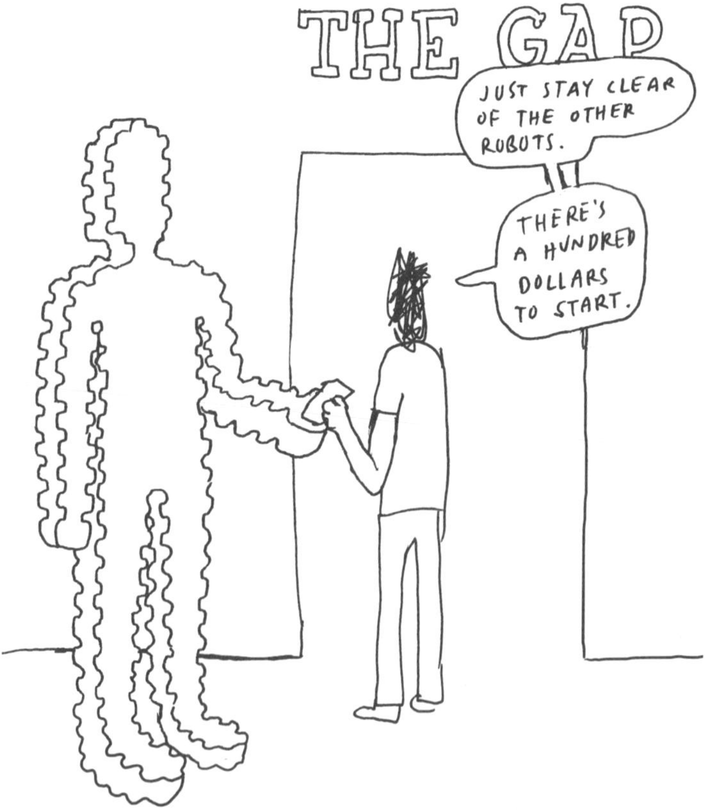
THE GAP
JUST STAY CLEAR OF THE OTHER ROBOTS.
THERE'S A HUNDRED DOLLARS TO START.

THE GAP

RESPONDING TO THE CRITICS

WE ARE GOING TO PAUSE IN OUR NARRATIVE, NOW, TO RESPOND TO SOME OF THE CRITICS WRITING ABOUT THE LAST ISSUE. THAT WOULD BE MONOLOGUES FOR THE QUOTE UN QUOTE COMING PLAGUE.

GO AHEAD.

..."THIS COMIC IS NOT FUNNY..."

WELL THAT'S EASY. FUCK YOU. I DON'T THINK YOU ARE FUNNY EITHER.

NEXT.

"...THIS BOOK IS AWESOME, BUT NO ONE WILL BUY IT BECAUSE THE DRAWING IS CRUDE AND OFF-PUTTING AT FIRST."
CRUDE?! GIVE ME A BREAK! IT TOOK ME ALL MY LIFE TO LEARN TO DRAW LIKE THIS! IT'S LIKE PICASSO. TO GET TO THE POINT WHERE HE COULD DRAW LIKE A COMPLETE RETARD HE FIRST HAD TO PAINT ALL THOSE FAGGY PINK CIRCUS PERFORMERS.

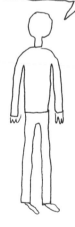

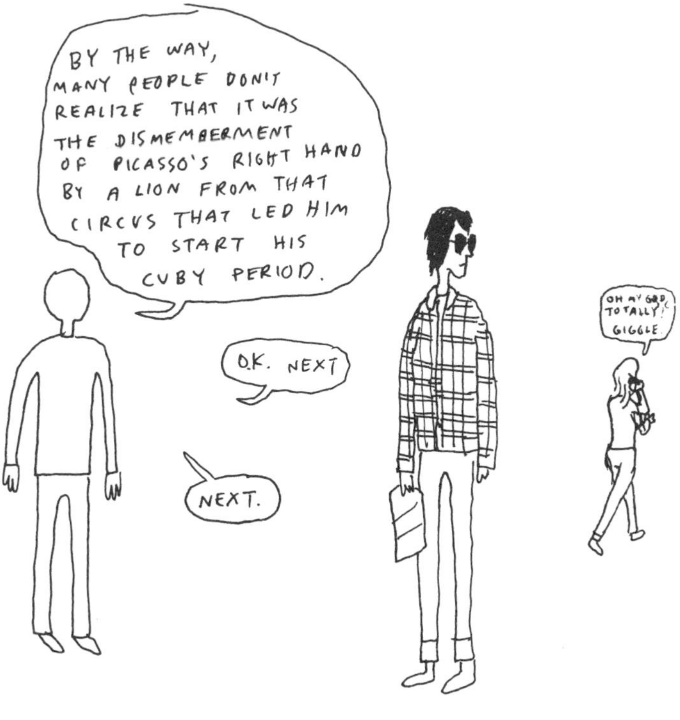
BY THE WAY, MANY PEOPLE DON'T REALIZE THAT IT WAS THE DISMEMBERMENT OF PICASSO'S RIGHT HAND BY A LION FROM THAT CIRCUS THAT LED HIM TO START HIS CUBY PERIOD.
OH MY GOD, TOTALLY! GIGGLE.
O.K. NEXT
NEXT.

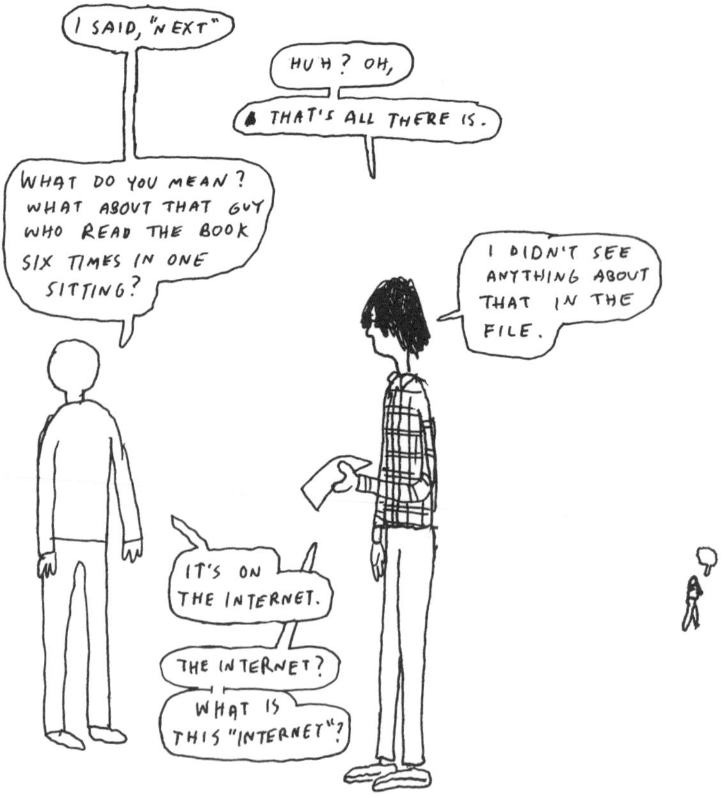
I SAID, "NEXT"
HUH? OH,
THAT'S ALL THERE IS.
WHAT DO YOU MEAN? WHAT ABOUT THAT GUY WHO READ THE BOOK SIX TIMES IN ONE SITTING?
I DIDN'T SEE ANYTHING ABOUT THAT IN THE FILE.
IT'S ON THE INTERNET.
THE INTERNET?
WHAT IS THIS "INTERNET"?

WHAT? DON'T YOU KNOW? IT'S... IT'S...
HMM, YES, WHAT IS THE INTERNET EXACTLY?
I'M JUST KIDDING, I'LL GO LOOK.

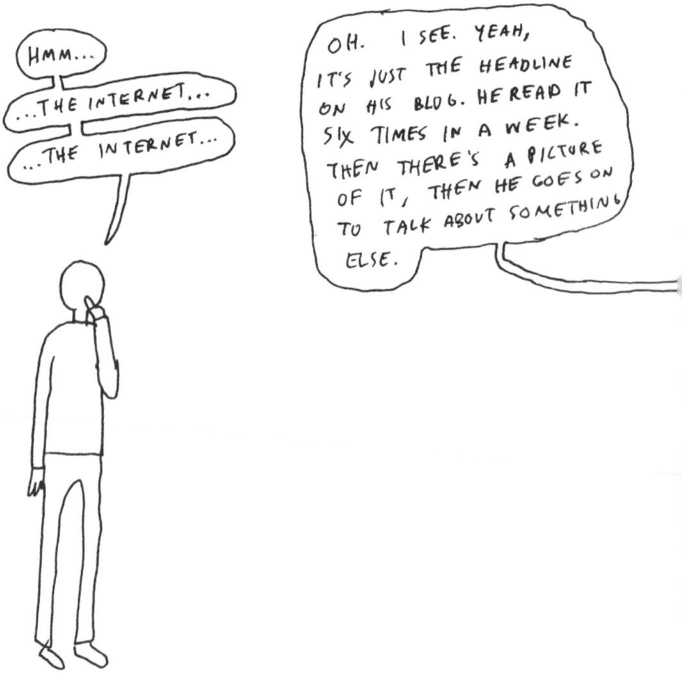
HMM...
...THE INTERNET...
...THE INTERNET...
OH. I SEE. YEAH, IT'S JUST THE HEADLINE ON HIS BLOG. HE READ IT SIX TIMES IN A WEEK. THEN THERE'S A PICTURE OF IT, THEN HE GOES ON TO TALK ABOUT SOMETHING ELSE.

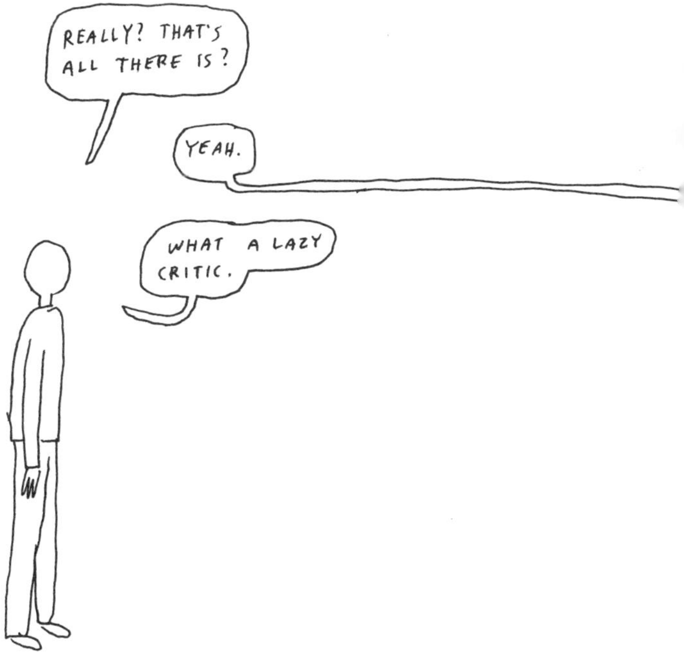
REALLY? THAT'S ALL THERE IS?
YEAH.
WHAT A LAZY CRITIC.

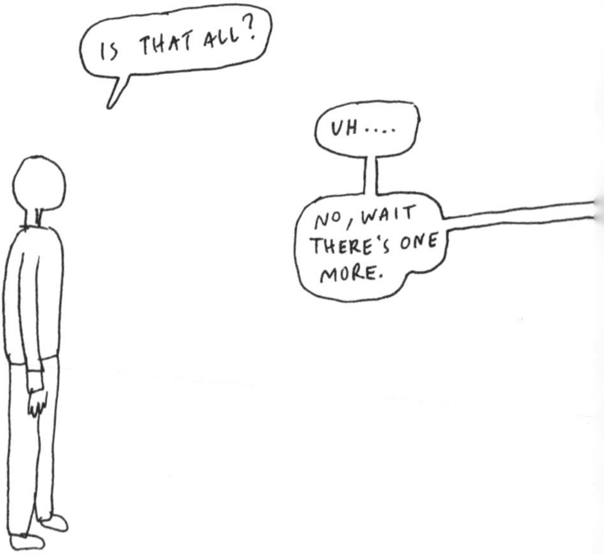
IS THAT ALL?
UH....
NO, WAIT THERE'S ONE MORE.

LET'S SEE... "ANDRE BRETON MEETS CHARLES SCHULZ"... "A DEPARTURE IN STYLE"... "DIFFICULT TO UNDERSTAND..." "FUNNY"... "POIGNANT"... "ACHIEVES A WONDROUS THING"... AND.... LET'S SEE... OH, "RANDOM AND INCOHERENT."
THAT'S IT.

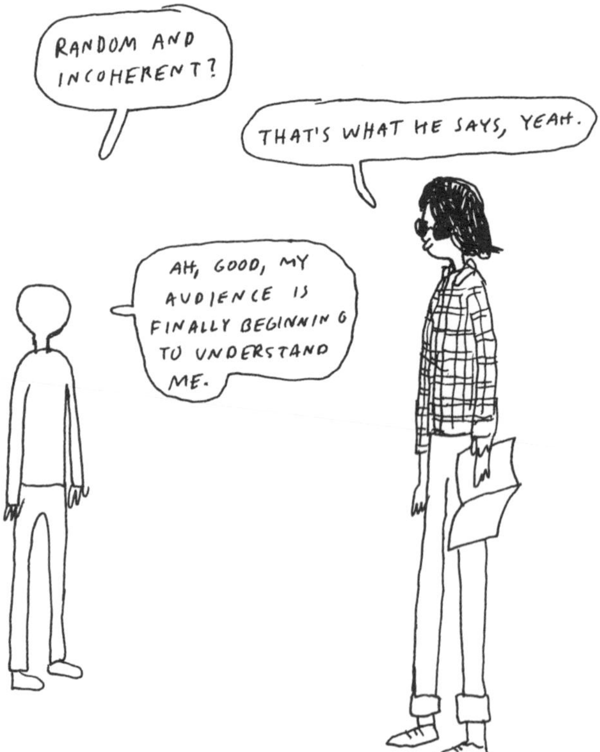
RANDOM AND INCOHERENT?
THAT'S WHAT HE SAYS, YEAH.
AH, GOOD, MY AUDIENCE IS FINALLY BEGINNING TO UNDERSTAND ME.

IN THAT CASE WE CAN BEGIN AGAIN.
PLEASE TURN THE PAGE.

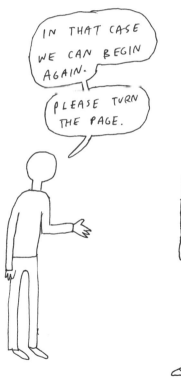

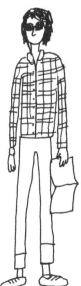

PART III

THIS IS MY IMPRESSION OF [redacted] SACCO AND VANZETTI

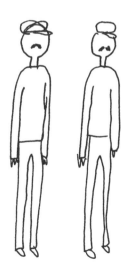

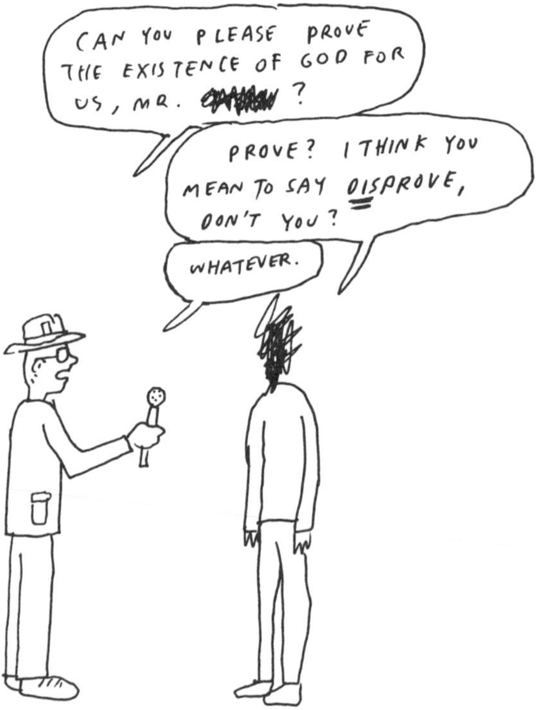
CAN YOU PLEASE PROVE THE EXISTENCE OF GOD FOR US, MR. [redacted] ?
PROVE? I THINK YOU MEAN TO SAY DISPROVE, DON'T YOU?
WHATEVER.

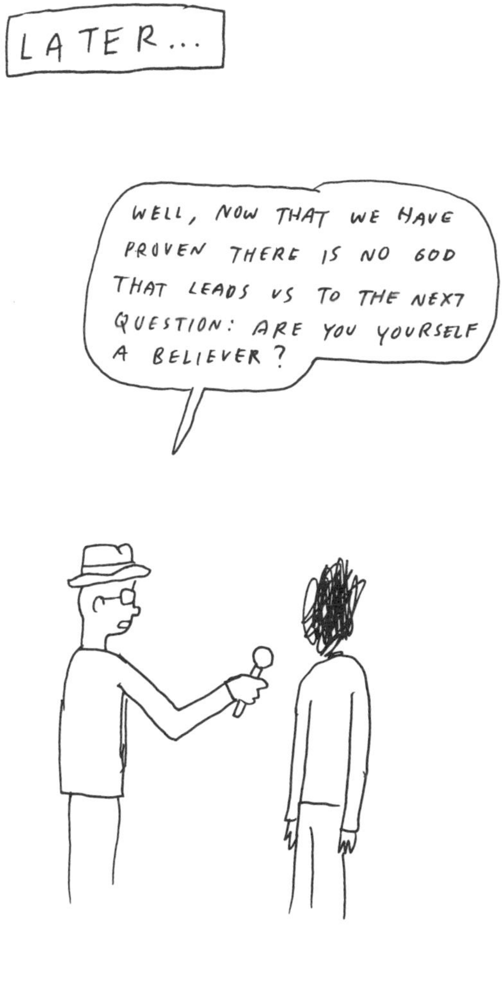
LATER...
WELL, NOW THAT WE HAVE PROVEN THERE IS NO GOD THAT LEADS US TO THE NEXT QUESTION: ARE YOU YOURSELF A BELIEVER?

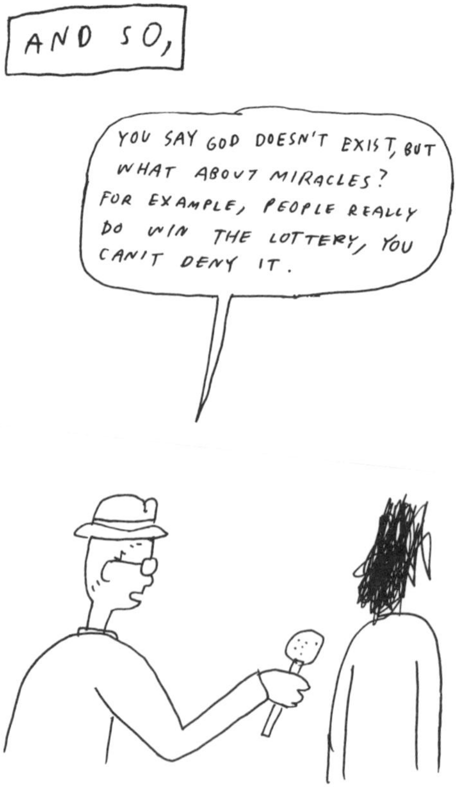
AND SO,
YOU SAY GOD DOESN'T EXIST, BUT WHAT ABOUT MIRACLES? FOR EXAMPLE, PEOPLE REALLY DO WIN THE LOTTERY, YOU CAN'T DENY IT.

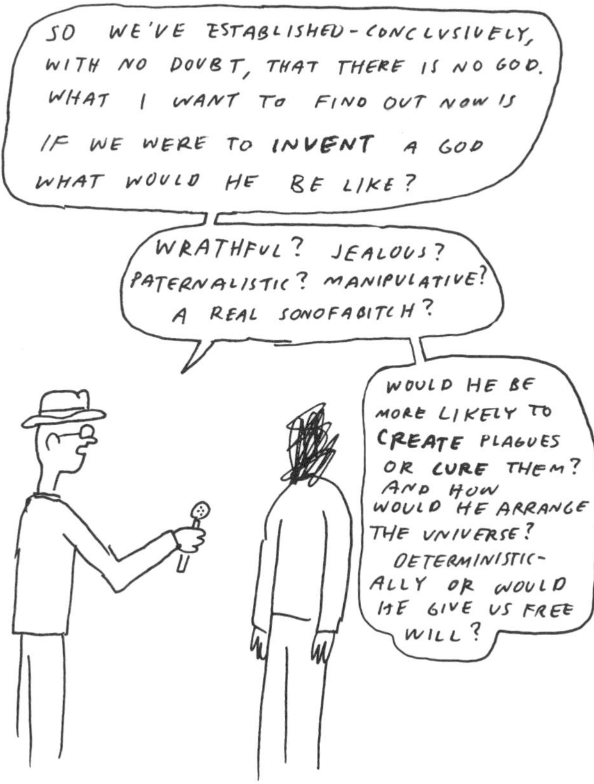
SO WE'VE ESTABLISHED - CONCLUSIVELY, WITH NO DOUBT, THAT THERE IS NO GOD. WHAT I WANT TO FIND OUT NOW IS IF WE WERE TO **INVENT** A GOD WHAT WOULD HE BE LIKE?
WRATHFUL? JEALOUS? PATERNALISTIC? MANIPULATIVE? A REAL SONOFABITCH?
WOULD HE BE MORE LIKELY TO **CREATE** PLAGUES OR **CURE** THEM? AND HOW WOULD HE ARRANGE THE UNIVERSE? DETERMINISTIC-ALLY OR WOULD HE GIVE US FREE WILL?

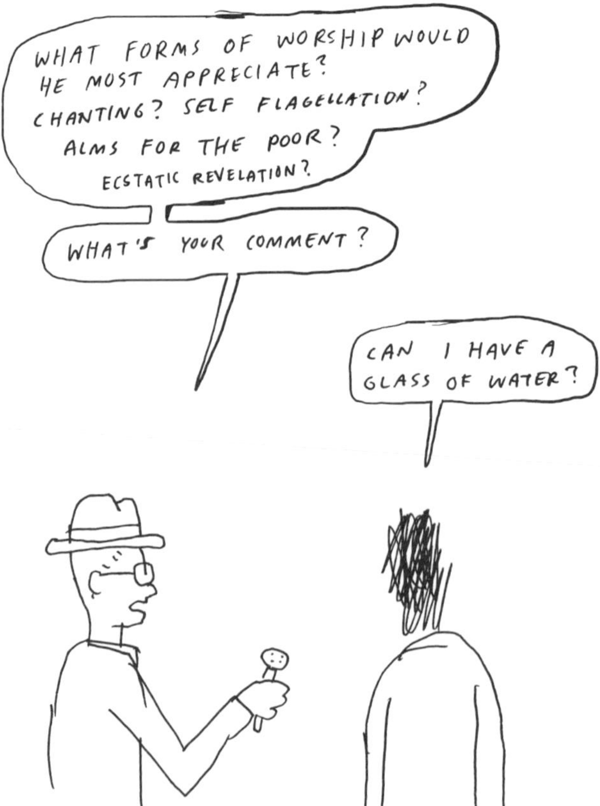
WHAT FORMS OF WORSHIP WOULD HE MOST APPRECIATE? CHANTING? SELF FLAGELLATION? ALMS FOR THE POOR? ECSTATIC REVELATION?
WHAT'S YOUR COMMENT?
CAN I HAVE A GLASS OF WATER?

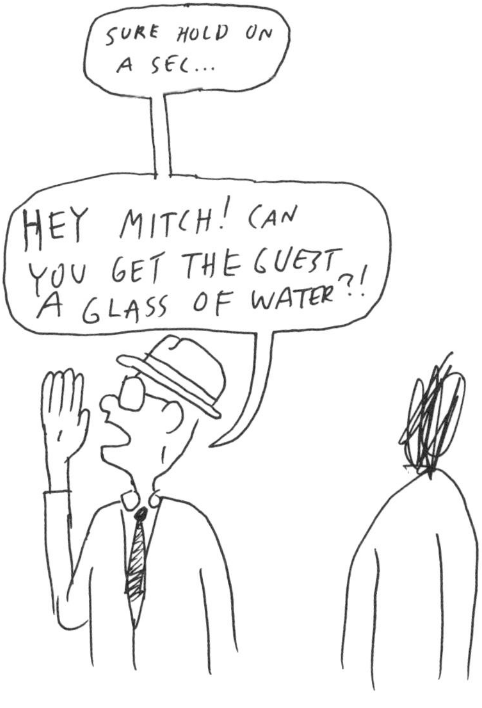
SURE HOLD ON A SEC...
HEY MITCH! CAN YOU GET THE GUEST A GLASS OF WATER?!

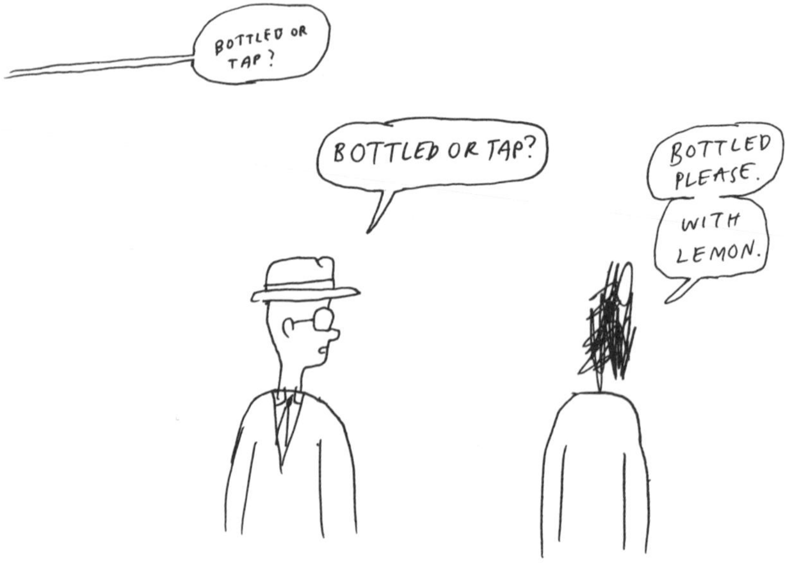
BOTTLED OR TAP?
BOTTLED OR TAP?
BOTTLED PLEASE.
WITH LEMON.

BOTTLED! WITH LEMON!

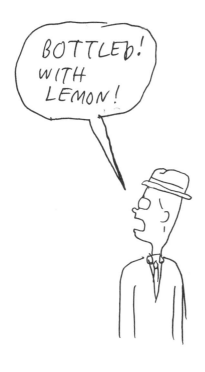

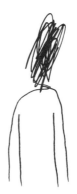

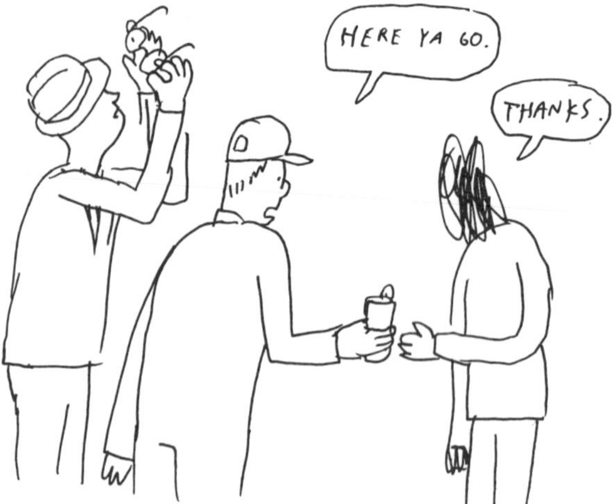
HERE YA GO.
THANKS.

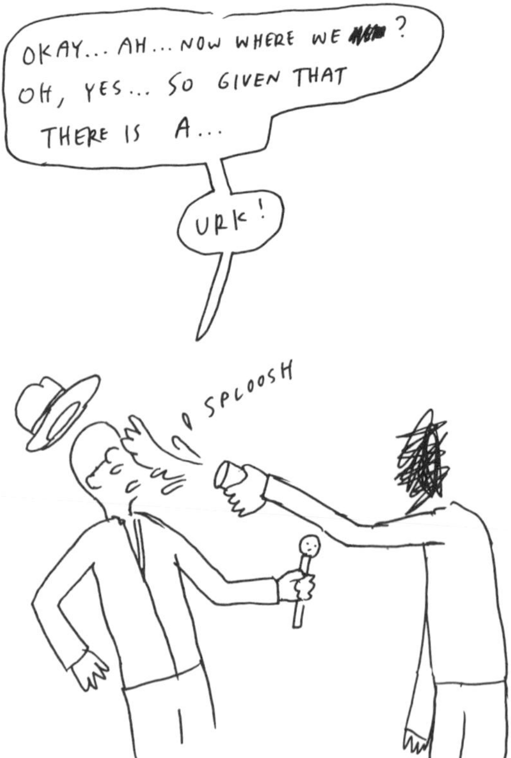
OKAY... AH... NOW WHERE WE ?
OH, YES... SO GIVEN THAT
THERE IS A...
URK!
SPLOOSH

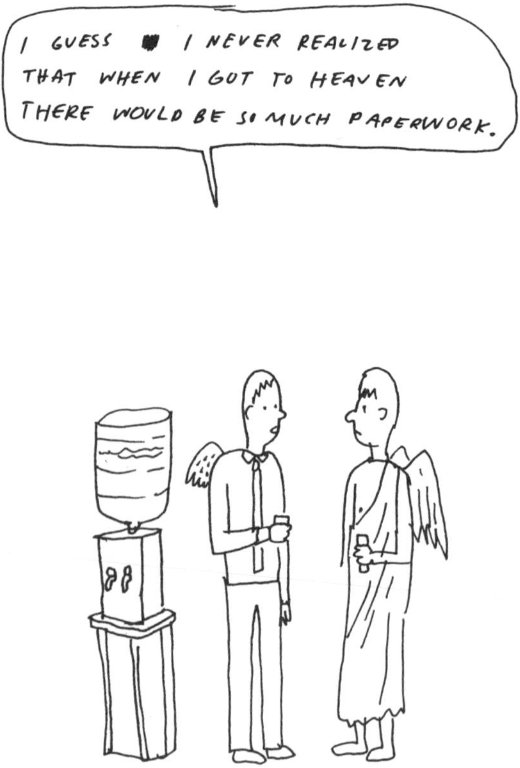
I GUESS I NEVER REALIZED THAT WHEN I GOT TO HEAVEN THERE WOULD BE SO MUCH PAPERWORK.

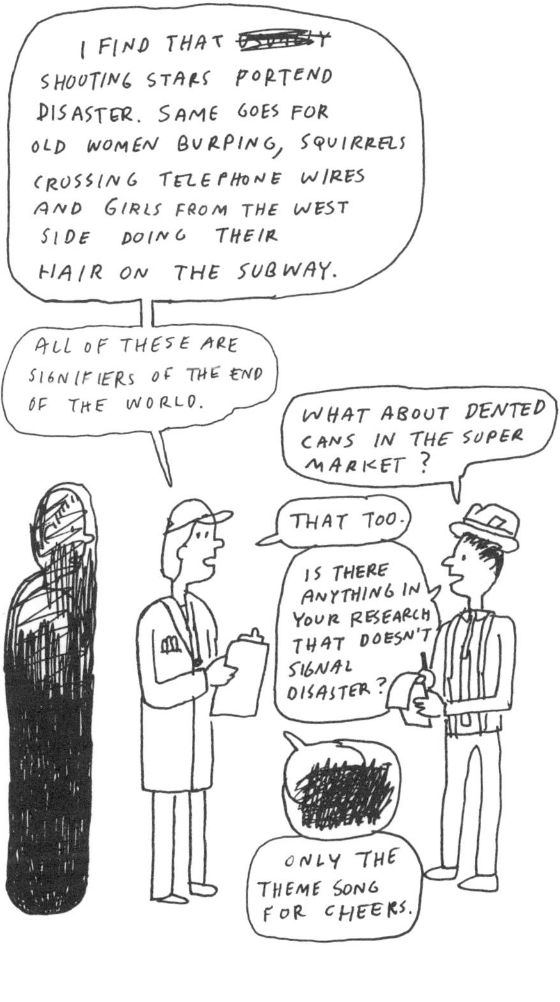
I FIND THAT SHOUTING STARS PORTEND DISASTER. SAME GOES FOR OLD WOMEN BURPING, SQUIRRELS CROSSING TELEPHONE WIRES AND GIRLS FROM THE WEST SIDE DOING THEIR HAIR ON THE SUBWAY.
ALL OF THESE ARE SIGNIFIERS OF THE END OF THE WORLD.
WHAT ABOUT DENTED CANS IN THE SUPER MARKET?
THAT TOO.
IS THERE ANYTHING IN YOUR RESEARCH THAT DOESN'T SIGNAL DISASTER?
ONLY THE THEME SONG FOR CHEERS.

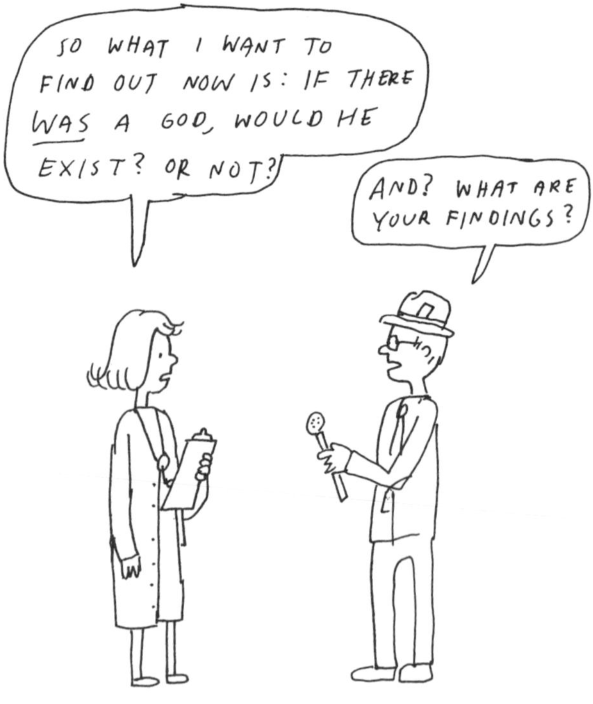
SO WHAT I WANT TO FIND OUT NOW IS: IF THERE WAS A GOD, WOULD HE EXIST? OR NOT?
AND? WHAT ARE YOUR FINDINGS?

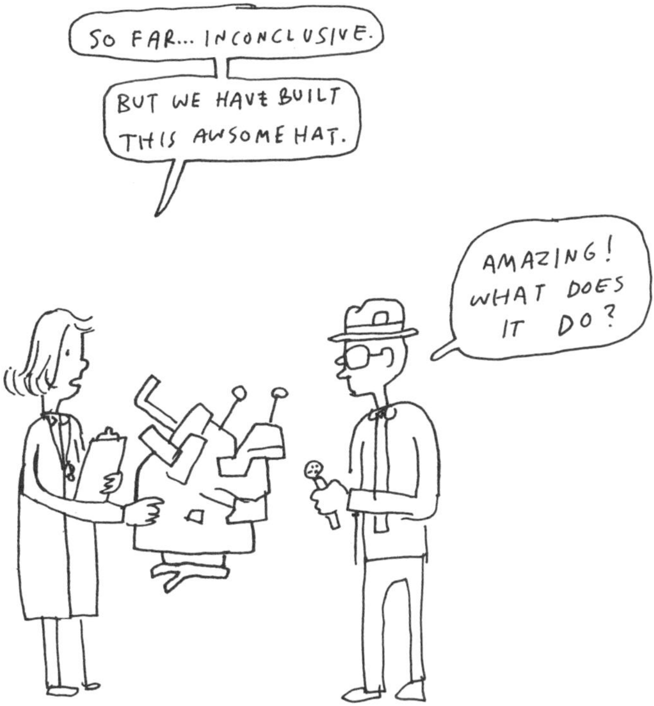
SO FAR... INCONCLUSIVE.
BUT WE HAVE BUILT THIS AWSOME HAT.
AMAZING! WHAT DOES IT DO?

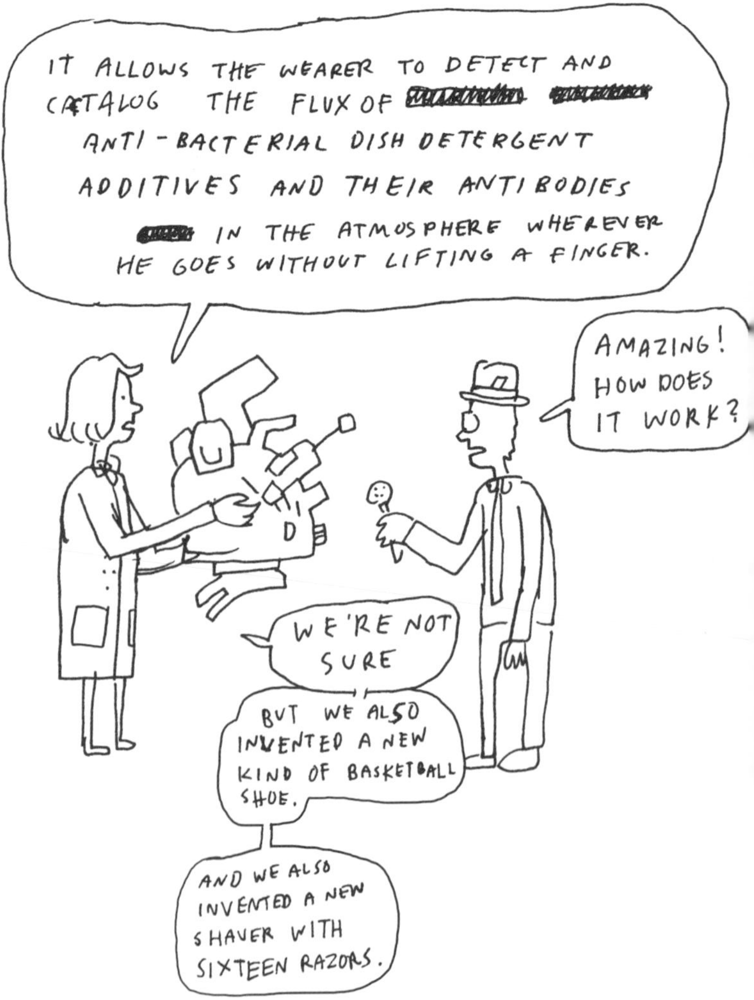
IT ALLOWS THE WEARER TO DETECT AND CATALOG THE FLUX OF [redacted] ANTI-BACTERIAL DISH DETERGENT ADDITIVES AND THEIR ANTIBODIES [redacted] IN THE ATMOSPHERE WHEREVER HE GOES WITHOUT LIFTING A FINGER.
AMAZING! HOW DOES IT WORK?
WE'RE NOT SURE
BUT WE ALSO INVENTED A NEW KIND OF BASKETBALL SHOE.
AND WE ALSO INVENTED A NEW SHAVER WITH SIXTEEN RAZORS.

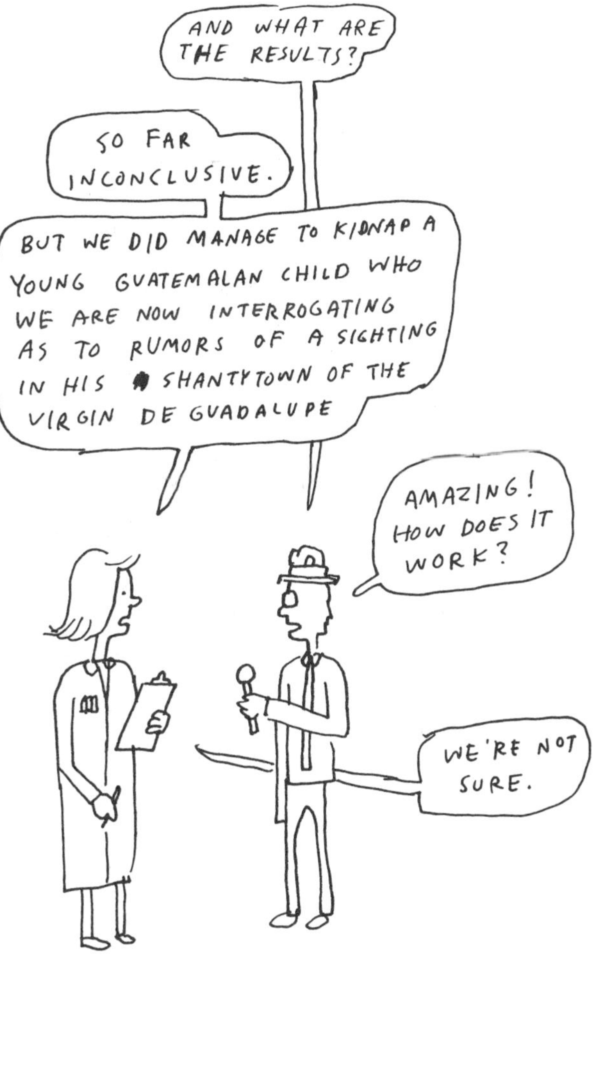
AND WHAT ARE THE RESULTS?
SO FAR INCONCLUSIVE.
BUT WE DID MANAGE TO KIDNAP A YOUNG GUATEMALAN CHILD WHO WE ARE NOW INTERROGATING AS TO RUMORS OF A SIGHTING IN HIS SHANTYTOWN OF THE VIRGIN DE GUADALUPE
AMAZING! HOW DOES IT WORK?
WE'RE NOT SURE.

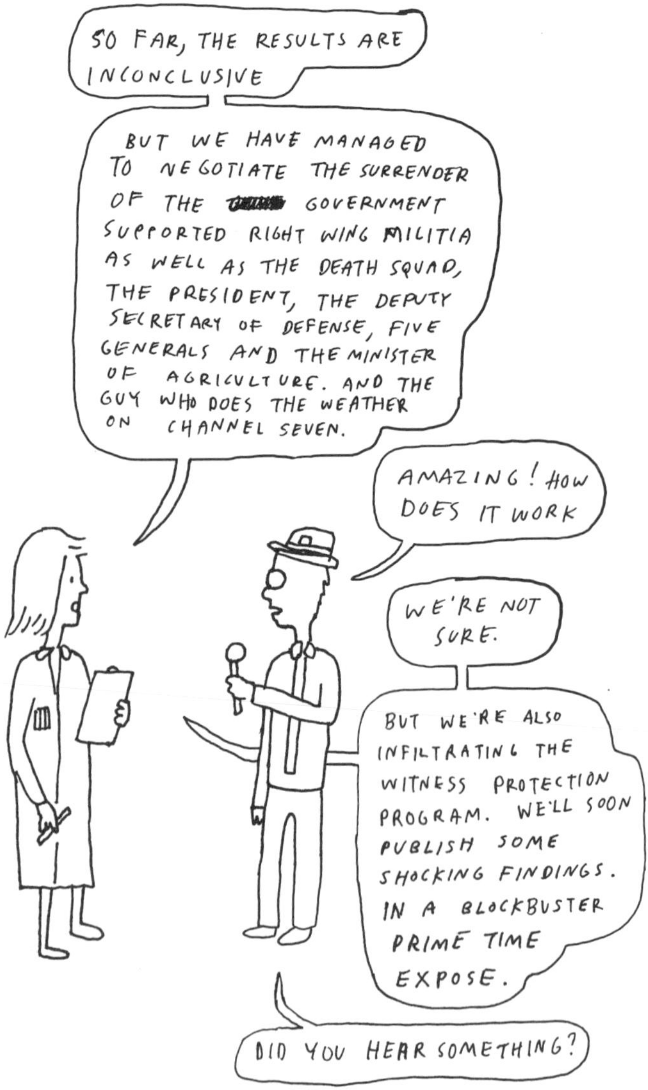
SO FAR, THE RESULTS ARE INCONCLUSIVE
BUT WE HAVE MANAGED TO NEGOTIATE THE SURRENDER OF THE [redacted] GOVERNMENT SUPPORTED RIGHT WING MILITIA AS WELL AS THE DEATH SQUAD, THE PRESIDENT, THE DEPUTY SECRETARY OF DEFENSE, FIVE GENERALS AND THE MINISTER OF AGRICULTURE. AND THE GUY WHO DOES THE WEATHER ON CHANNEL SEVEN.
AMAZING! HOW DOES IT WORK
WE'RE NOT SURE.
BUT WE'RE ALSO INFILTRATING THE WITNESS PROTECTION PROGRAM. WE'LL SOON PUBLISH SOME SHOCKING FINDINGS. IN A BLOCKBUSTER PRIME TIME EXPOSE.
DID YOU HEAR SOMETHING?

OH, MAYBE IT'S MY CELLPHONE... HOLD ON, I BETTER TAKE THIS.

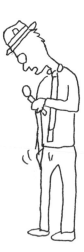

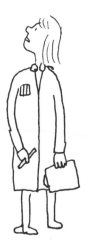

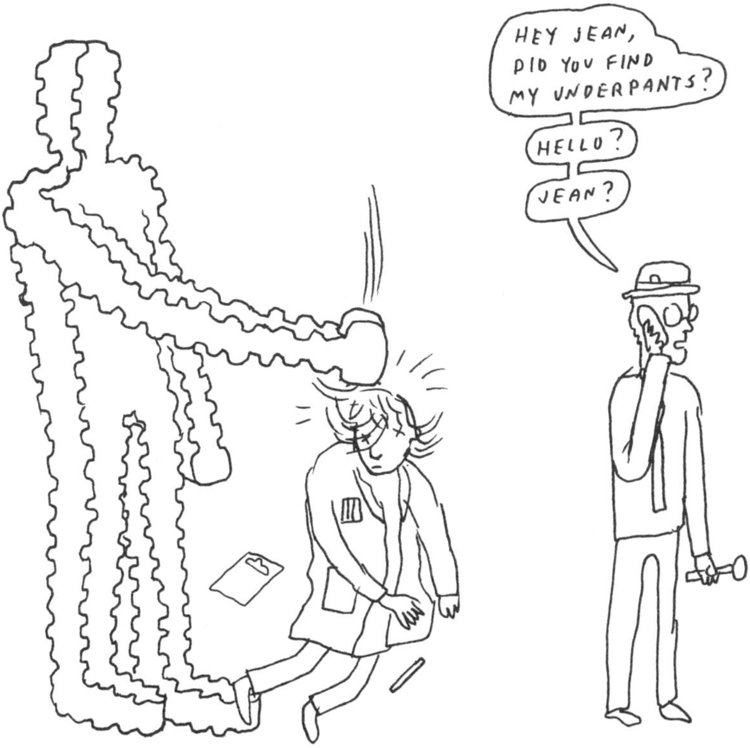
HEY JEAN,
DID YOU FIND
MY UNDERPANTS?
HELLO?
JEAN?

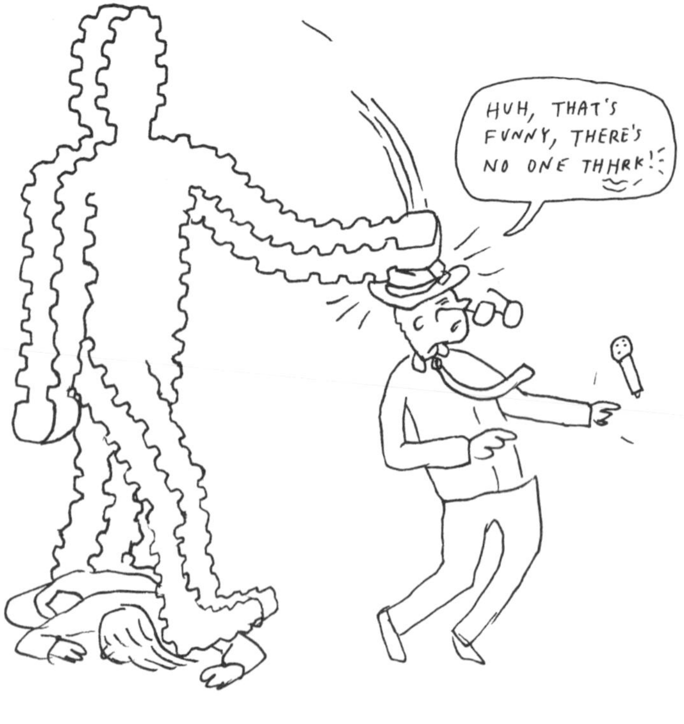
HUH, THAT'S FUNNY, THERE'S NO ONE THHRK!

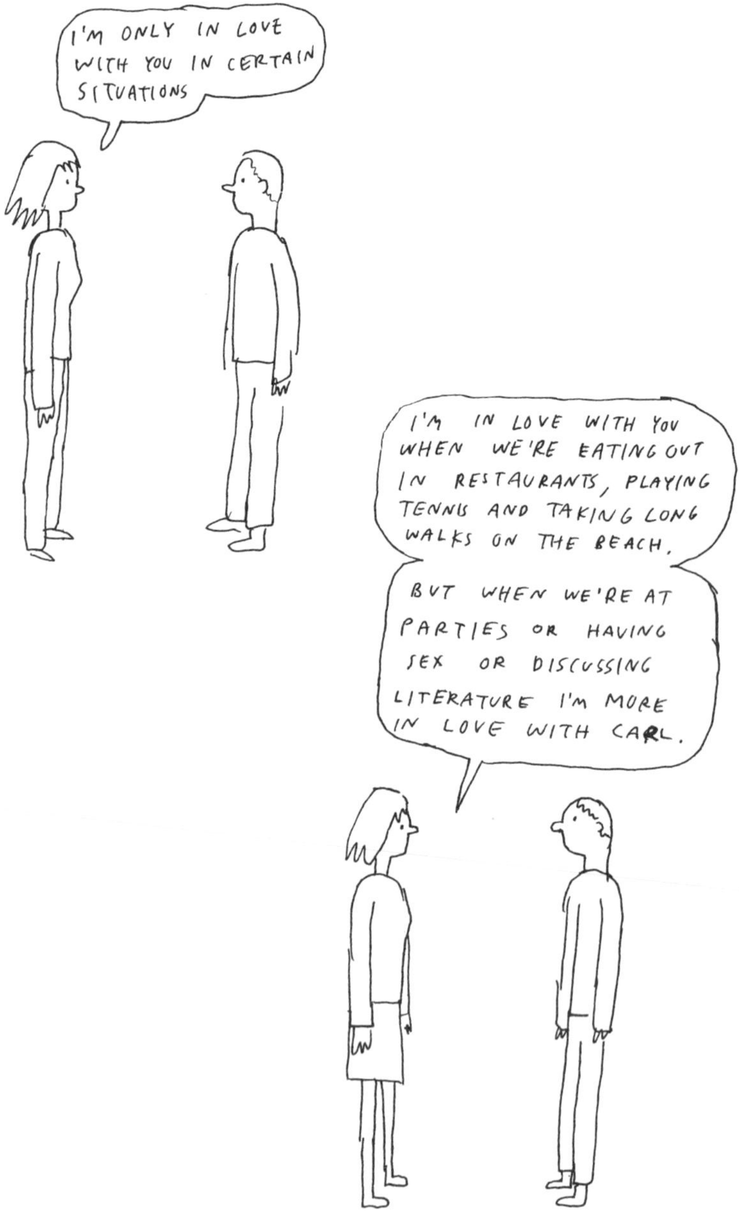
I'M ONLY IN LOVE WITH YOU IN CERTAIN SITUATIONS
I'M IN LOVE WITH YOU WHEN WE'RE EATING OUT IN RESTAURANTS, PLAYING TENNIS AND TAKING LONG WALKS ON THE BEACH.
BUT WHEN WE'RE AT PARTIES OR HAVING SEX OR DISCUSSING LITERATURE I'M MORE IN LOVE WITH CARL.

HOWEVER WHEN I'M ON THE TRAIN OR DRIVING THE CAR I FEEL MORE SECURE AND INDE- PENDENT. SO WITH THE LONG COMMUTE TO THIS NEW JOB, AND THE STATE OF THE ECONOMY, I WON'T HAVE TIME TO HAVE SEX, DISCUSS LITERATURE, OR TAKE WALKS ON THE BEACH, SO I'VE DECIDED TO BREAK UP WITH BOTH OF YOU.

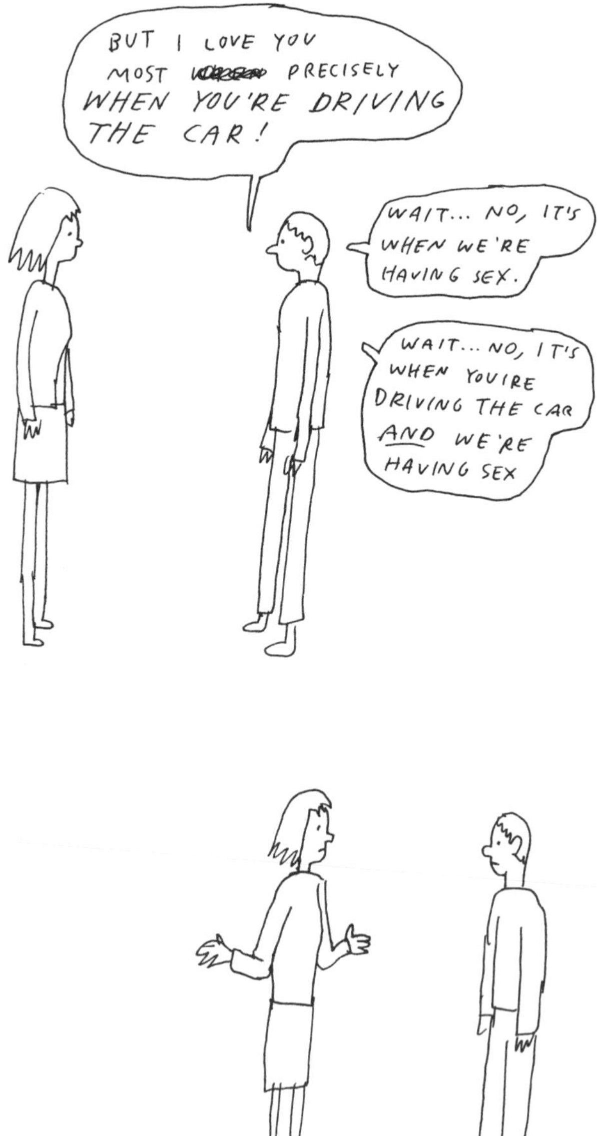
BUT I LOVE YOU MOST PRECISELY WHEN YOU'RE DRIVING THE CAR!
WAIT... NO, IT'S WHEN WE'RE HAVING SEX.
WAIT... NO, IT'S WHEN YOU'RE DRIVING THE CAR AND WE'RE HAVING SEX

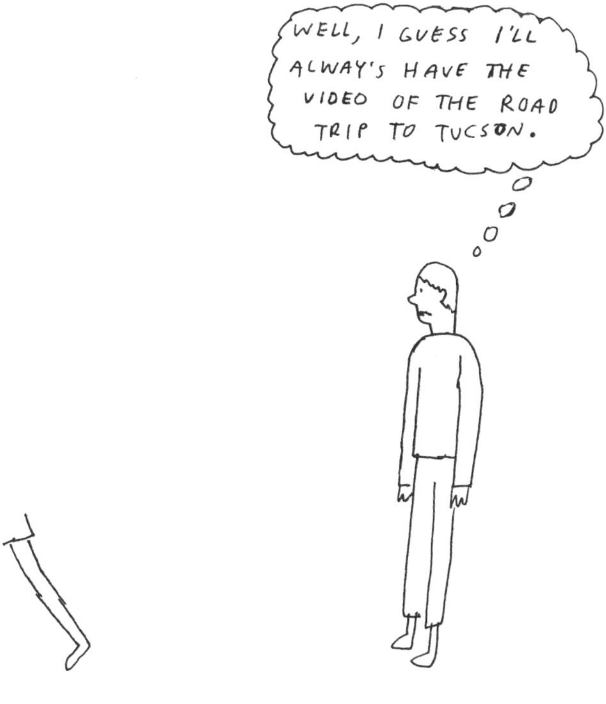
WELL, I GUESS I'LL ALWAY'S HAVE THE VIDEO OF THE ROAD TRIP TO TUCSON.

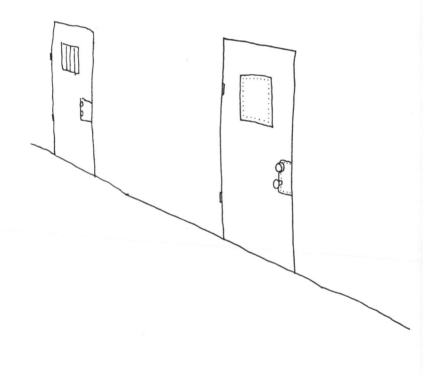

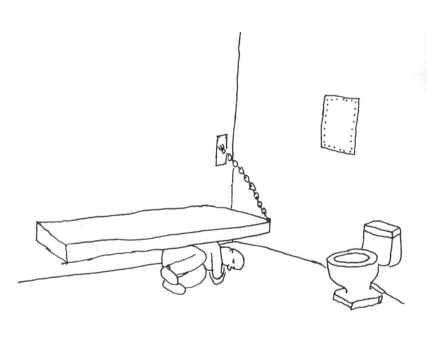

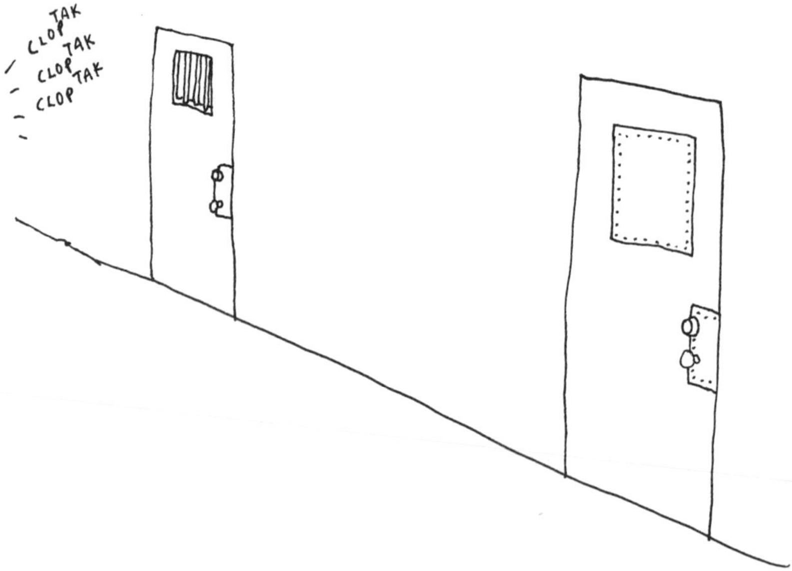
CLOP TAK
CLOP TAK
CLOP TAK

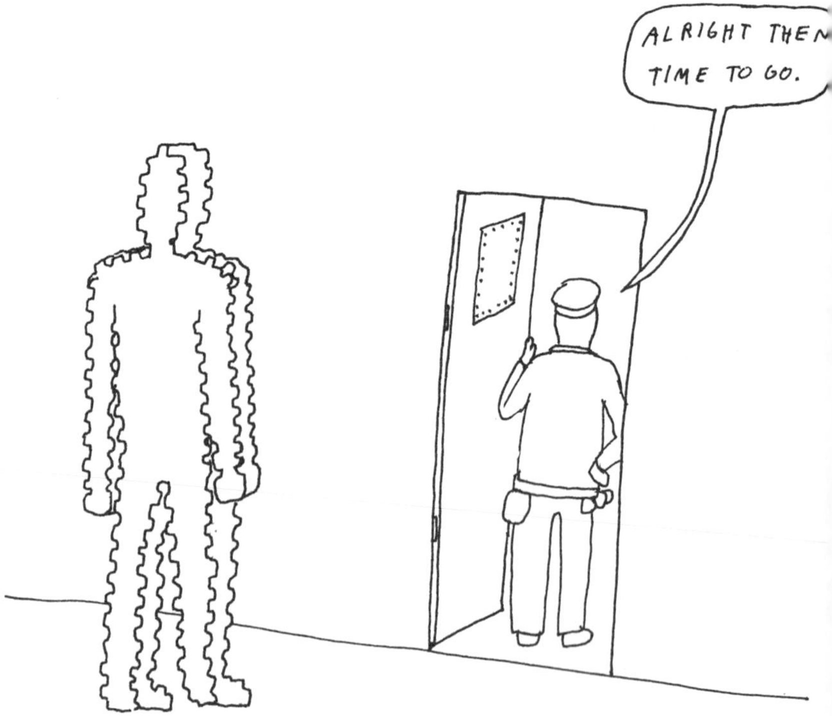
ALRIGHT THEN
TIME TO GO.

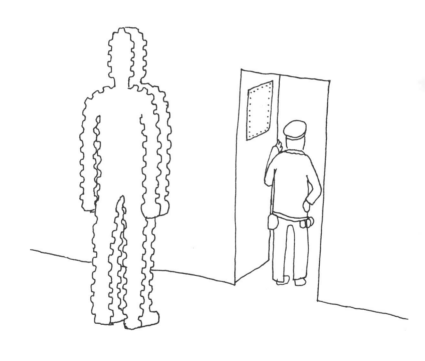

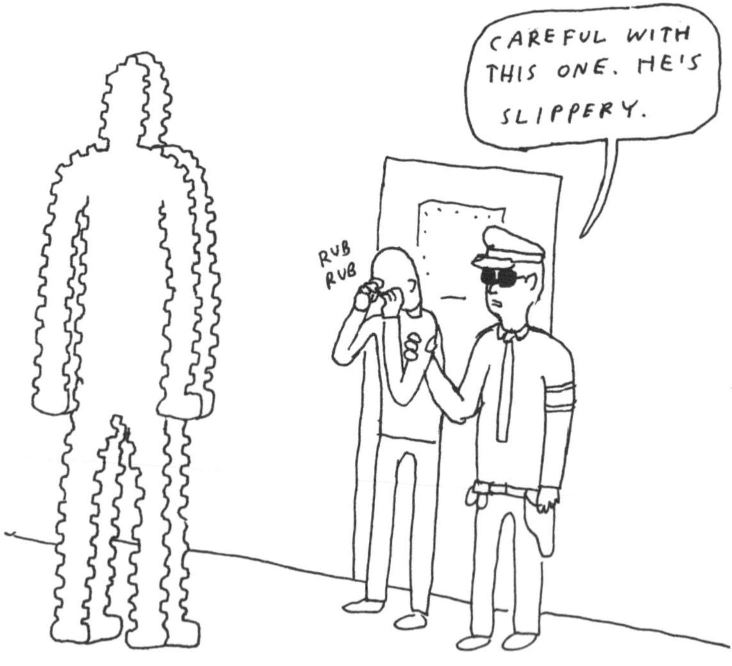
RUB RUB
CAREFUL WITH THIS ONE. HE'S SLIPPERY.

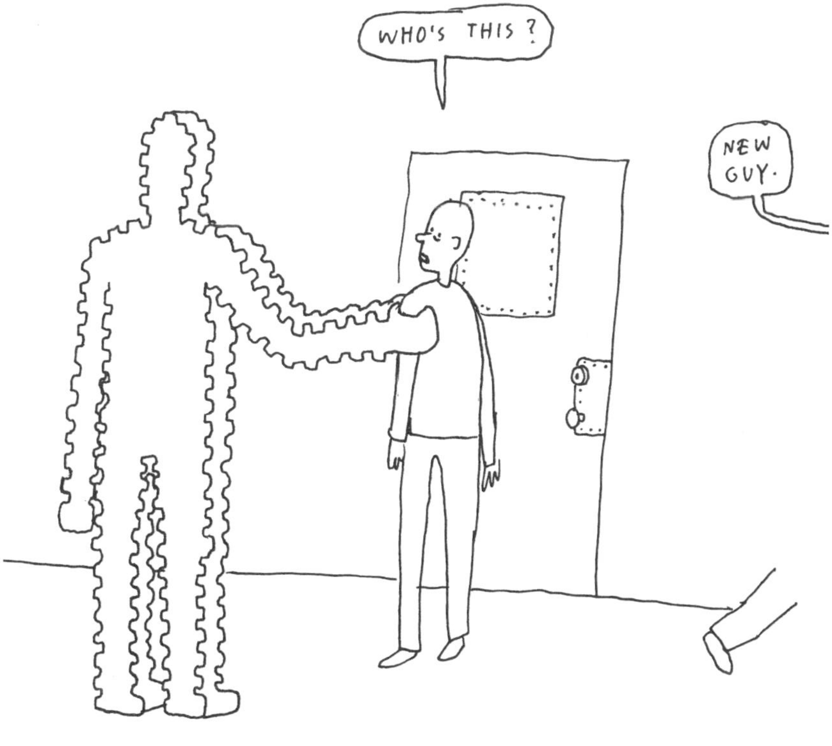
WHO'S THIS?
NEW GUY.

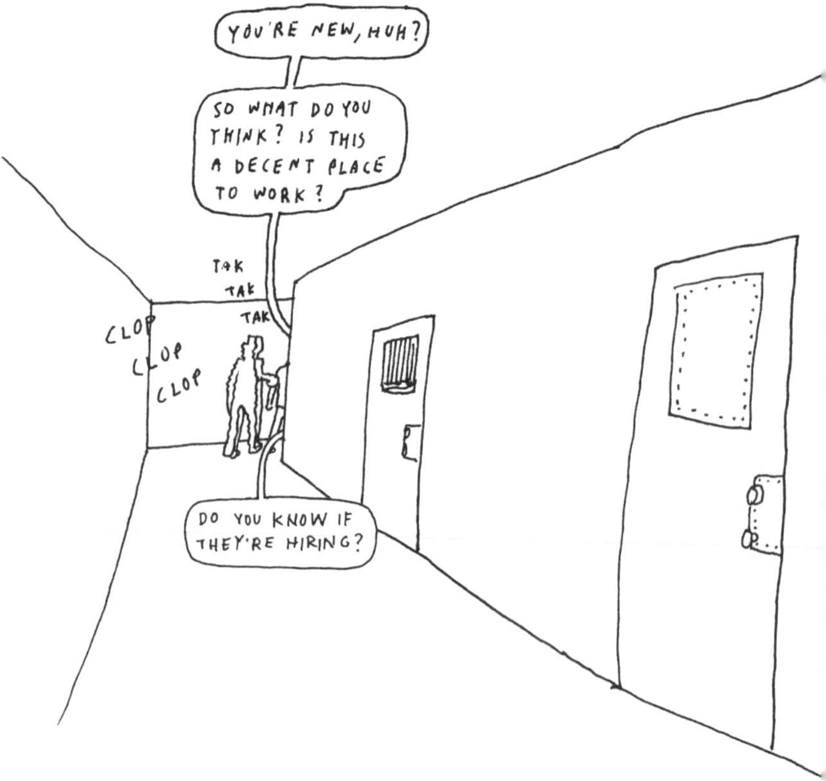
YOU'RE NEW, HUH?
SO WHAT DO YOU THINK? IS THIS A DECENT PLACE TO WORK?
TAK
TAK
TAK
CLOP
CLOP
CLOP
DO YOU KNOW IF THEY'RE HIRING?

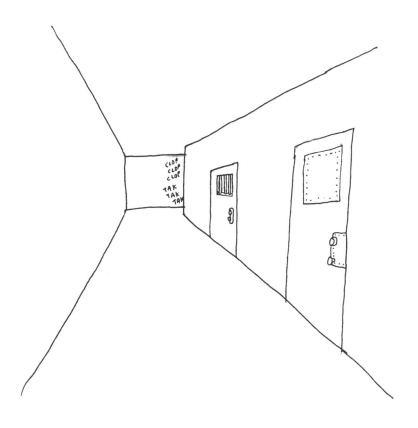

CLOP
CLOP
CLOP

TAK
TAK
TAK

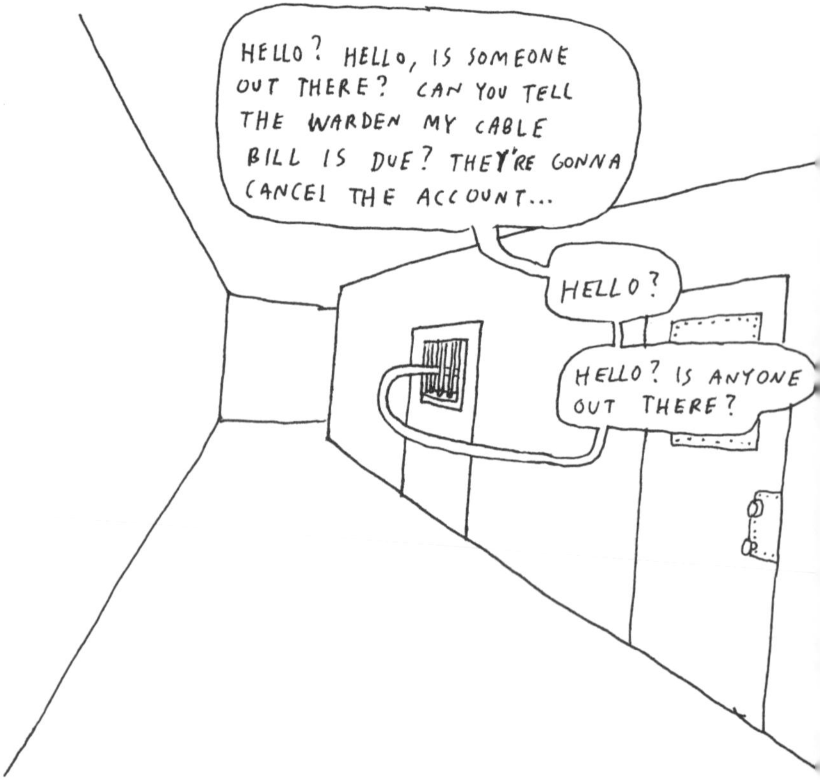
HELLO? HELLO, IS SOMEONE OUT THERE? CAN YOU TELL THE WARDEN MY CABLE BILL IS DUE? THEY'RE GONNA CANCEL THE ACCOUNT...
HELLO?
HELLO? IS ANYONE OUT THERE?

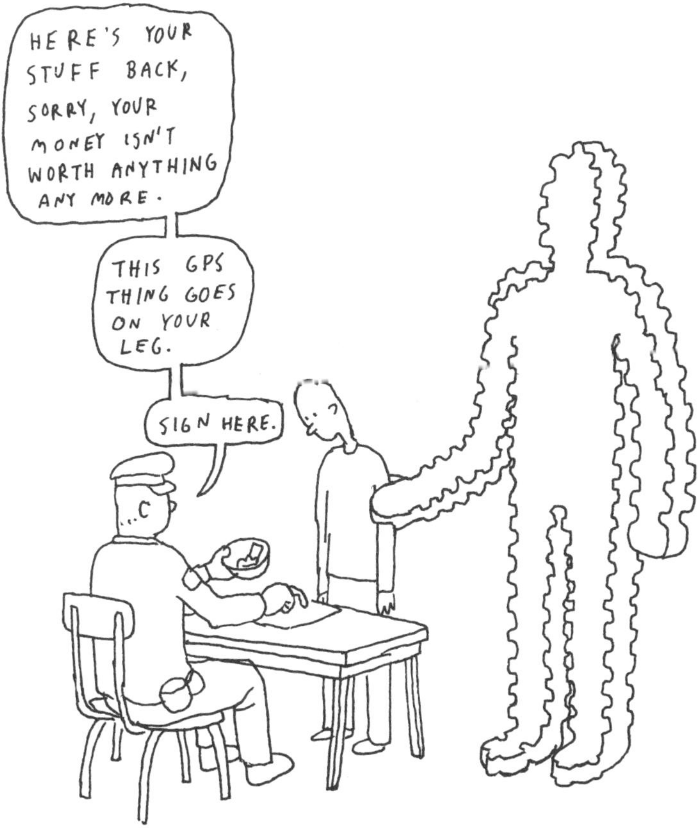
HERE'S YOUR STUFF BACK, SORRY, YOUR MONEY ISN'T WORTH ANYTHING ANY MORE.
THIS GPS THING GOES ON YOUR LEG.
SIGN HERE.

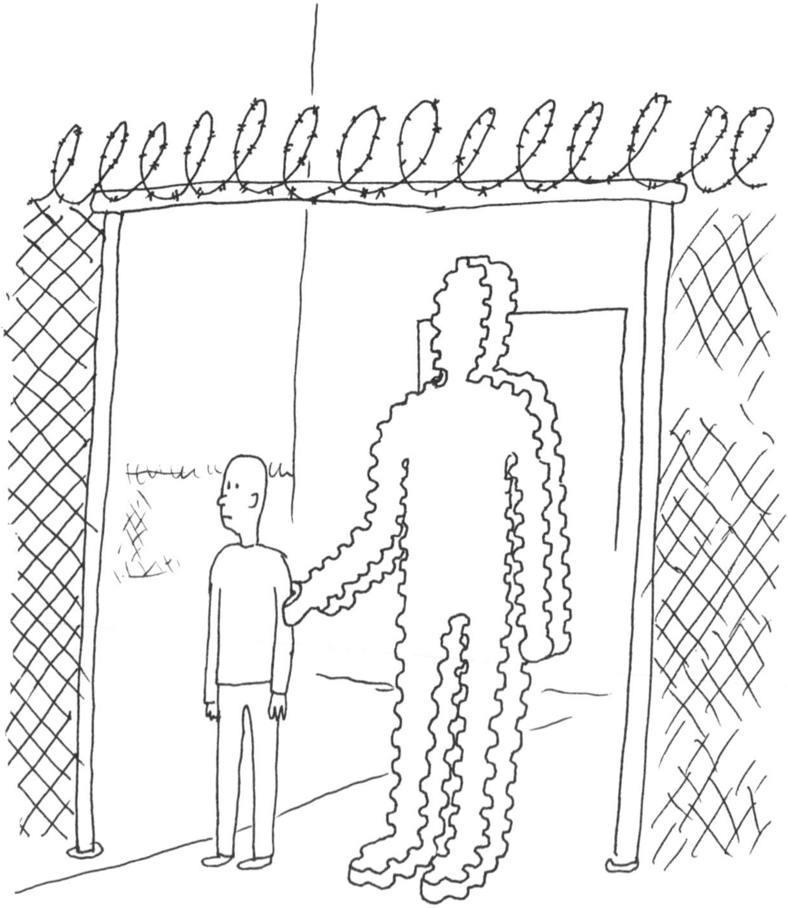

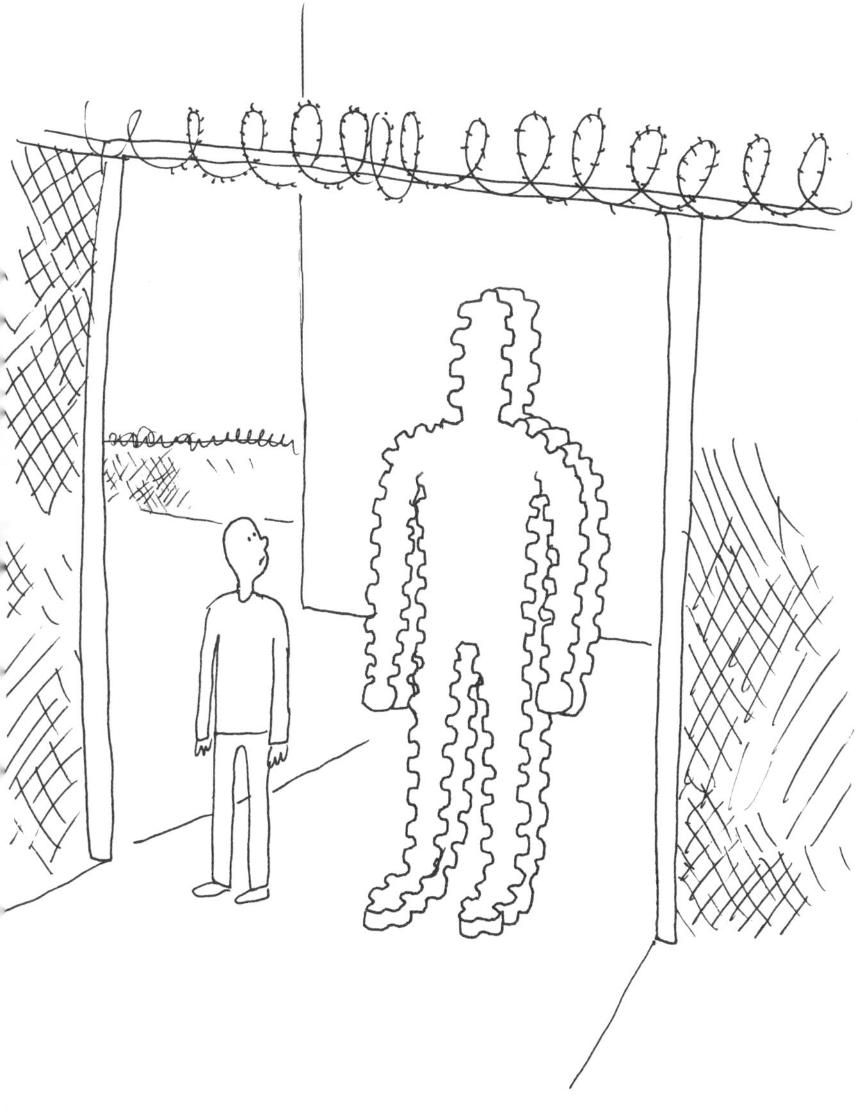

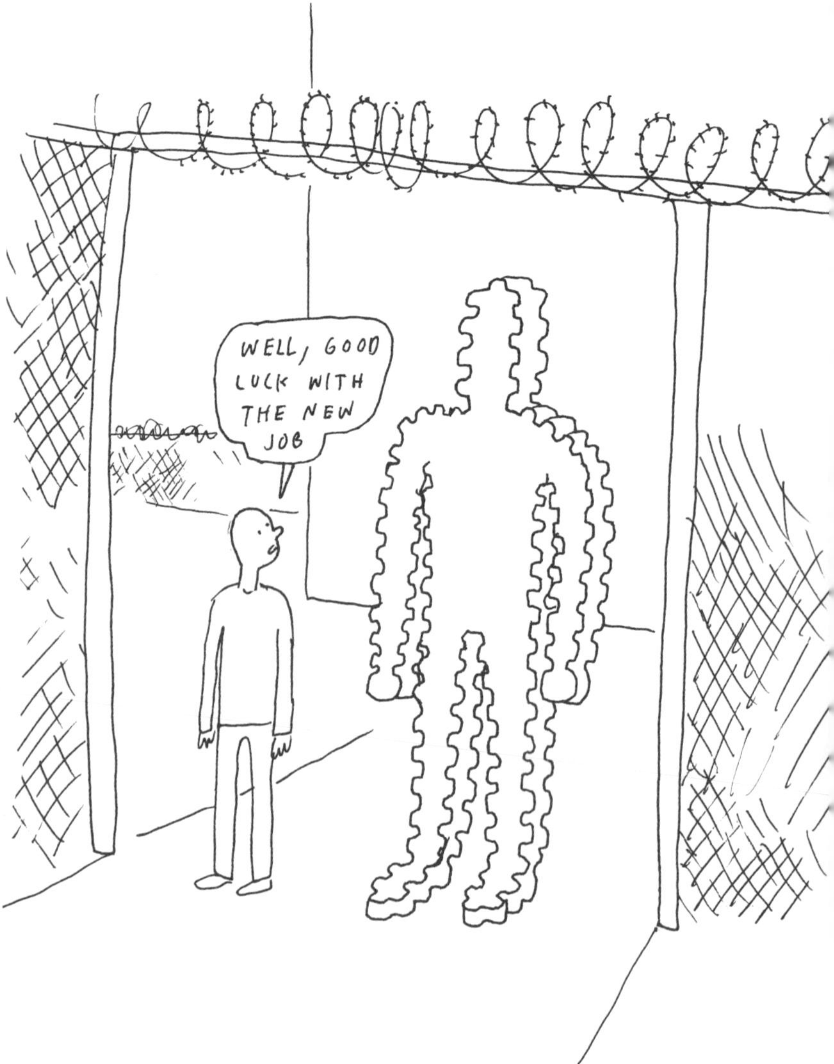
WELL, GOOD LUCK WITH THE NEW JOB

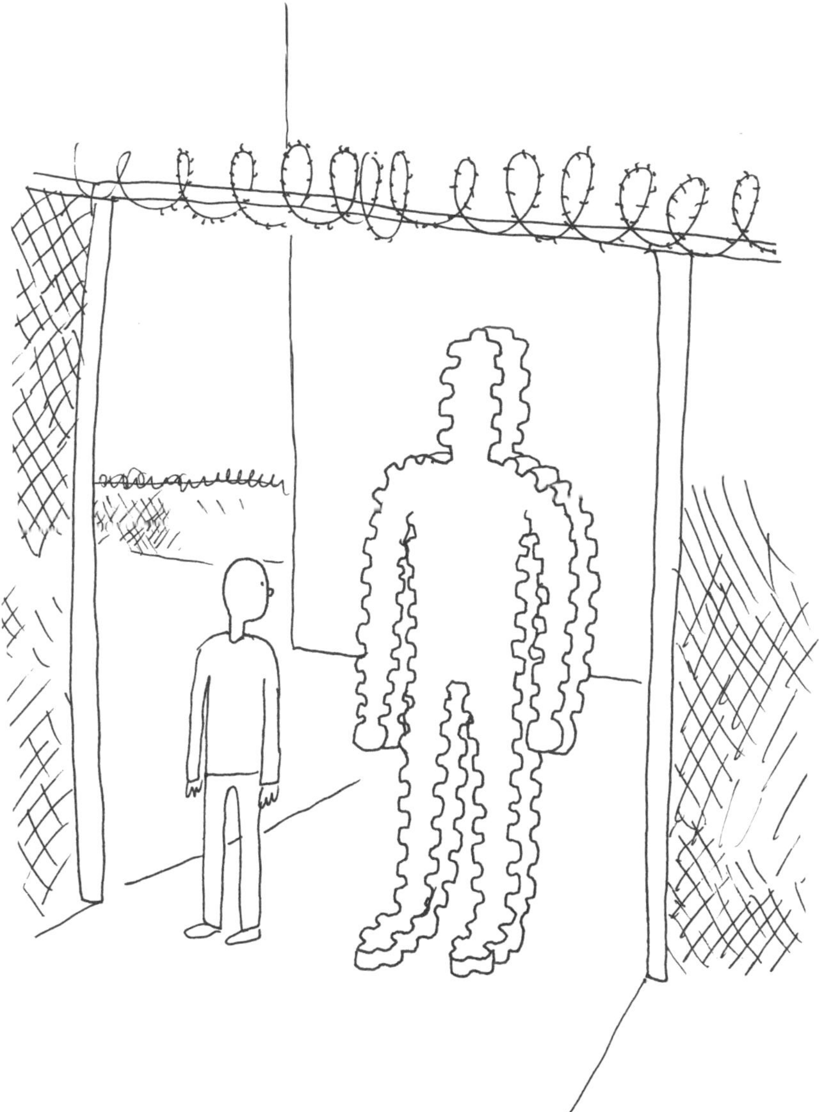

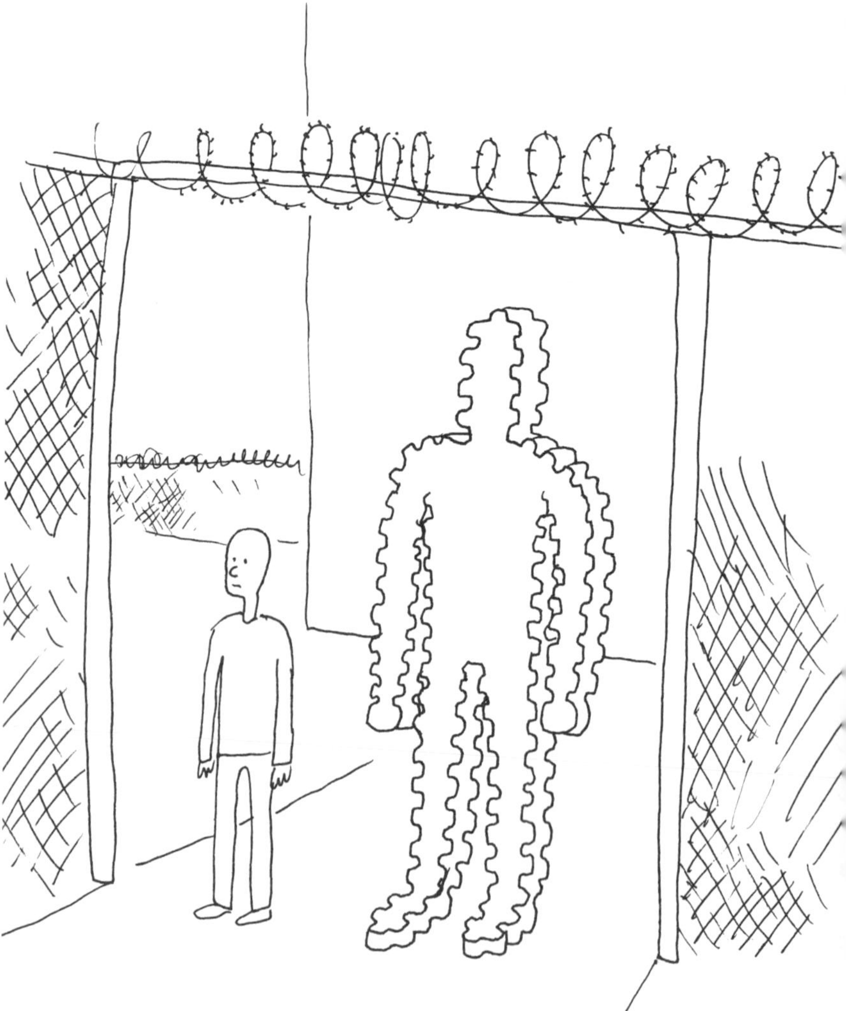

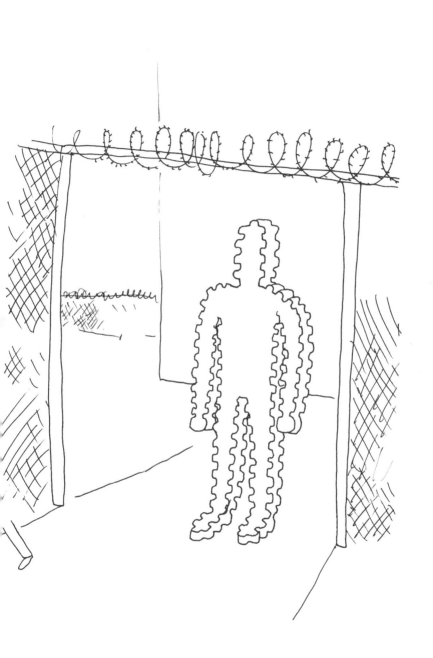

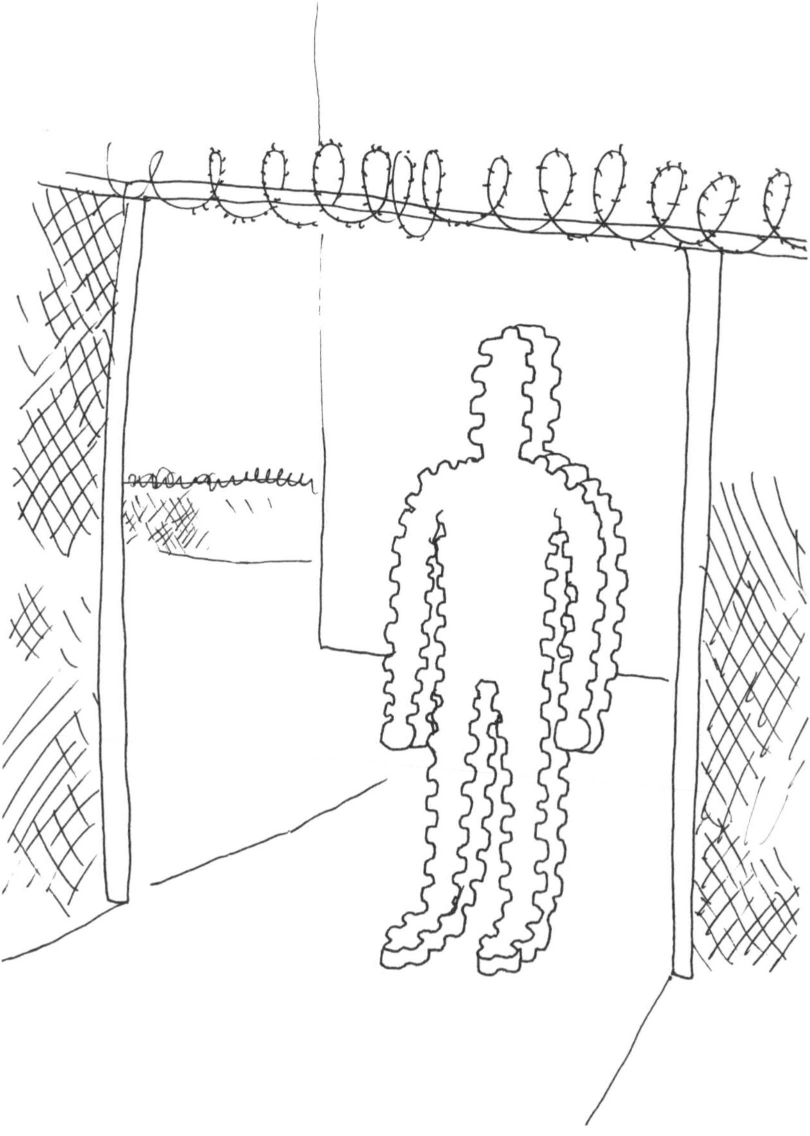

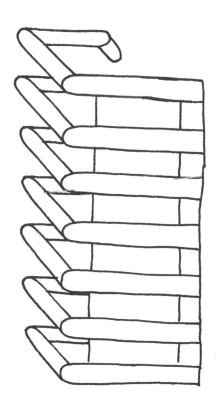

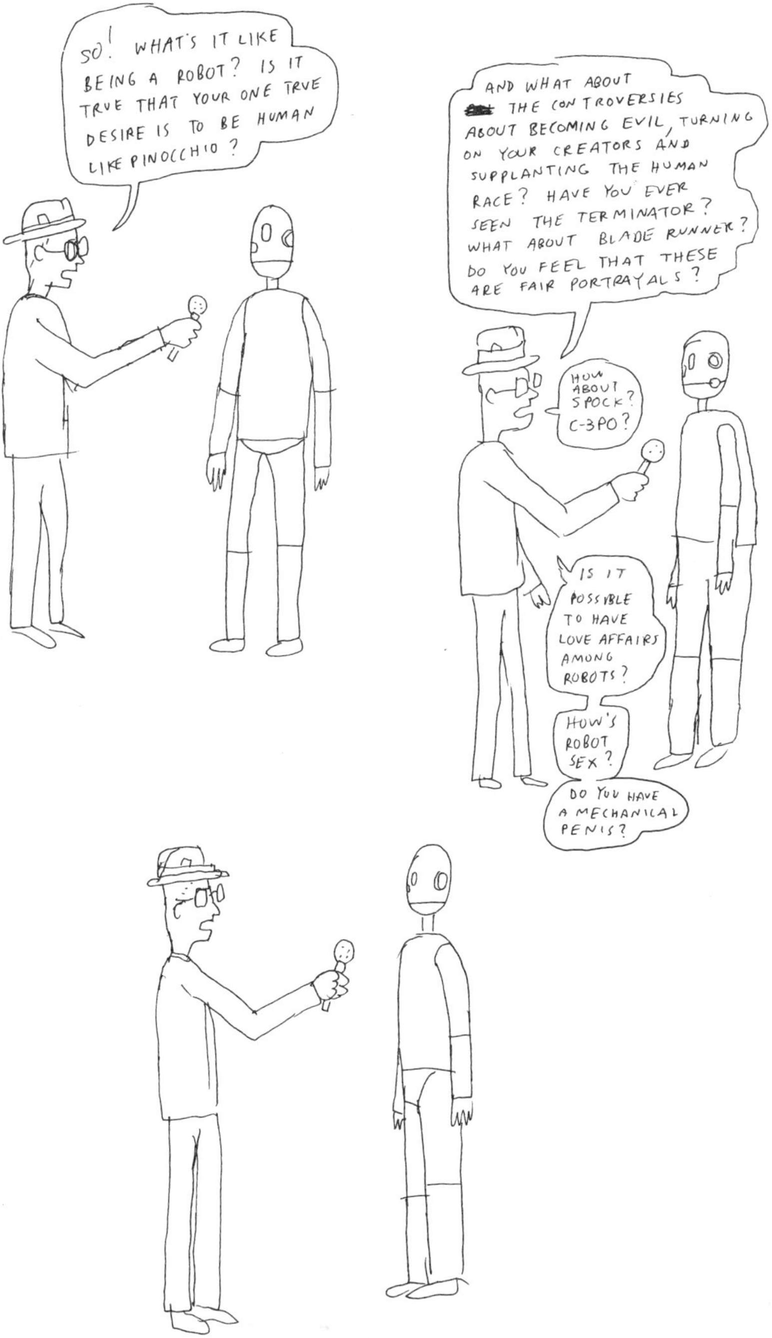
SO! WHAT'S IT LIKE BEING A ROBOT? IS IT TRUE THAT YOUR ONE TRUE DESIRE IS TO BE HUMAN LIKE PINOCCHIO?
AND WHAT ABOUT THE CONTROVERSIES ABOUT BECOMING EVIL, TURNING ON YOUR CREATORS AND SUPPLANTING THE HUMAN RACE? HAVE YOU EVER SEEN THE TERMINATOR? WHAT ABOUT BLADE RUNNER? DO YOU FEEL THAT THESE ARE FAIR PORTRAYALS?
HOW ABOUT SPOCK? C-3PO?
IS IT POSSIBLE TO HAVE LOVE AFFAIRS AMONG ROBOTS?
HOW'S ROBOT SEX?
DO YOU HAVE A MECHANICAL PENIS?

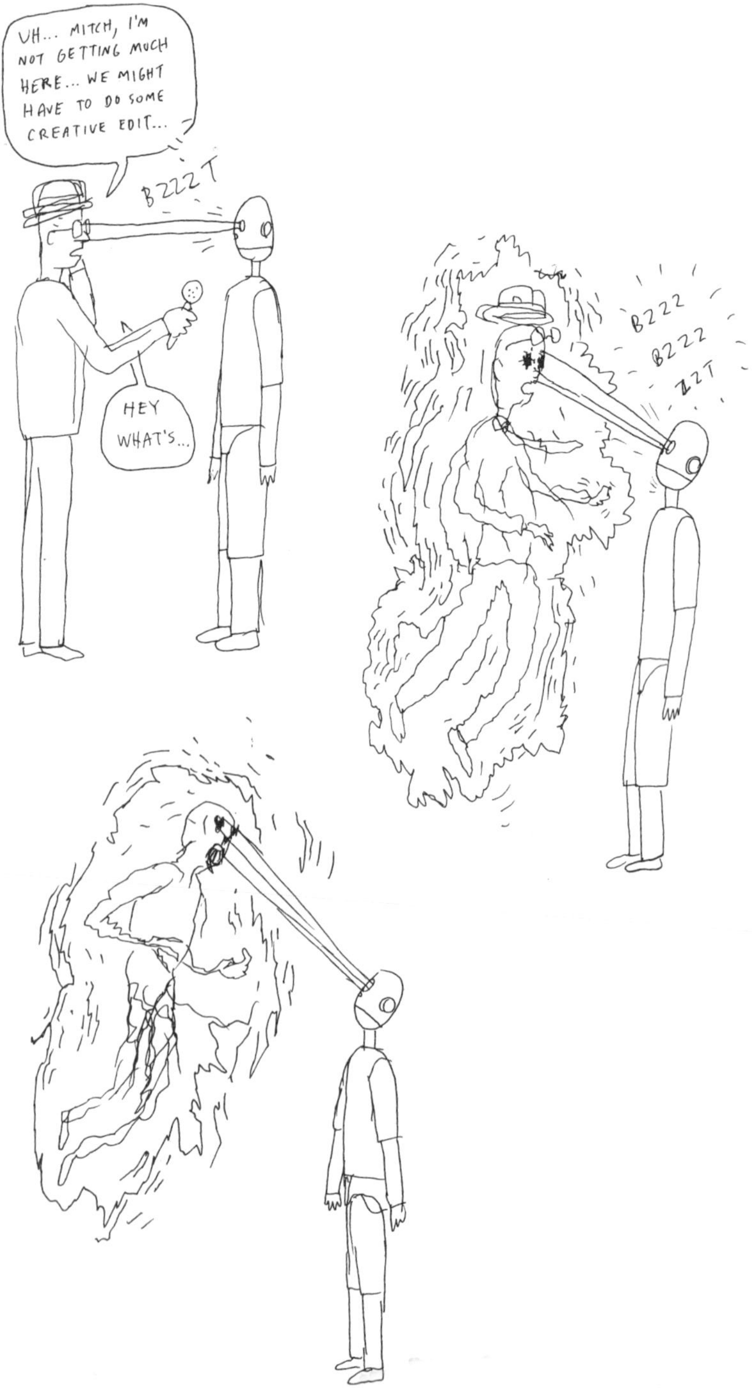
UH... MITCH, I'M NOT GETTING MUCH HERE... WE MIGHT HAVE TO DO SOME CREATIVE EDIT...
BZZZT
HEY WHAT'S...
BZZZ BZZZ ZZT

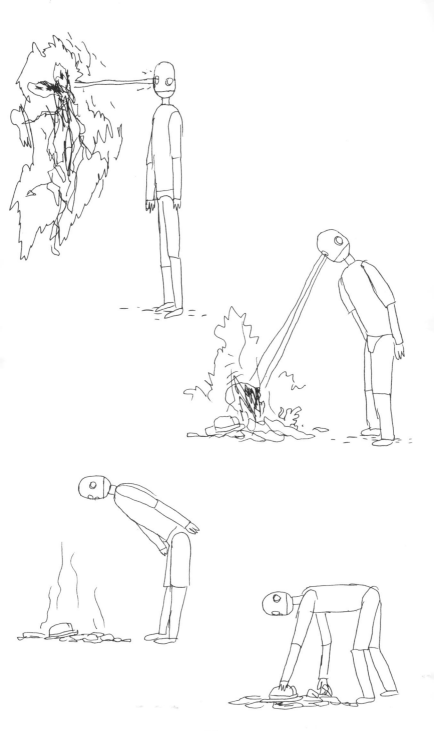

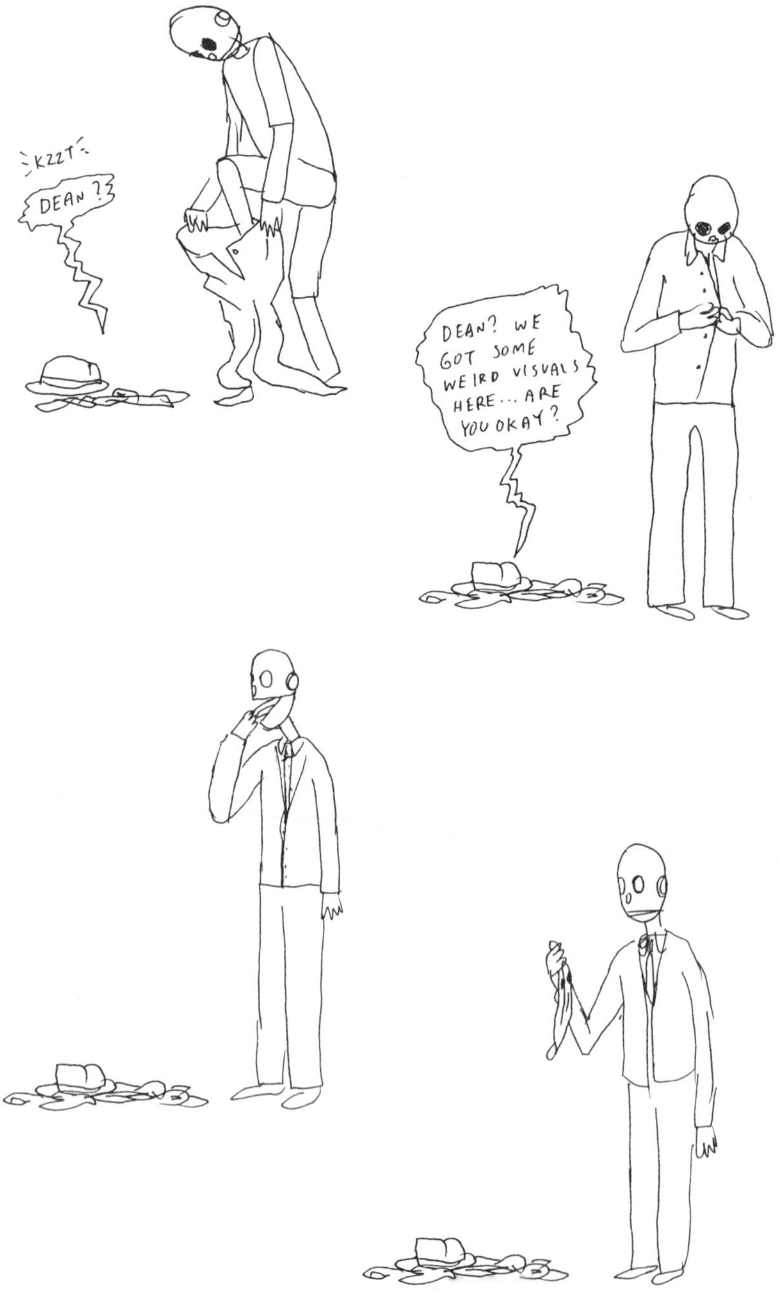
KZZT
DEAN?
DEAN? WE GOT SOME WEIRD VISUALS HERE... ARE YOU OKAY?

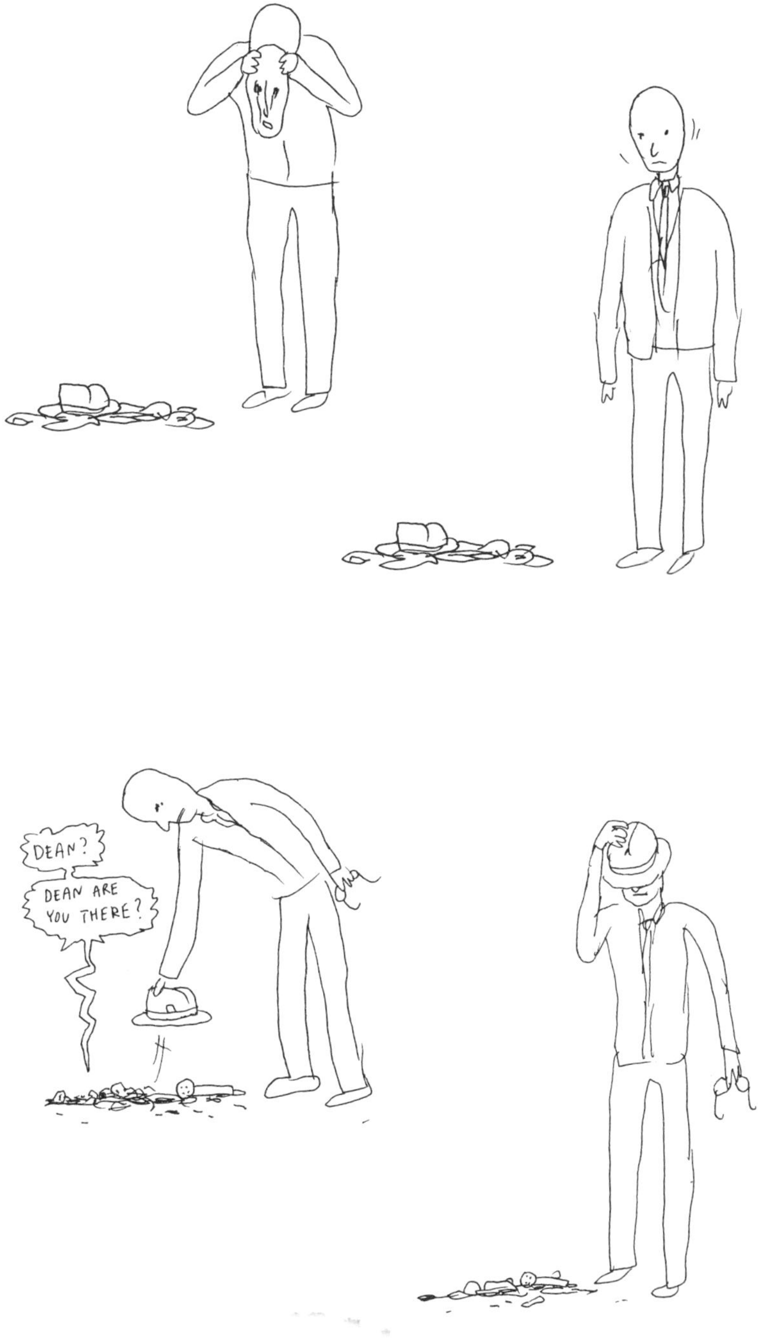
DEAN?
DEAN ARE YOU THERE?

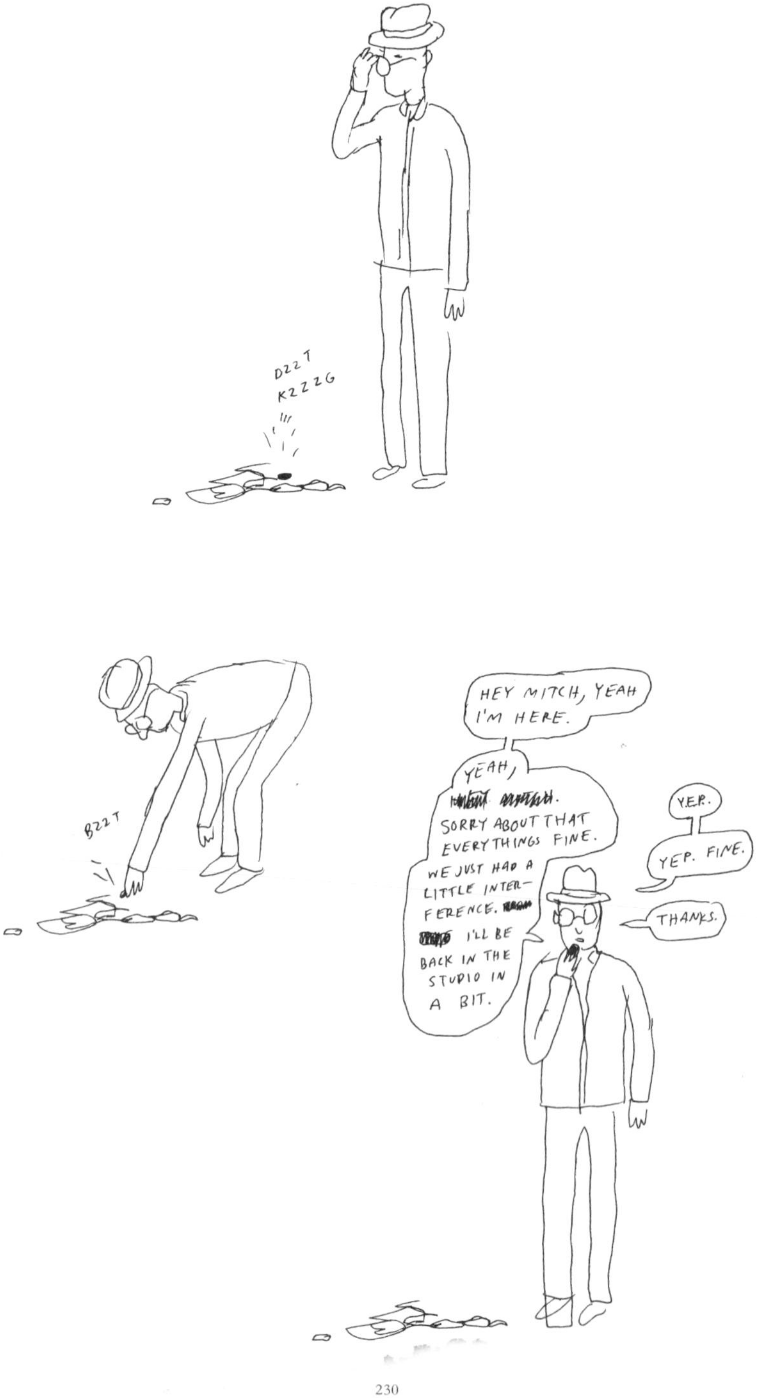
DZZT
KZZZG
BZZT
HEY MITCH, YEAH I'M HERE.
YEAH, SORRY ABOUT THAT EVERYTHINGS FINE. WE JUST HAD A LITTLE INTER-FERENCE. I'LL BE BACK IN THE STUDIO IN A BIT.
YEP.
YEP. FINE.
THANKS.

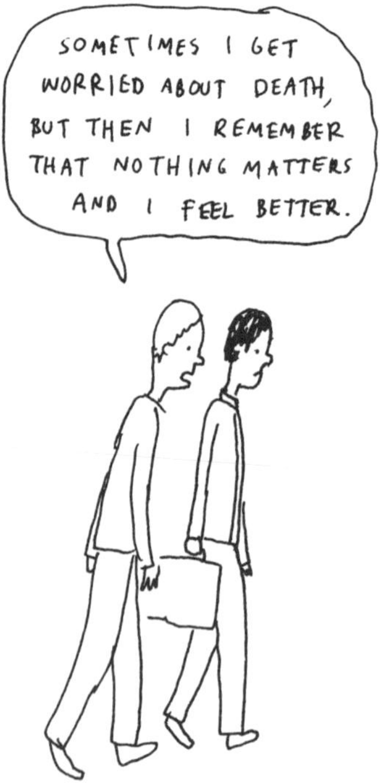
SOMETIMES I GET WORRIED ABOUT DEATH, BUT THEN I REMEMBER THAT NOTHING MATTERS AND I FEEL BETTER.

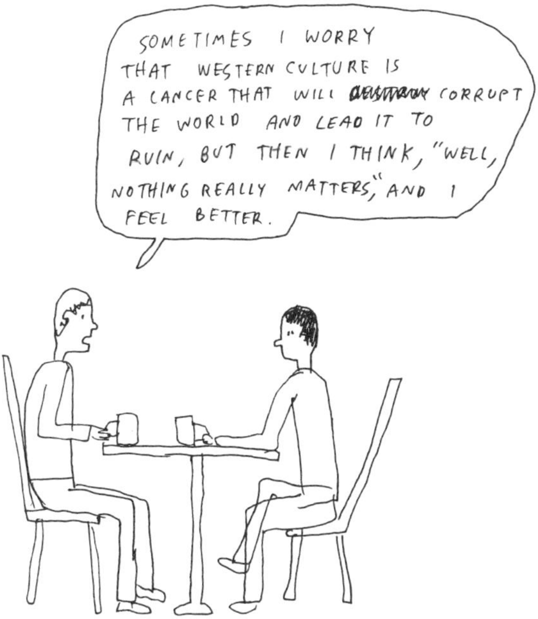
SOMETIMES I WORRY THAT WESTERN CULTURE IS A CANCER THAT WILL CORRUPT THE WORLD AND LEAD IT TO RUIN, BUT THEN I THINK, "WELL, NOTHING REALLY MATTERS," AND I FEEL BETTER.

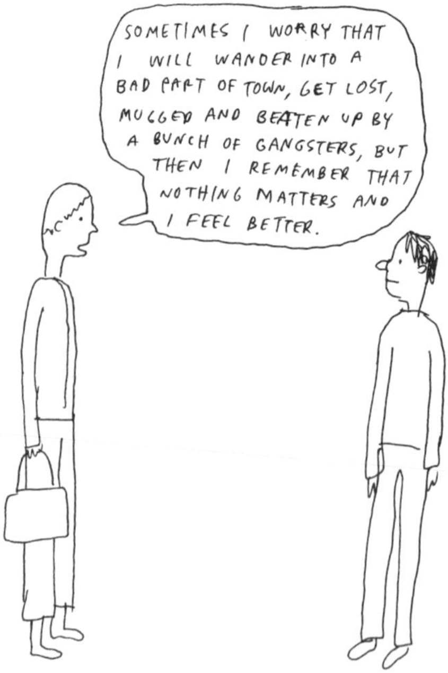
SOMETIMES I WORRY THAT I WILL WANDER INTO A BAD PART OF TOWN, GET LOST, MUGGED AND BEATEN UP BY A BUNCH OF GANGSTERS, BUT THEN I REMEMBER THAT NOTHING MATTERS AND I FEEL BETTER.

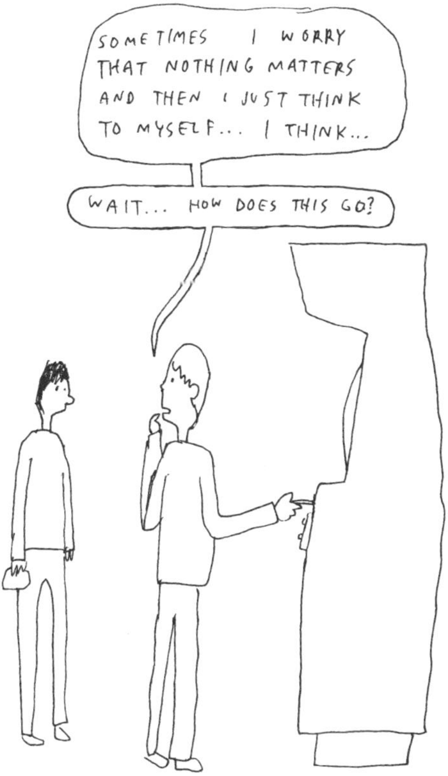
SOMETIMES I WORRY THAT NOTHING MATTERS AND THEN I JUST THINK TO MYSELF... I THINK...
WAIT... HOW DOES THIS GO?

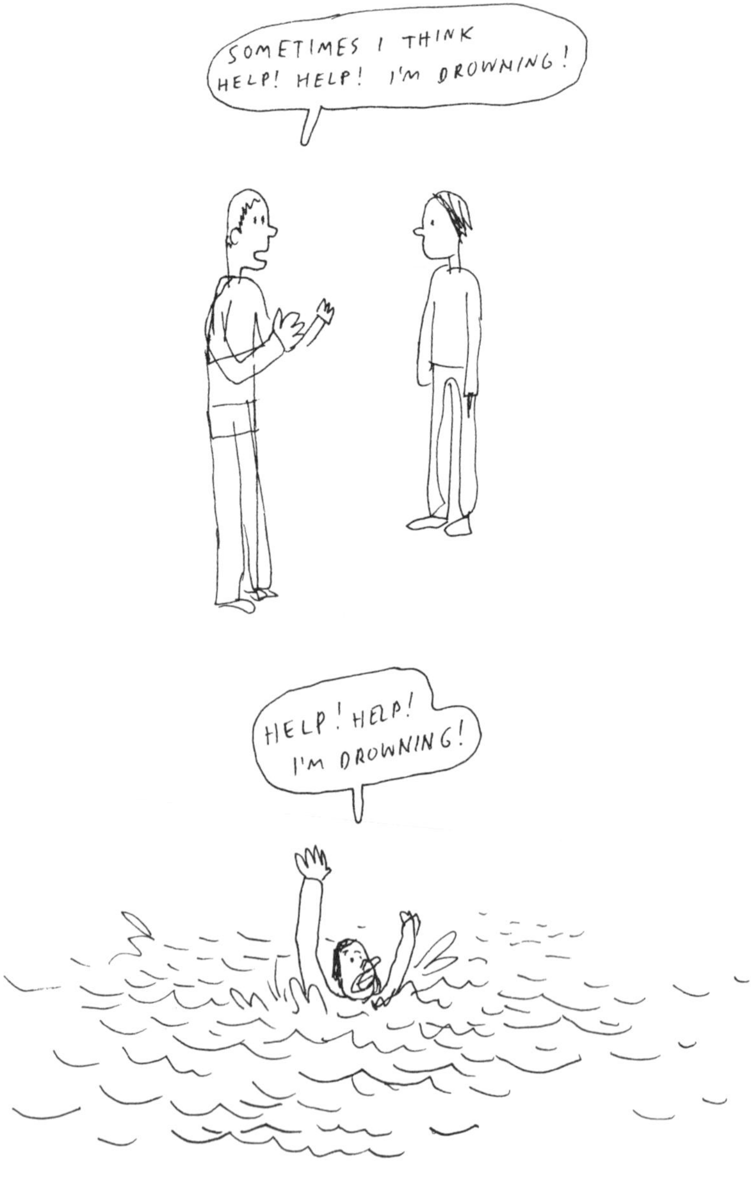
SOMETIMES I THINK HELP! HELP! I'M DROWNING!
HELP! HELP! I'M DROWNING!

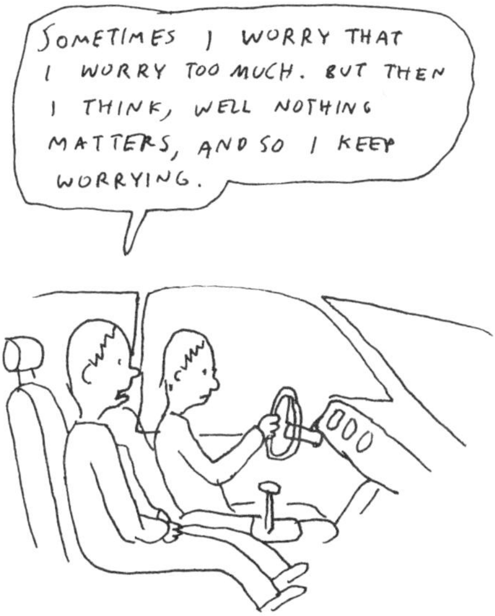
SOMETIMES I WORRY THAT I WORRY TOO MUCH. BUT THEN I THINK, WELL NOTHING MATTERS, AND SO I KEEP WORRYING.

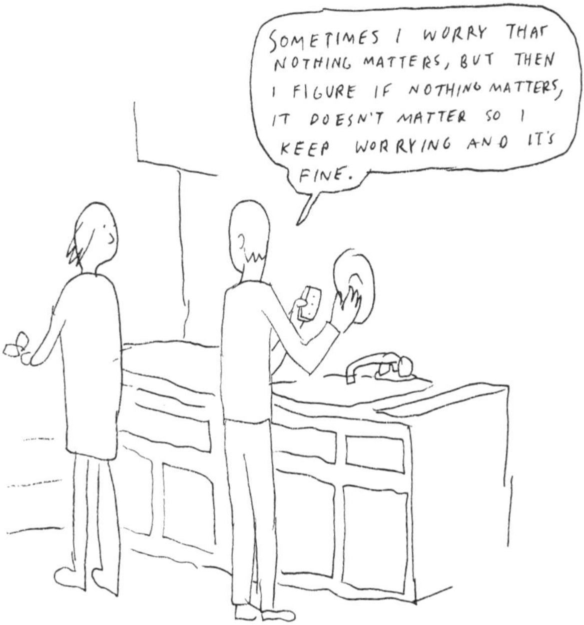
SOMETIMES I WORRY THAT NOTHING MATTERS, BUT THEN I FIGURE IF NOTHING MATTERS, IT DOESN'T MATTER SO I KEEP WORRYING AND IT'S FINE.

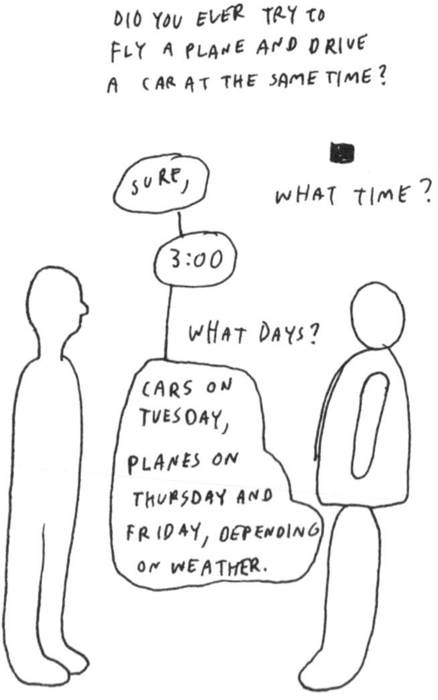
DID YOU EVER TRY TO FLY A PLANE AND DRIVE A CAR AT THE SAME TIME?
SURE,
WHAT TIME?
3:00
WHAT DAYS?
CARS ON TUESDAY, PLANES ON THURSDAY AND FRIDAY, DEPENDING ON WEATHER.

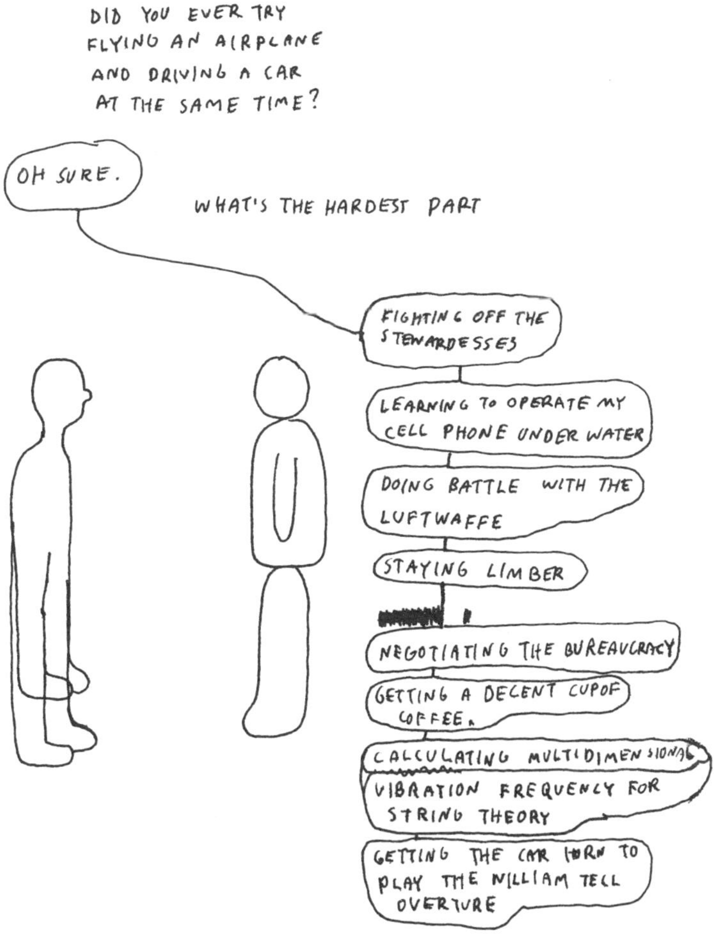
DID YOU EVER TRY FLYING AN AIRPLANE AND DRIVING A CAR AT THE SAME TIME?
OH SURE.
WHAT'S THE HARDEST PART
FIGHTING OFF THE STEWARDESSES
LEARNING TO OPERATE MY CELL PHONE UNDER WATER
DOING BATTLE WITH THE LUFTWAFFE
STAYING LIMBER
NEGOTIATING THE BUREAUCRACY
GETTING A DECENT CUPOF COFFEE.
CALCULATING MULTIDIMENSIONAL VIBRATION FREQUENCY FOR STRING THEORY
GETTING THE CAR HORN TO PLAY THE WILLIAM TELL OVERTURE

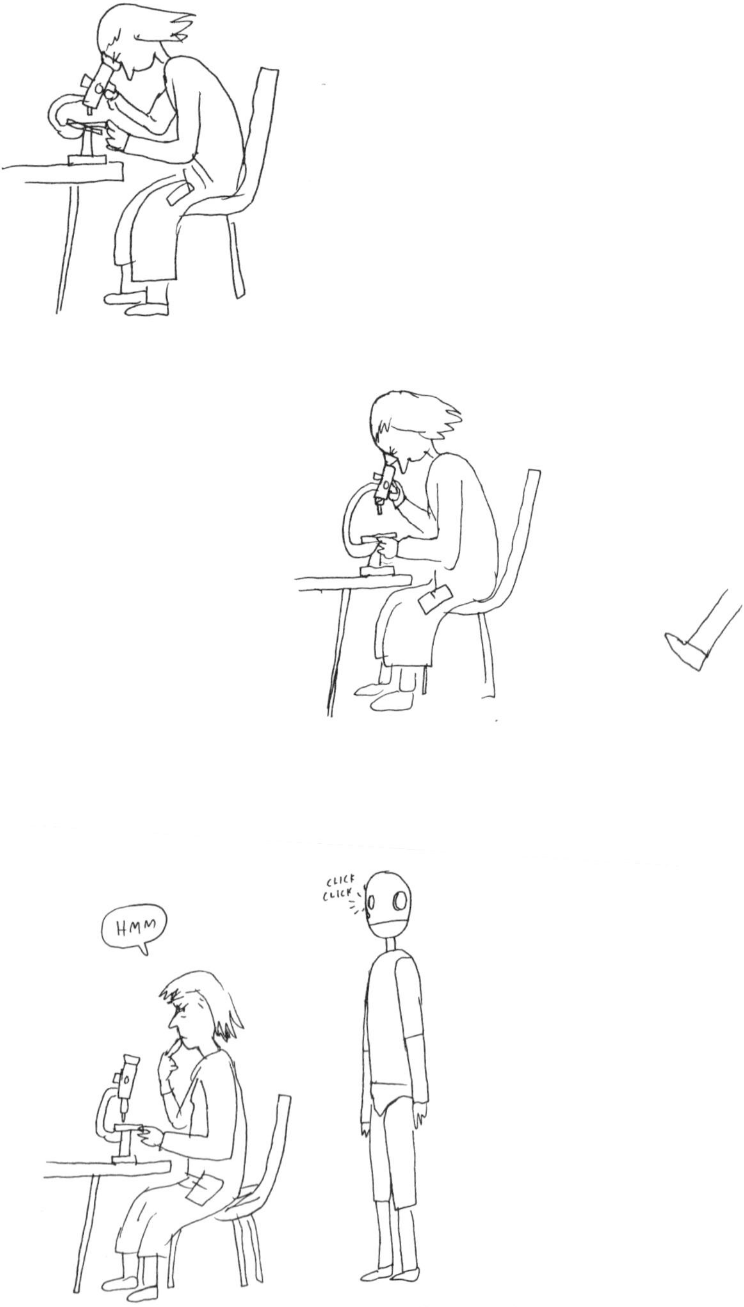
CLICK
CLICK
HMM

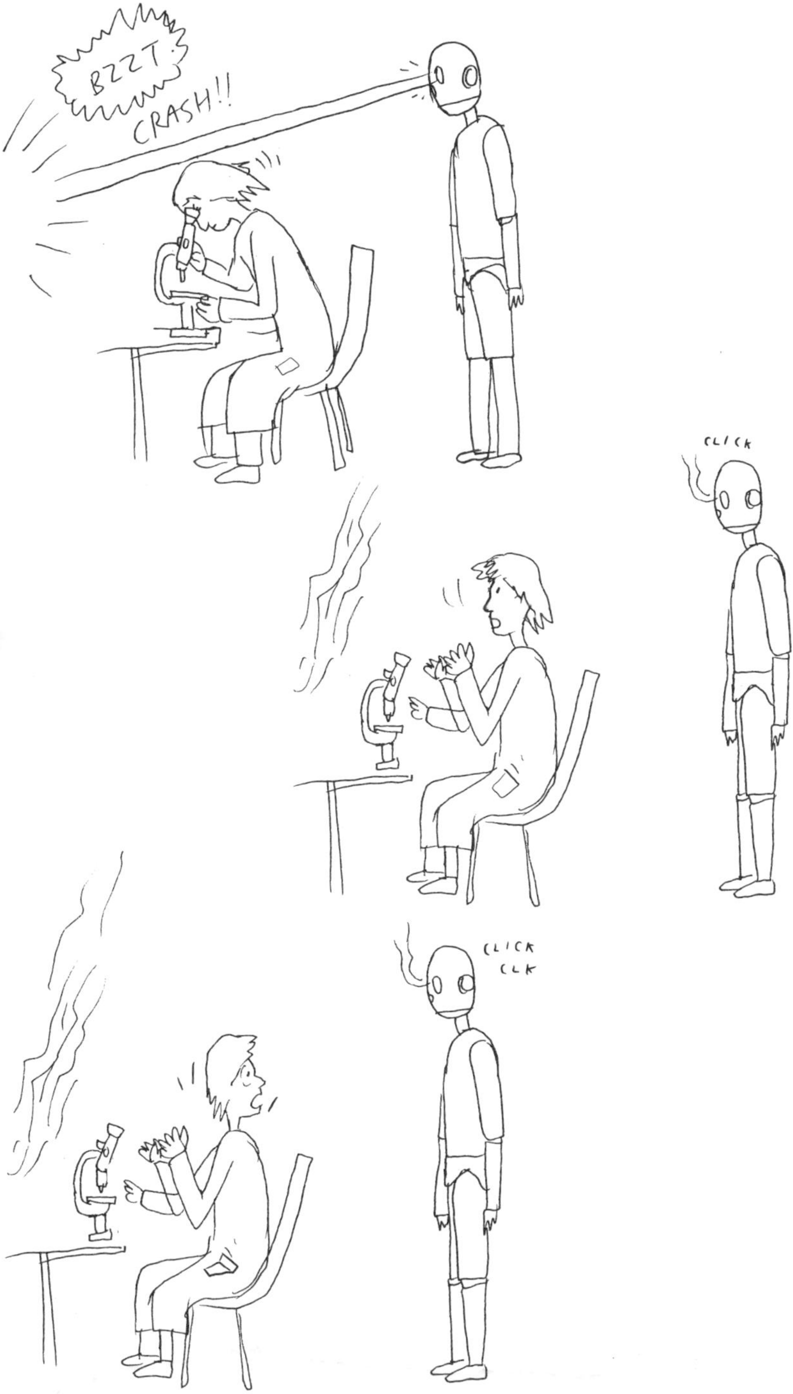
BZZT
CRASH!!
CLICK
CLICK
CLK

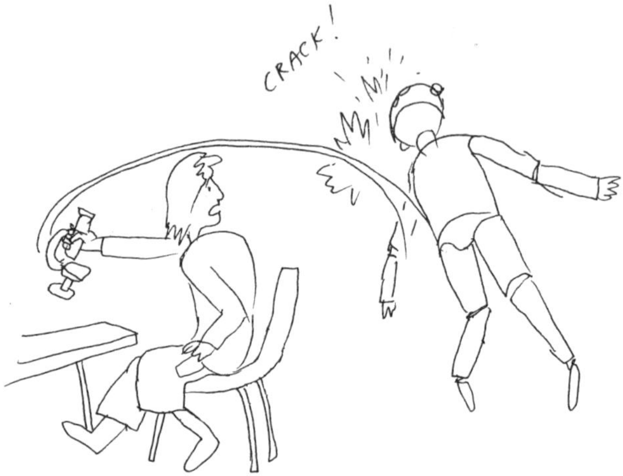
CRACK!

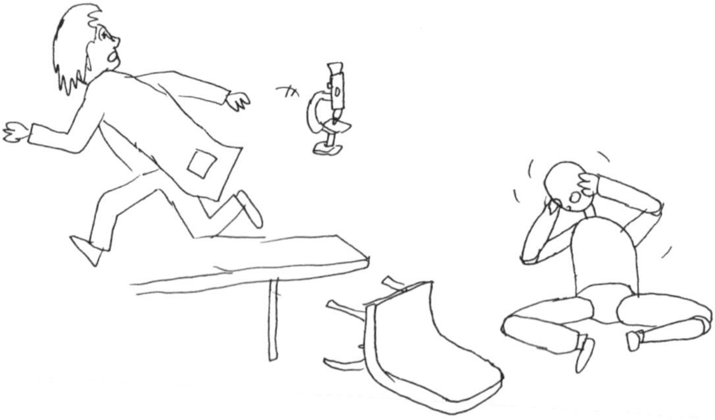

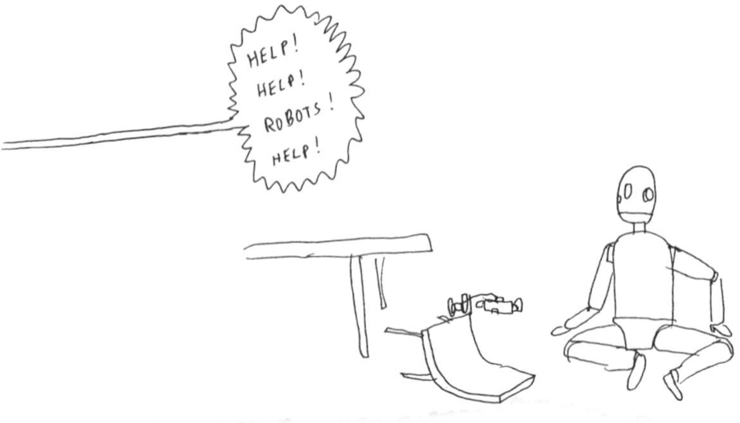
HELP!
HELP!
ROBOTS!
HELP!

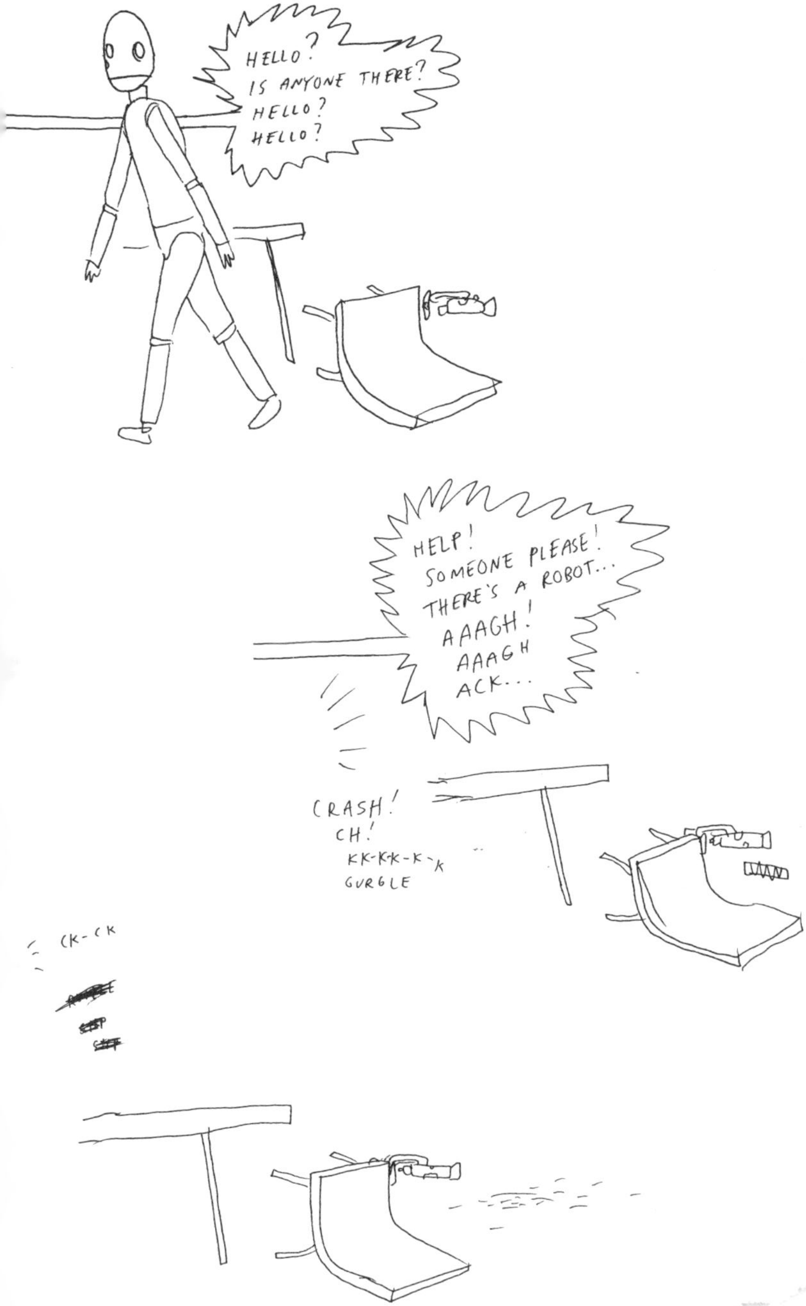
HELLO?
IS ANYONE THERE?
HELLO?
HELLO?
HELP!
SOMEONE PLEASE!
THERE'S A ROBOT...
AAAGH!
AAAGH
ACK...
CRASH!
CH!
KK-K-K-K-K
GURGLE
CK-CK

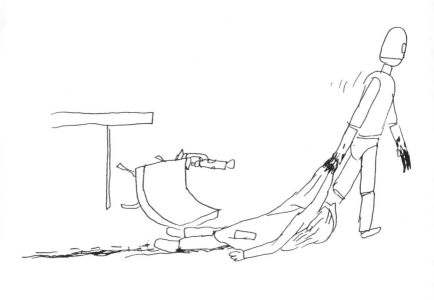

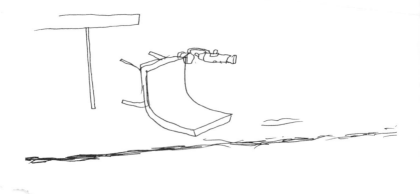

MUGGINGS

ACTUALLY, YES, I DID HAVE A BAD CHILDHOOD BUT THIS IS MORE ABOUT MY RETIREMENT.

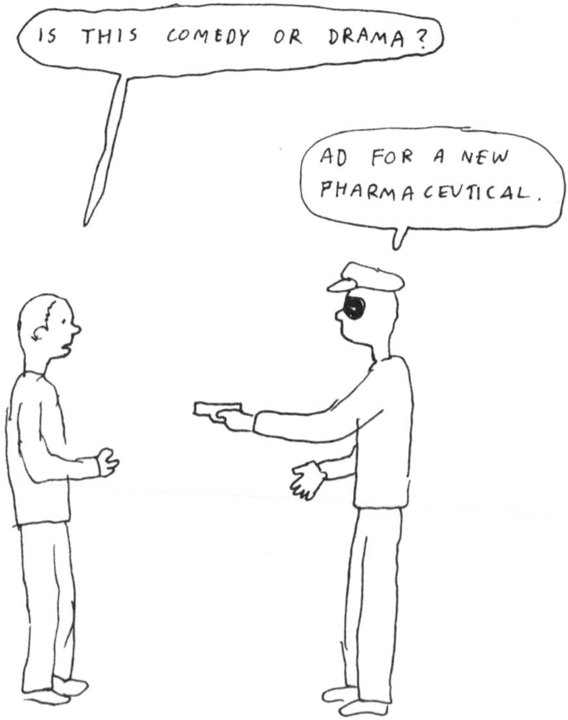
IS THIS COMEDY OR DRAMA?
AD FOR A NEW PHARMACEUTICAL.

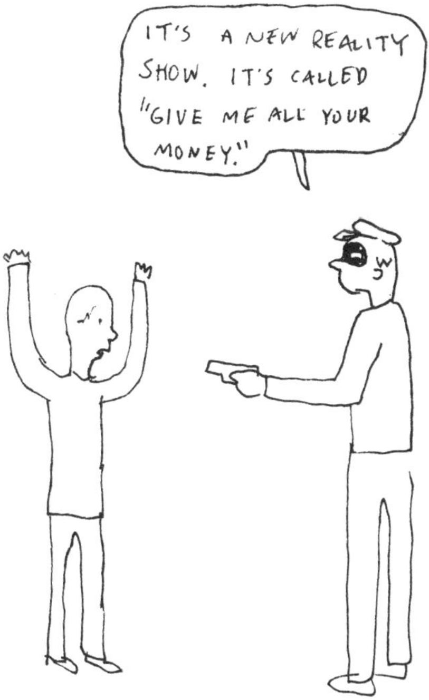
IT'S A NEW REALITY SHOW. IT'S CALLED "GIVE ME ALL YOUR MONEY."

CAN YOU HOLD ON FOR A MINUTE? I HAVE TO PEE.
CAN YOU HOLD ON A MINUTE? I HAVE TO CHECK MY EMAIL.

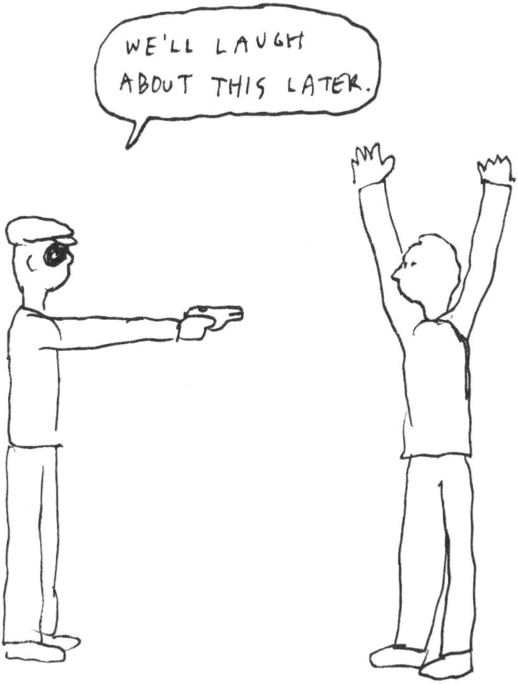
WE'LL LAUGH ABOUT THIS LATER.

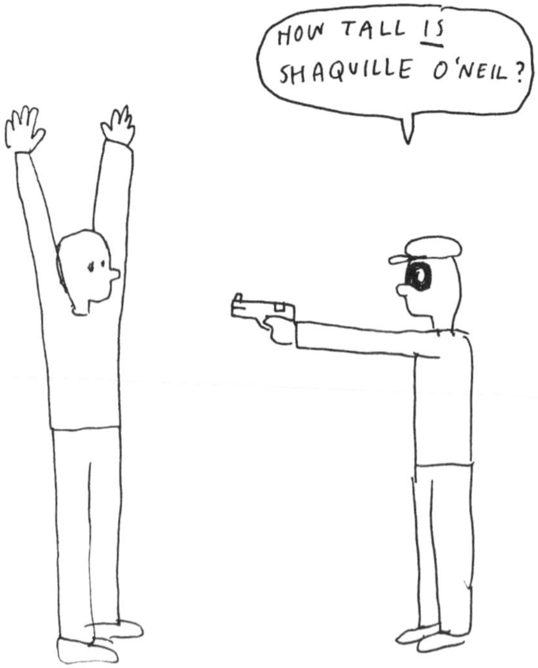
HOW TALL IS SHAQUILLE O'NEIL?

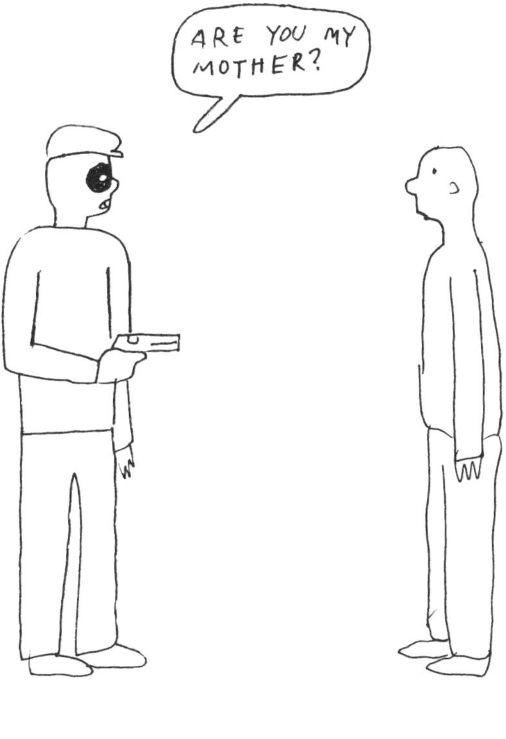
ARE YOU MY MOTHER?

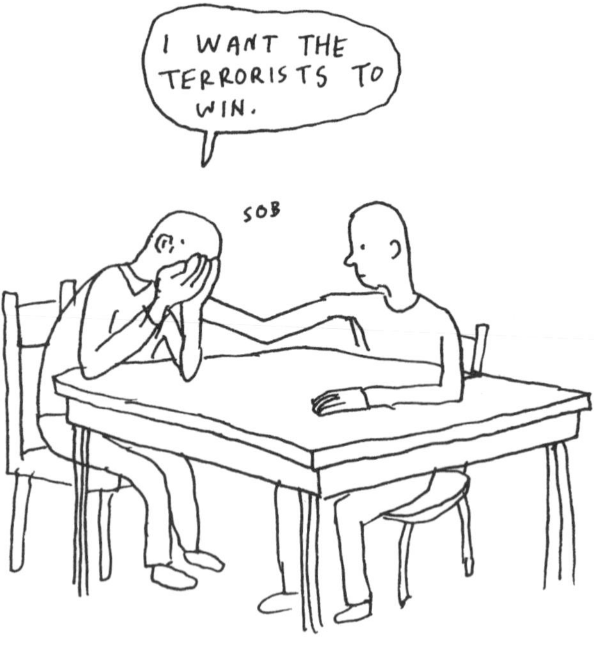
I WANT THE TERRORISTS TO WIN.
SOB

THIS IS AWKWARD.

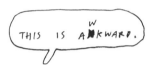

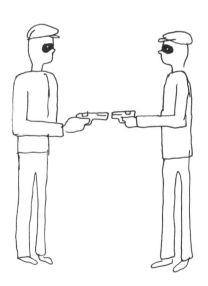

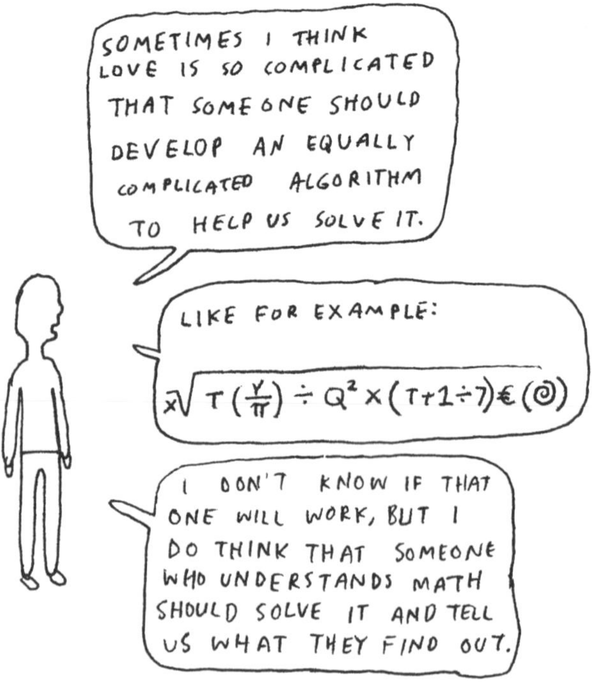

SOMETIMES I THINK
LOVE IS SO COMPLICATED
THAT SOMEONE SHOULD
DEVELOP AN EQUALLY
COMPLICATED ALGORITHM
TO HELP US SOLVE IT.

LIKE FOR EXAMPLE:

$$x\sqrt{T\left(\frac{y}{\pi}\right) \div Q^2 \times (T+1 \div 7) \in (\textcircled{\textit{o}})}$$

I DON'T KNOW IF THAT
ONE WILL WORK, BUT I
DO THINK THAT SOMEONE
WHO UNDERSTANDS MATH
SHOULD SOLVE IT AND TELL
US WHAT THEY FIND OUT.

EVERYTHING I NEEDED TO KNOW I LEARNED FROM BEATING PEOPLE UP AND MAKING THEM TELL ME.

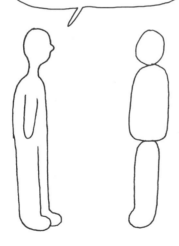

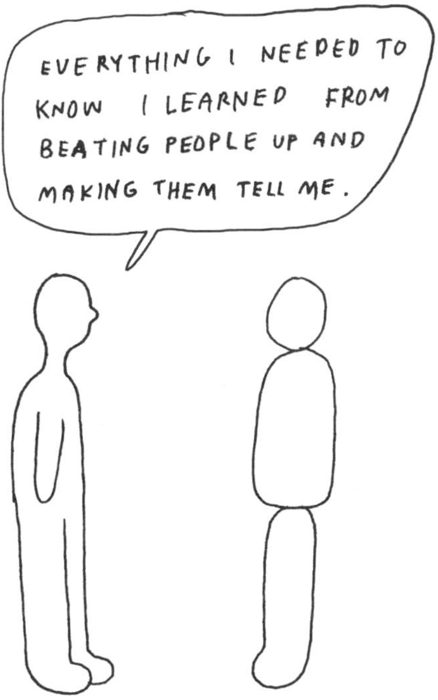

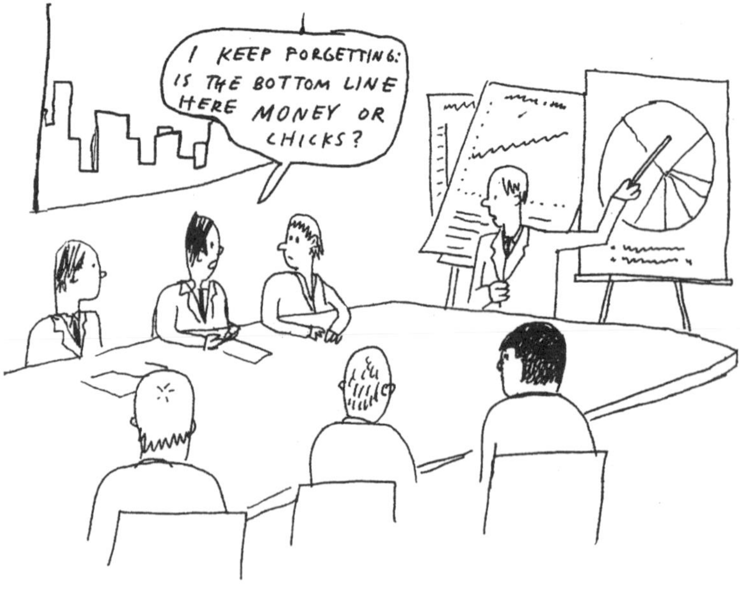
I KEEP FORGETTING: IS THE BOTTOM LINE HERE MONEY OR CHICKS?

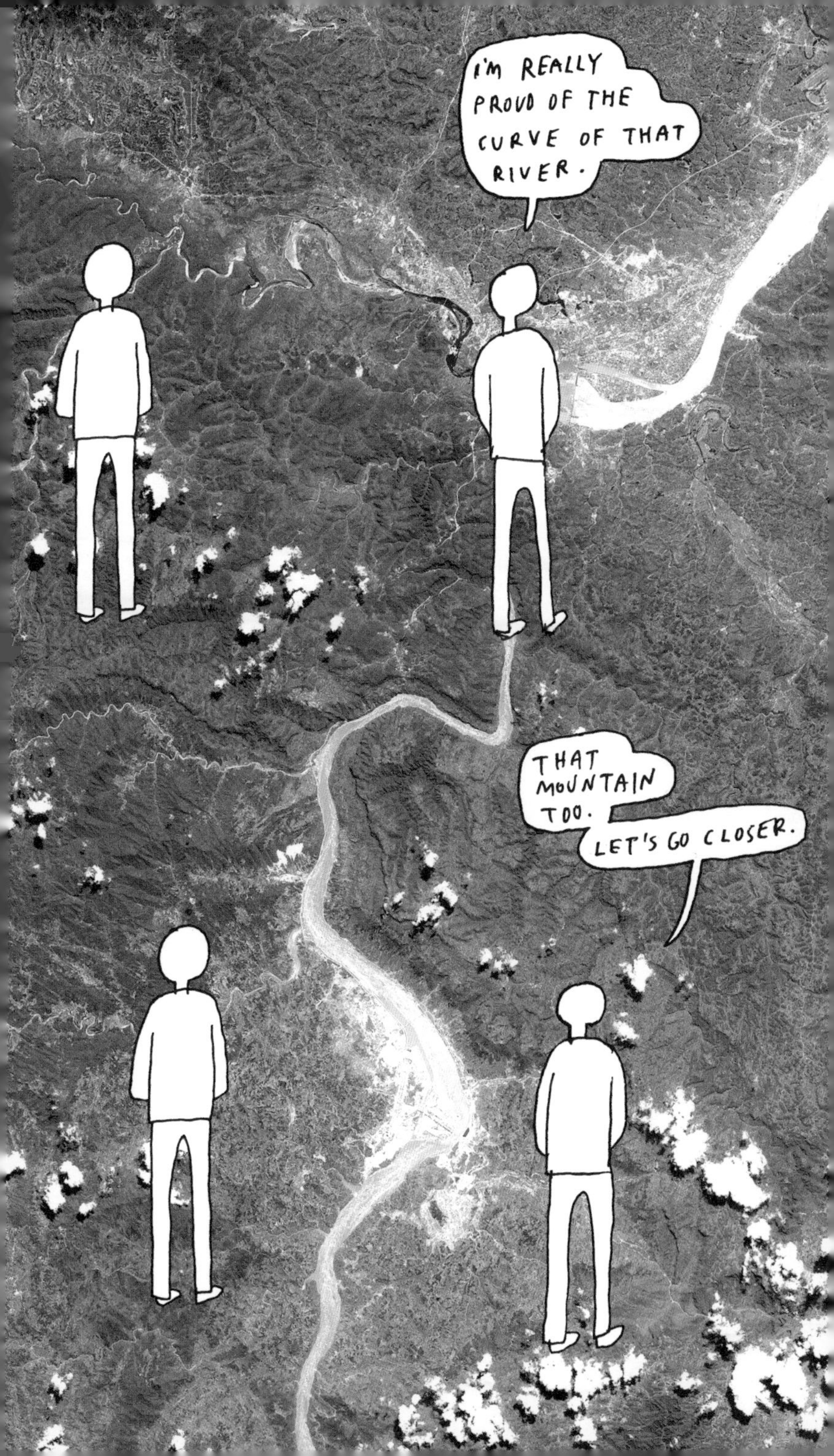
I'M REALLY PROUD OF THE CURVE OF THAT RIVER.
THAT MOUNTAIN TOO.
LET'S GO CLOSER.

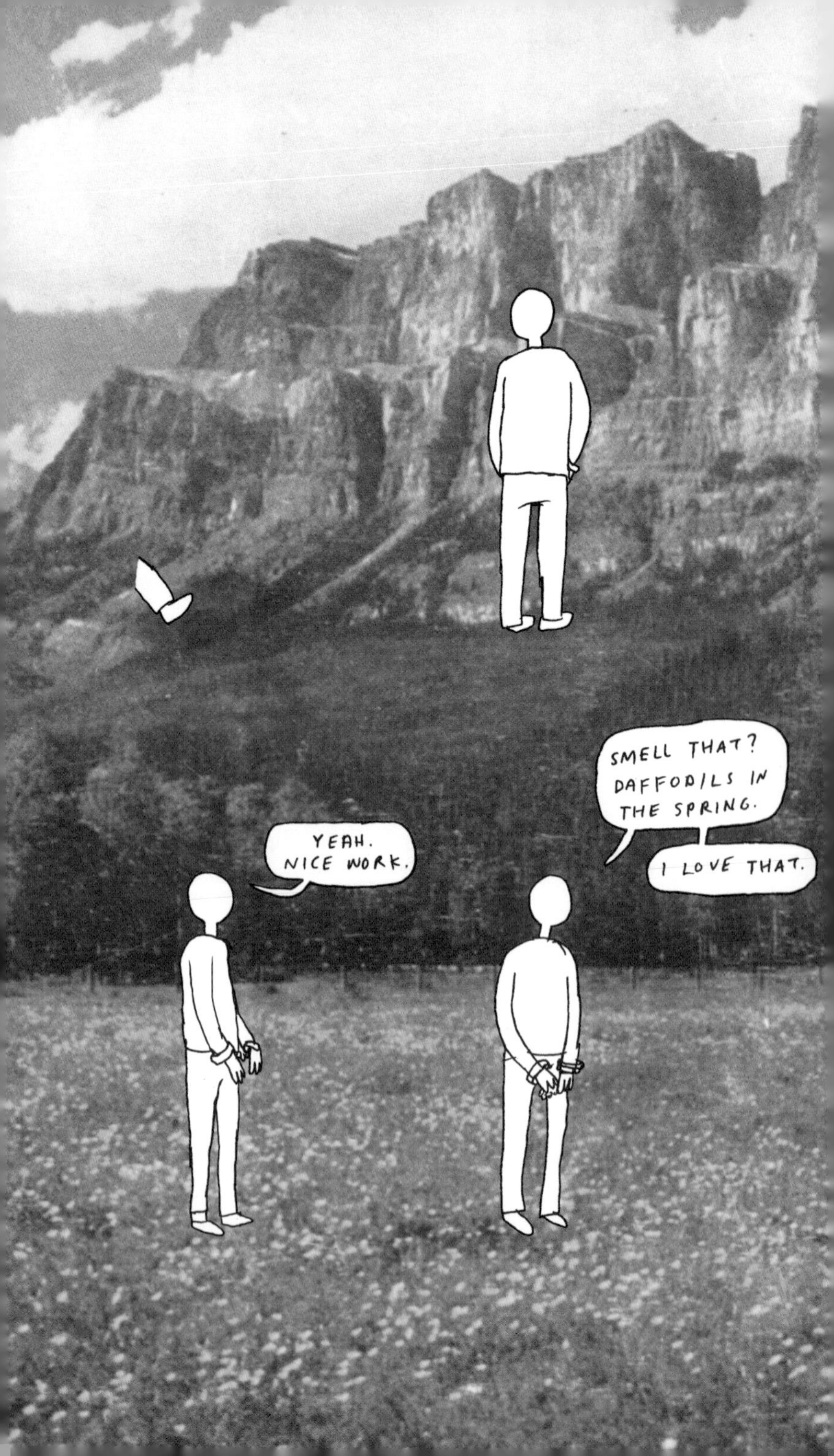
SMELL THAT? DAFFODILS IN THE SPRING.
I LOVE THAT.
YEAH. NICE WORK.

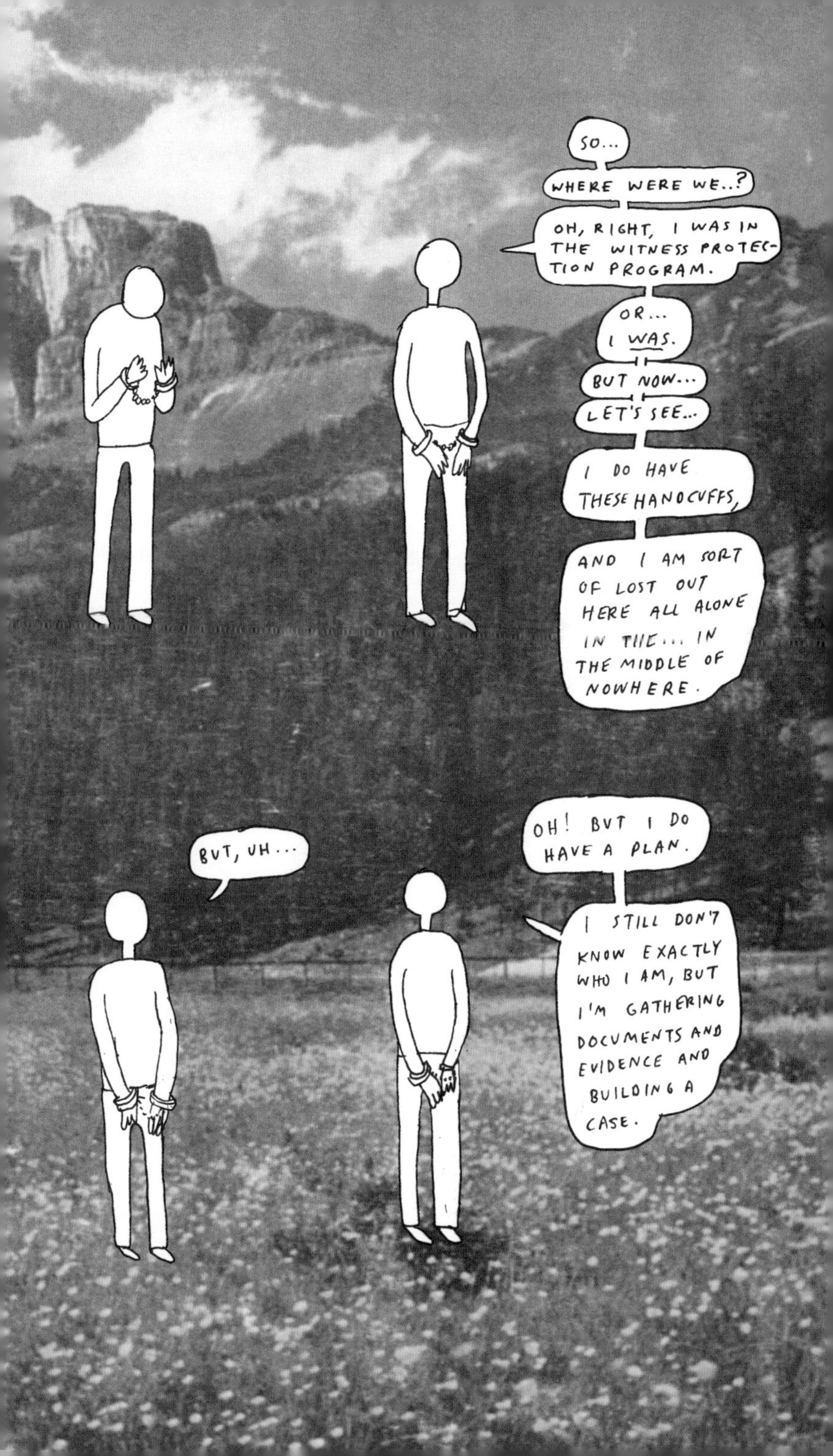
SO...
WHERE WERE WE...?
OH, RIGHT, I WAS IN THE WITNESS PROTECTION PROGRAM.
OR... I WAS.
BUT NOW...
LET'S SEE...
I DO HAVE THESE HANDCUFFS,
AND I AM SORT OF LOST OUT HERE ALL ALONE IN THE... IN THE MIDDLE OF NOWHERE.
BUT, UH...
OH! BUT I DO HAVE A PLAN.
I STILL DON'T KNOW EXACTLY WHO I AM, BUT I'M GATHERING DOCUMENTS AND EVIDENCE AND BUILDING A CASE.

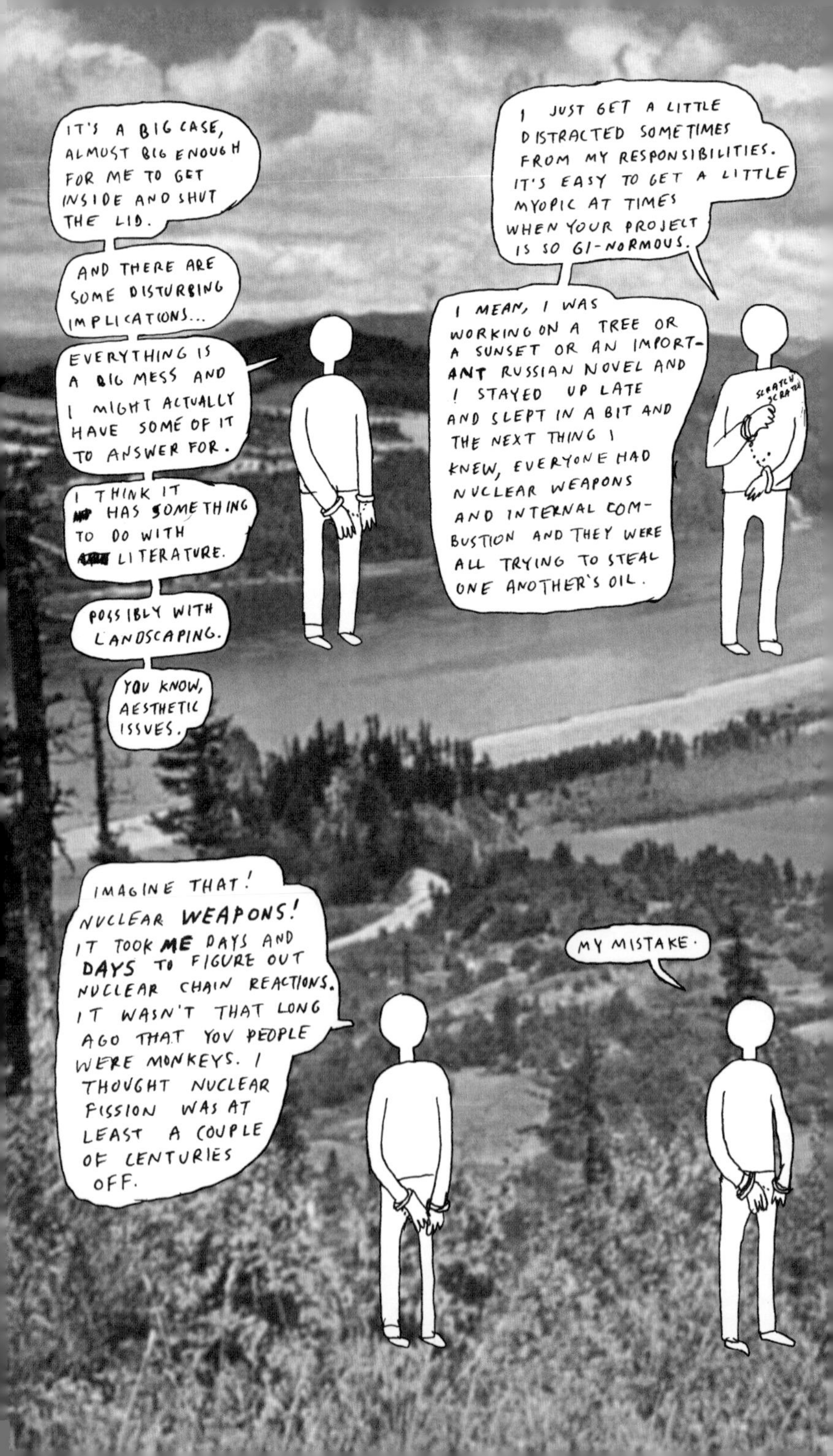
IT'S A BIG CASE, ALMOST BIG ENOUGH FOR ME TO GET INSIDE AND SHUT THE LID.
AND THERE ARE SOME DISTURBING IMPLICATIONS...
EVERYTHING IS A BIG MESS AND I MIGHT ACTUALLY HAVE SOME OF IT TO ANSWER FOR.
I THINK IT [redacted] HAS SOMETHING TO DO WITH [redacted] LITERATURE.
POSSIBLY WITH LANDSCAPING.
YOU KNOW, AESTHETIC ISSUES.
I JUST GET A LITTLE DISTRACTED SOMETIMES FROM MY RESPONSIBILITIES. IT'S EASY TO GET A LITTLE MYOPIC AT TIMES WHEN YOUR PROJECT IS SO GI-NORMOUS.
I MEAN, I WAS WORKING ON A TREE OR A SUNSET OR AN IMPORT-ANT RUSSIAN NOVEL AND I STAYED UP LATE AND SLEPT IN A BIT AND THE NEXT THING I KNEW, EVERYONE HAD NUCLEAR WEAPONS AND INTERNAL COM-BUSTION AND THEY WERE ALL TRYING TO STEAL ONE ANOTHER'S OIL.
SCRATCH SCRATCH
IMAGINE THAT! NUCLEAR WEAPONS! IT TOOK ME DAYS AND DAYS TO FIGURE OUT NUCLEAR CHAIN REACTIONS. IT WASN'T THAT LONG AGO THAT YOU PEOPLE WERE MONKEYS. I THOUGHT NUCLEAR FISSION WAS AT LEAST A COUPLE OF CENTURIES OFF.
MY MISTAKE.

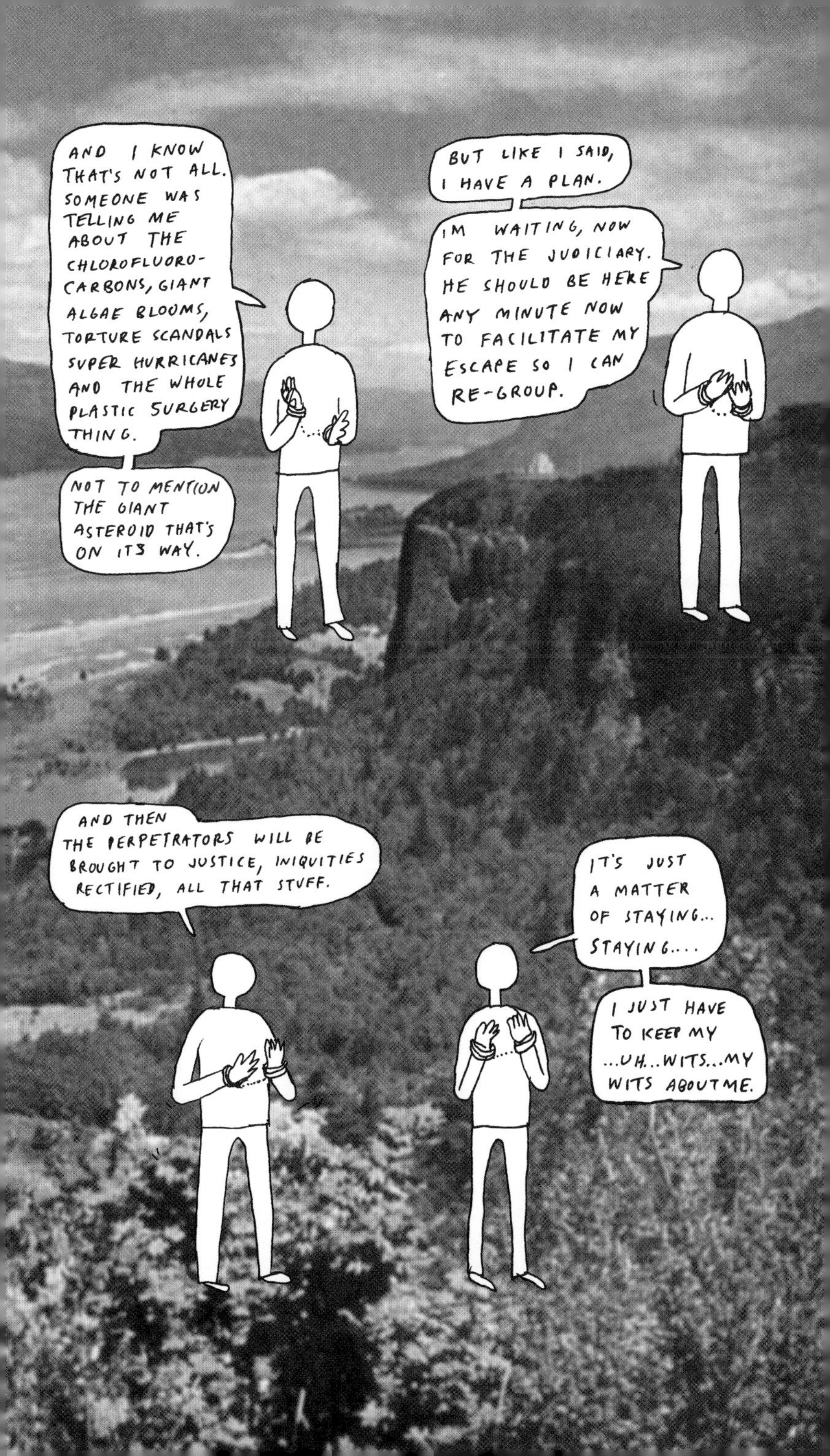
AND I KNOW THAT'S NOT ALL. SOMEONE WAS TELLING ME ABOUT THE CHLOROFLUORO-CARBONS, GIANT ALGAE BLOOMS, TORTURE SCANDALS SUPER HURRICANES AND THE WHOLE PLASTIC SURGERY THING.
NOT TO MENTION THE GIANT ASTEROID THAT'S ON ITS WAY.
BUT LIKE I SAID, I HAVE A PLAN.
IM WAITING, NOW FOR THE JUDICIARY. HE SHOULD BE HERE ANY MINUTE NOW TO FACILITATE MY ESCAPE SO I CAN RE-GROUP.
AND THEN THE PERPETRATORS WILL BE BROUGHT TO JUSTICE, INIQUITIES RECTIFIED, ALL THAT STUFF.
IT'S JUST A MATTER OF STAYING... STAYING....
I JUST HAVE TO KEEP MY ...UH...WITS...MY WITS ABOUTME.

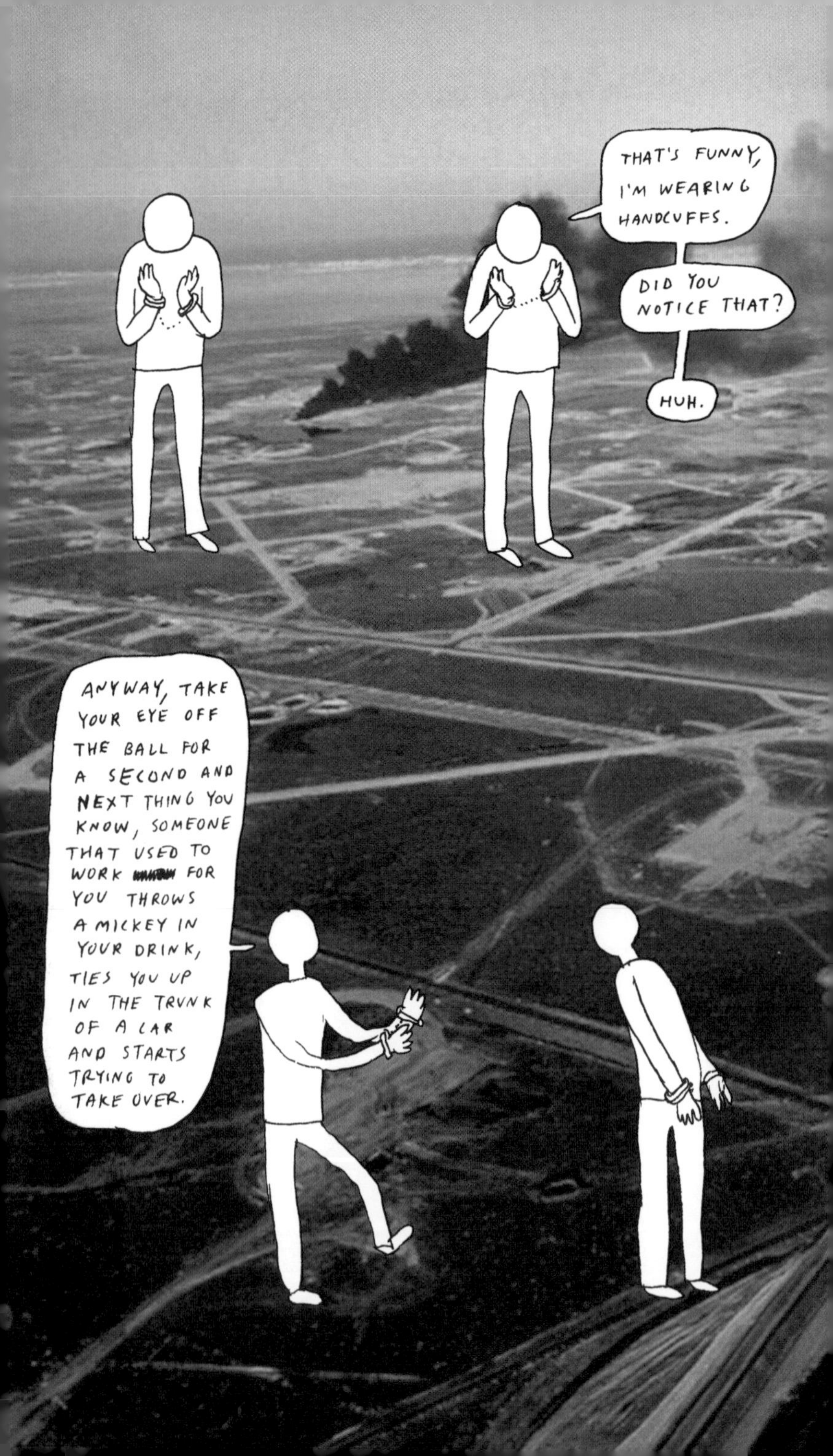
THAT'S FUNNY, I'M WEARING HANDCUFFS.
DID YOU NOTICE THAT?
HUH.
ANYWAY, TAKE YOUR EYE OFF THE BALL FOR A SECOND AND NEXT THING YOU KNOW, SOMEONE THAT USED TO WORK FOR YOU THROWS A MICKEY IN YOUR DRINK, TIES YOU UP IN THE TRUNK OF A CAR AND STARTS TRYING TO TAKE OVER.

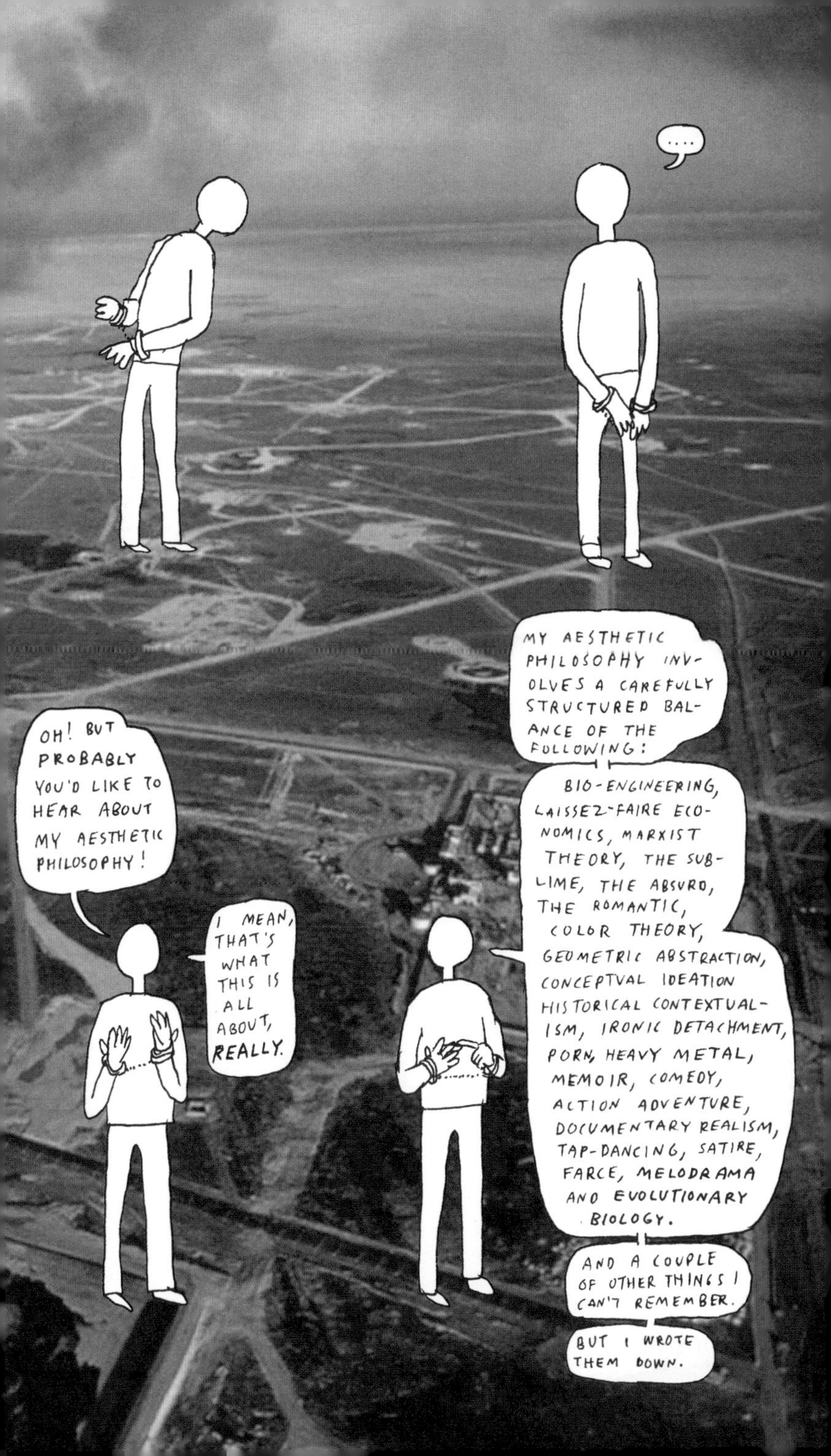
....
OH! BUT PROBABLY YOU'D LIKE TO HEAR ABOUT MY AESTHETIC PHILOSOPHY!
I MEAN, THAT'S WHAT THIS IS ALL ABOUT, **REALLY**.
MY AESTHETIC PHILOSOPHY INVOLVES A CAREFULLY STRUCTURED BALANCE OF THE FOLLOWING:
BIO-ENGINEERING, LAISSEZ-FAIRE ECONOMICS, MARXIST THEORY, THE SUBLIME, THE ABSURD, THE ROMANTIC, COLOR THEORY, GEOMETRIC ABSTRACTION, CONCEPTUAL IDEATION HISTORICAL CONTEXTUALISM, IRONIC DETACHMENT, PORN, HEAVY METAL, MEMOIR, COMEDY, ACTION ADVENTURE, DOCUMENTARY REALISM, TAP-DANCING, SATIRE, FARCE, MELODRAMA AND EVOLUTIONARY BIOLOGY.
AND A COUPLE OF OTHER THINGS I CAN'T REMEMBER.
BUT I WROTE THEM DOWN.

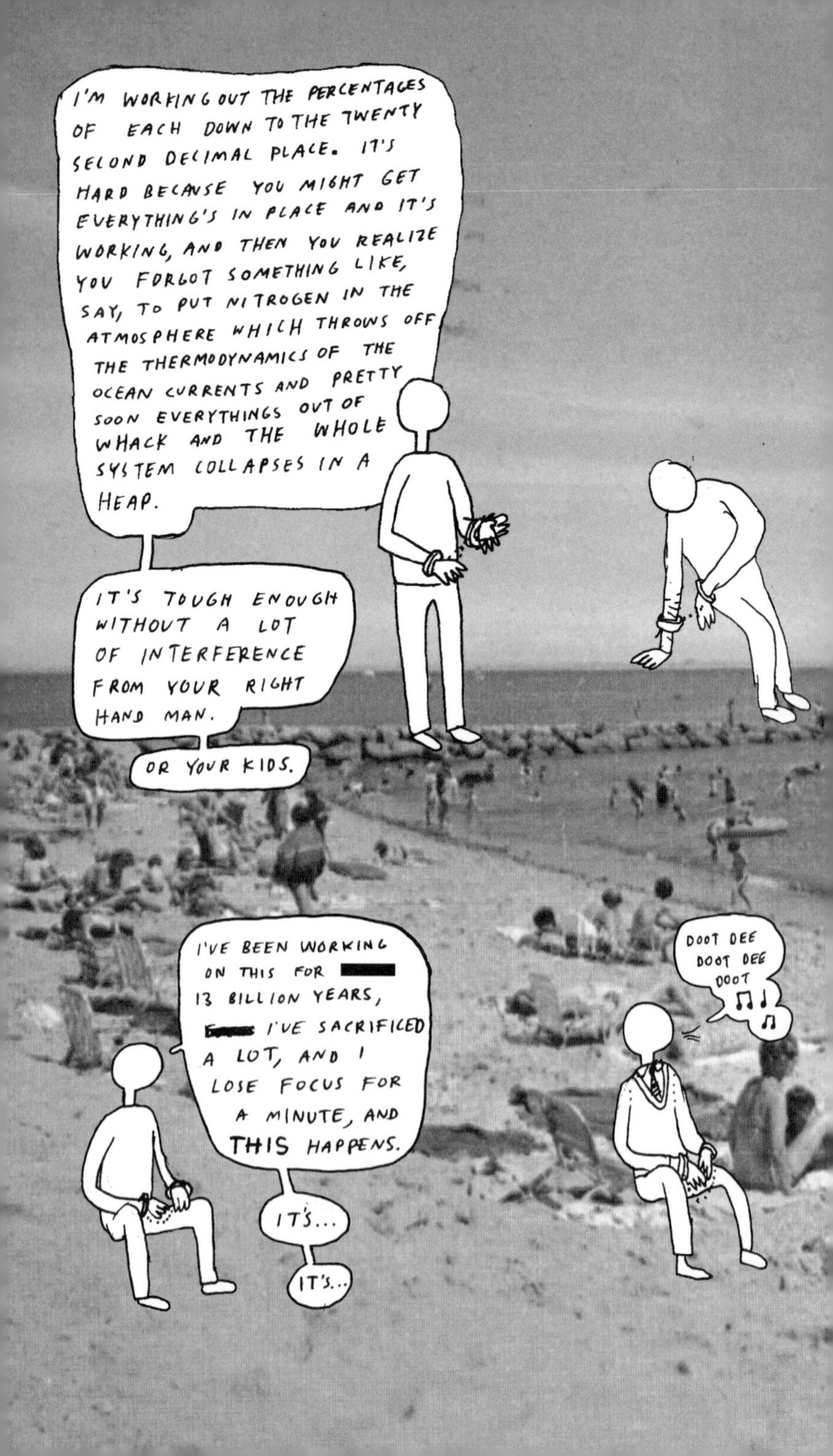
I'M WORKING OUT THE PERCENTAGES OF EACH DOWN TO THE TWENTY SECOND DECIMAL PLACE. IT'S HARD BECAUSE YOU MIGHT GET EVERYTHING'S IN PLACE AND IT'S WORKING, AND THEN YOU REALIZE YOU FORGOT SOMETHING LIKE, SAY, TO PUT NITROGEN IN THE ATMOSPHERE WHICH THROWS OFF THE THERMODYNAMICS OF THE OCEAN CURRENTS AND PRETTY SOON EVERYTHINGS OUT OF WHACK AND THE WHOLE SYSTEM COLLAPSES IN A HEAP.
IT'S TOUGH ENOUGH WITHOUT A LOT OF INTERFERENCE FROM YOUR RIGHT HAND MAN.
OR YOUR KIDS.
I'VE BEEN WORKING ON THIS FOR [redacted] 13 BILLION YEARS, [redacted] I'VE SACRIFICED A LOT, AND I LOSE FOCUS FOR A MINUTE, AND THIS HAPPENS.
IT'S...
IT'S...
DOOT DEE DOOT DEE DOOT

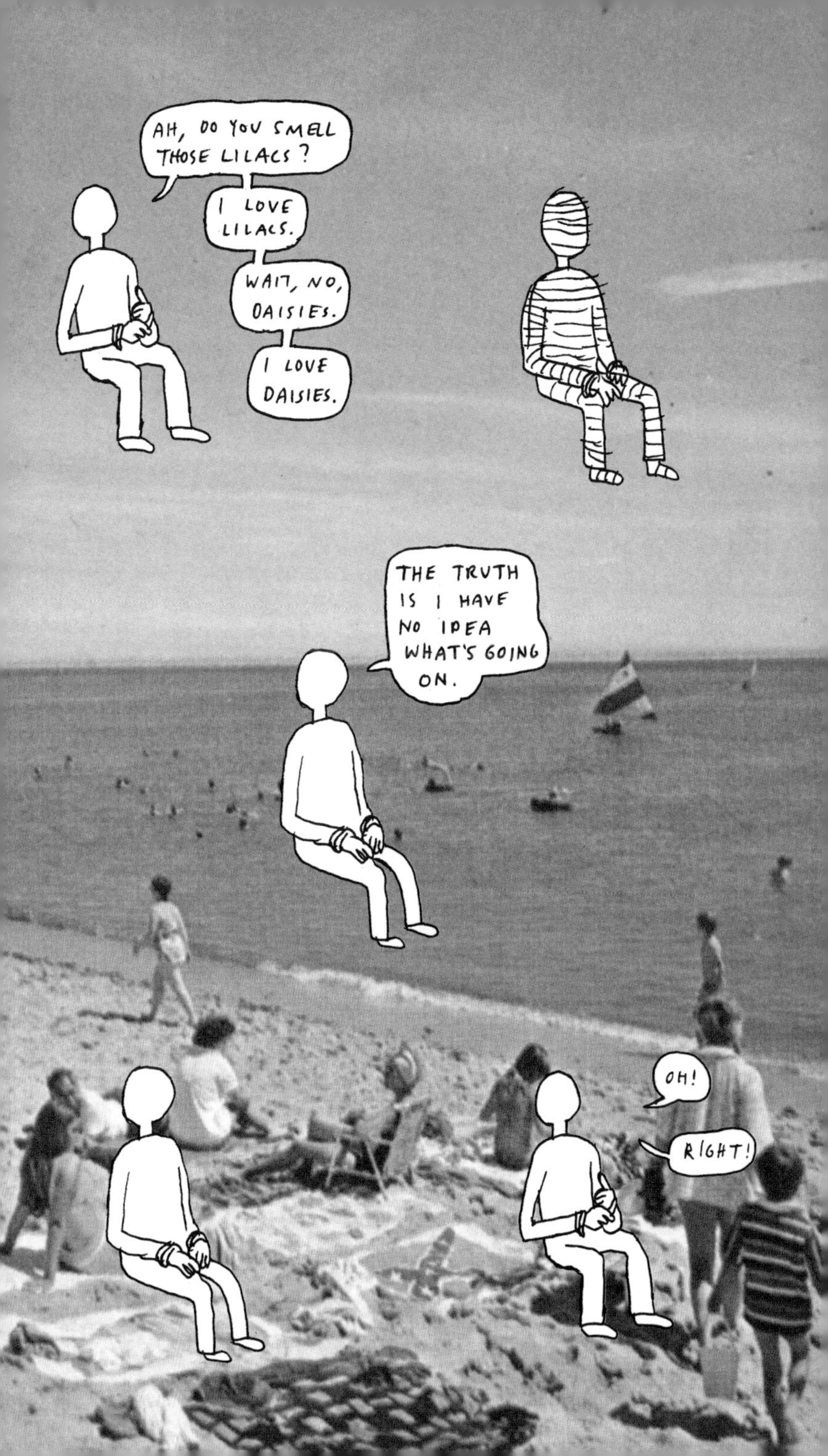
AH, DO YOU SMELL THOSE LILACS?
I LOVE LILACS.
WAIT, NO, DAISIES.
I LOVE DAISIES.
THE TRUTH IS I HAVE NO IDEA WHAT'S GOING ON.
OH!
RIGHT!

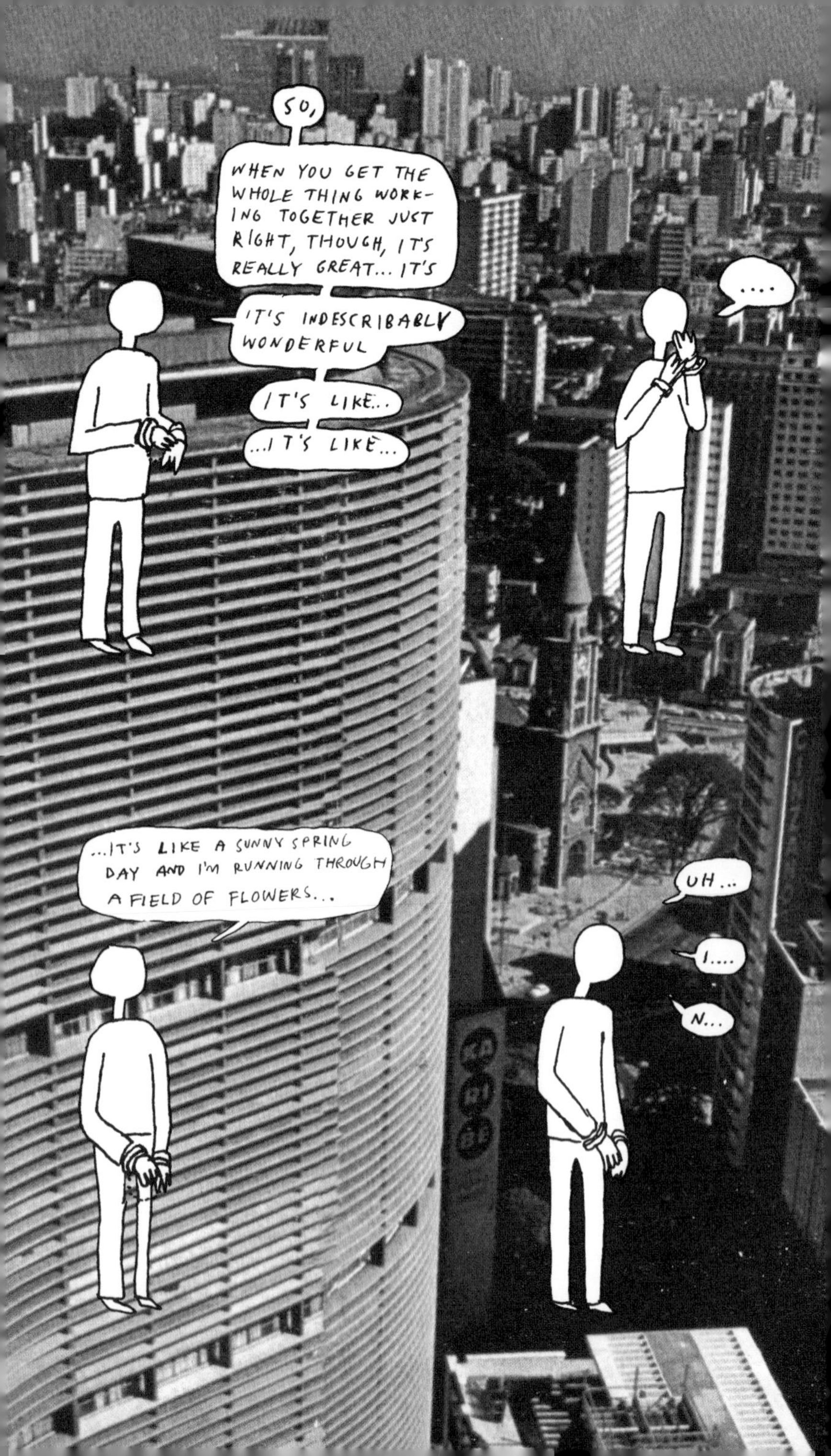
SO,
WHEN YOU GET THE WHOLE THING WORKING TOGETHER JUST RIGHT, THOUGH, IT'S REALLY GREAT... IT'S
IT'S INDESCRIBABLY WONDERFUL
IT'S LIKE..
...IT'S LIKE...
....
...IT'S LIKE A SUNNY SPRING DAY AND I'M RUNNING THROUGH A FIELD OF FLOWERS...
UH...
I....
N...

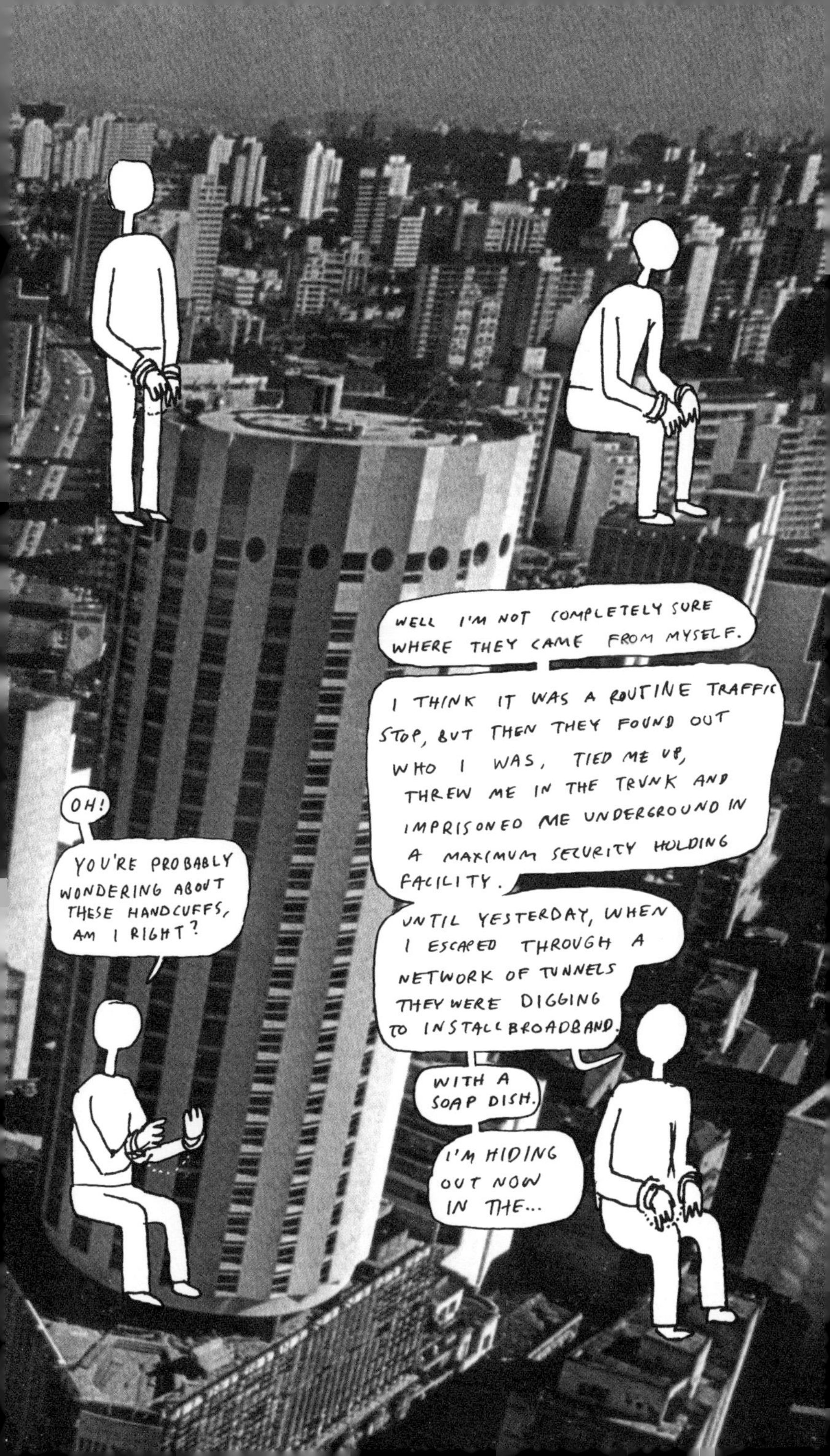

OH!
YOU'RE PROBABLY WONDERING ABOUT THESE HANDCUFFS, AM I RIGHT?
WELL I'M NOT COMPLETELY SURE WHERE THEY CAME FROM MYSELF.
I THINK IT WAS A ROUTINE TRAFFIC STOP, BUT THEN THEY FOUND OUT WHO I WAS, TIED ME UP, THREW ME IN THE TRUNK AND IMPRISONED ME UNDERGROUND IN A MAXIMUM SECURITY HOLDING FACILITY.
UNTIL YESTERDAY, WHEN I ESCAPED THROUGH A NETWORK OF TUNNELS THEY WERE DIGGING TO INSTALL BROADBAND.
WITH A SOAP DISH.
I'M HIDING OUT NOW IN THE...

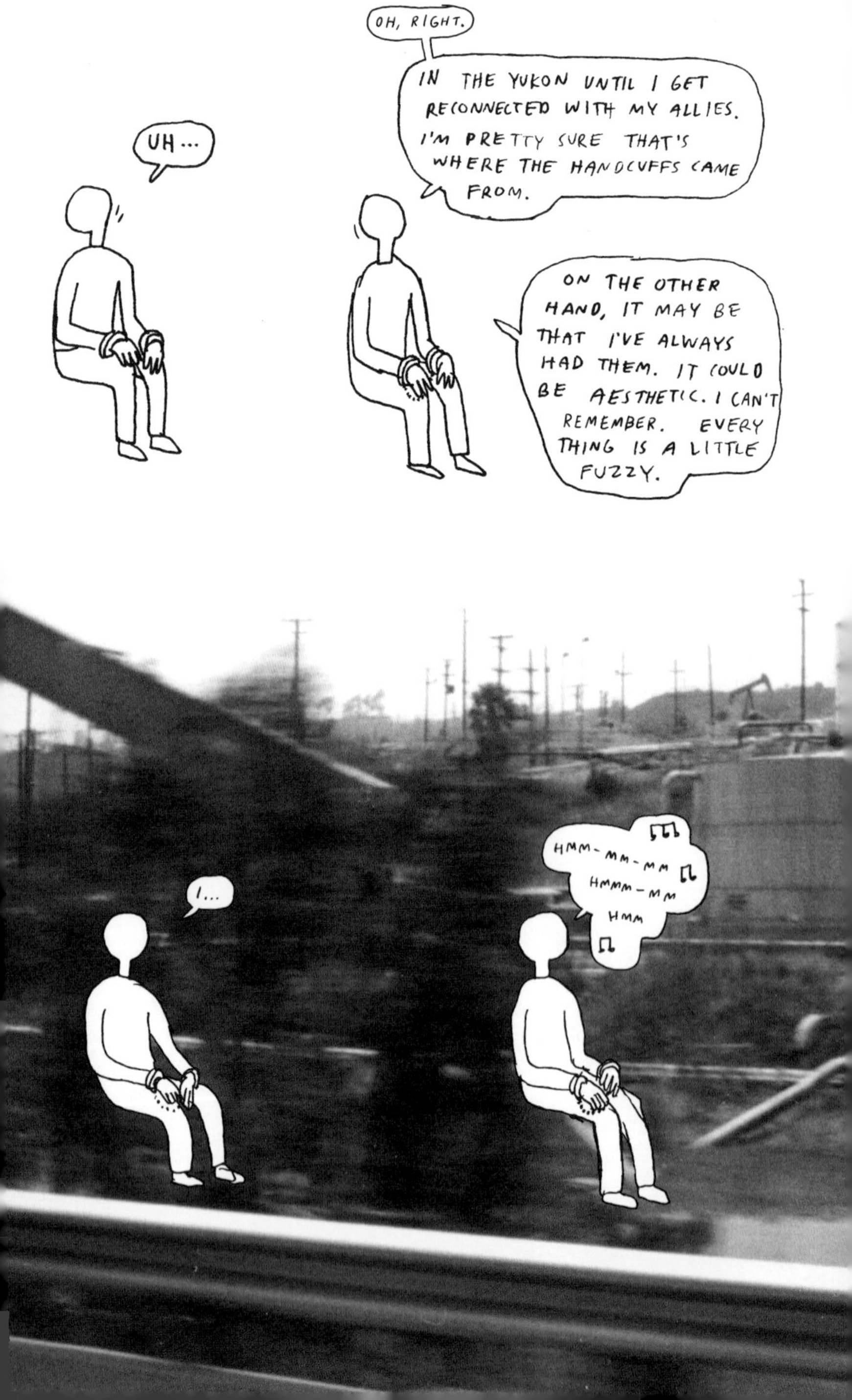
UH...
OH, RIGHT.
IN THE YUKON UNTIL I GET RECONNECTED WITH MY ALLIES. I'M PRETTY SURE THAT'S WHERE THE HANDCUFFS CAME FROM.
ON THE OTHER HAND, IT MAY BE THAT I'VE ALWAYS HAD THEM. IT COULD BE AESTHETIC. I CAN'T REMEMBER. EVERY THING IS A LITTLE FUZZY.
I...
HMM-MM-MM HMMM-MM HMM

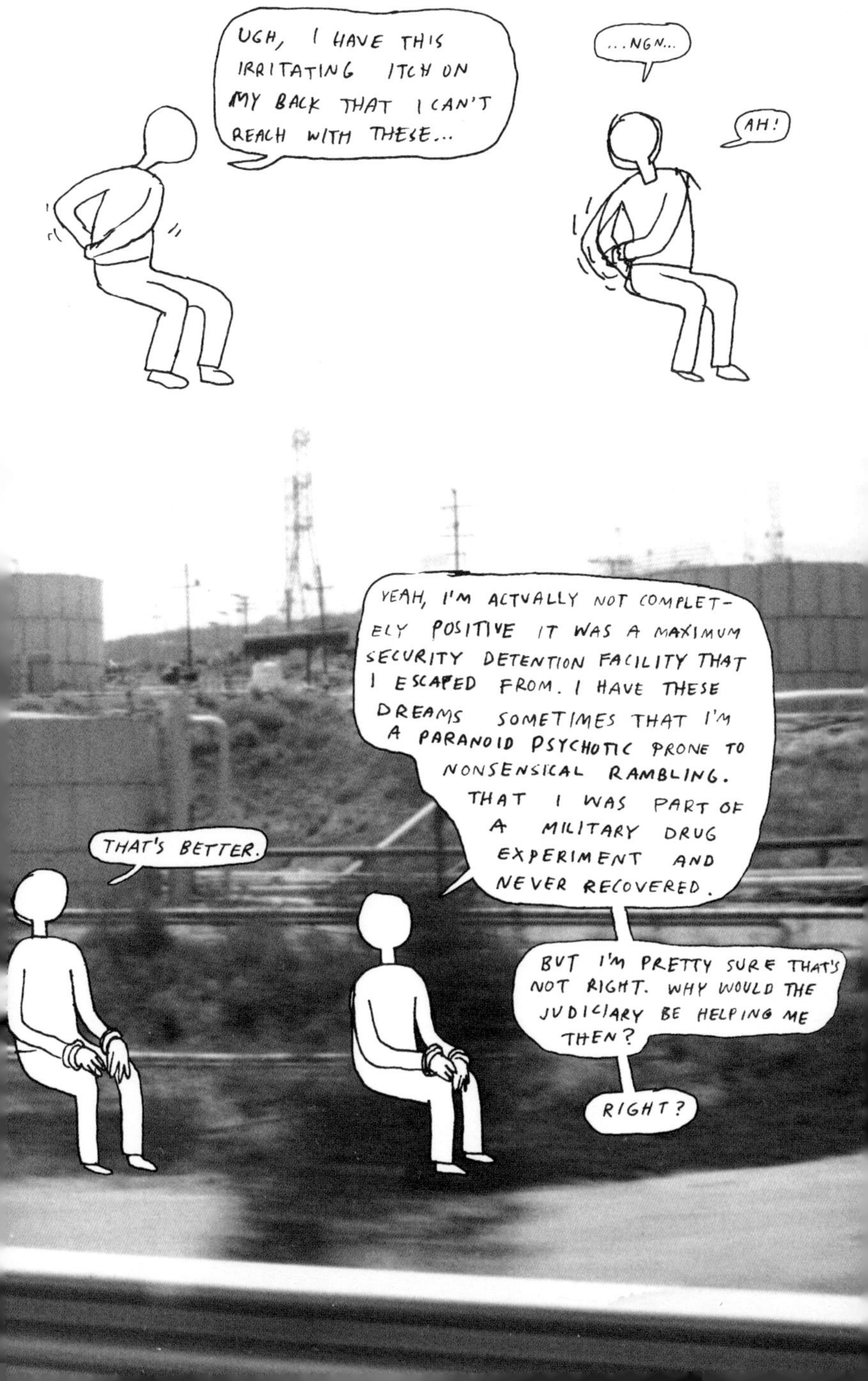
UGH, I HAVE THIS IRRITATING ITCH ON MY BACK THAT I CAN'T REACH WITH THESE...
...NGN...
AH!
THAT'S BETTER.
YEAH, I'M ACTUALLY NOT COMPLETELY POSITIVE IT WAS A MAXIMUM SECURITY DETENTION FACILITY THAT I ESCAPED FROM. I HAVE THESE DREAMS SOMETIMES THAT I'M A PARANOID PSYCHOTIC PRONE TO NONSENSICAL RAMBLING. THAT I WAS PART OF A MILITARY DRUG EXPERIMENT AND NEVER RECOVERED.
BUT I'M PRETTY SURE THAT'S NOT RIGHT. WHY WOULD THE JUDICIARY BE HELPING ME THEN?
RIGHT?

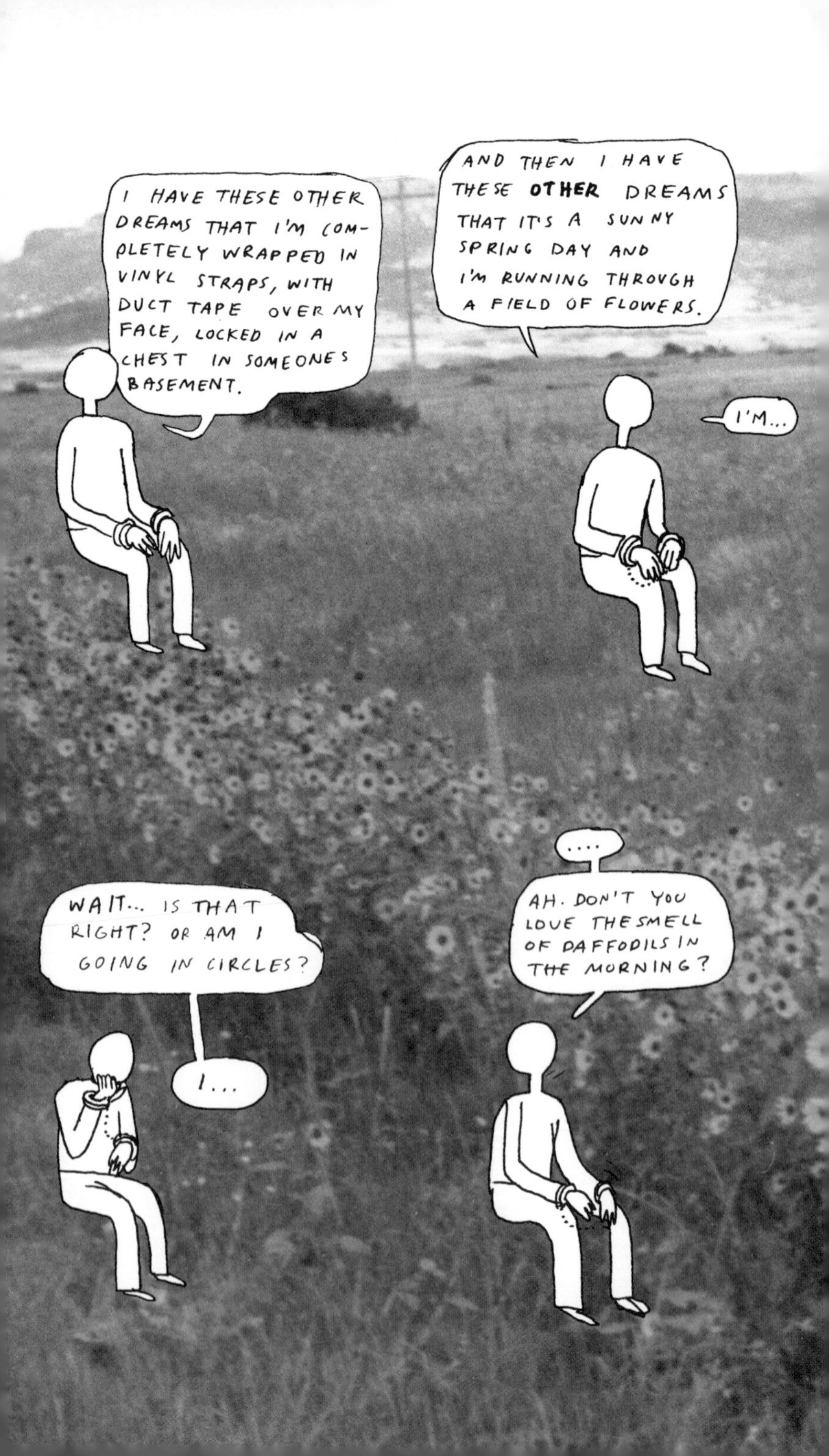
I HAVE THESE OTHER DREAMS THAT I'M COMPLETELY WRAPPED IN VINYL STRAPS, WITH DUCT TAPE OVER MY FACE, LOCKED IN A CHEST IN SOMEONES BASEMENT.
AND THEN I HAVE THESE **OTHER** DREAMS THAT IT'S A SUNNY SPRING DAY AND I'M RUNNING THROUGH A FIELD OF FLOWERS.
I'M...
WAIT... IS THAT RIGHT? OR AM I GOING IN CIRCLES?
I...
....
AH. DON'T YOU LOVE THE SMELL OF DAFFODILS IN THE MORNING?

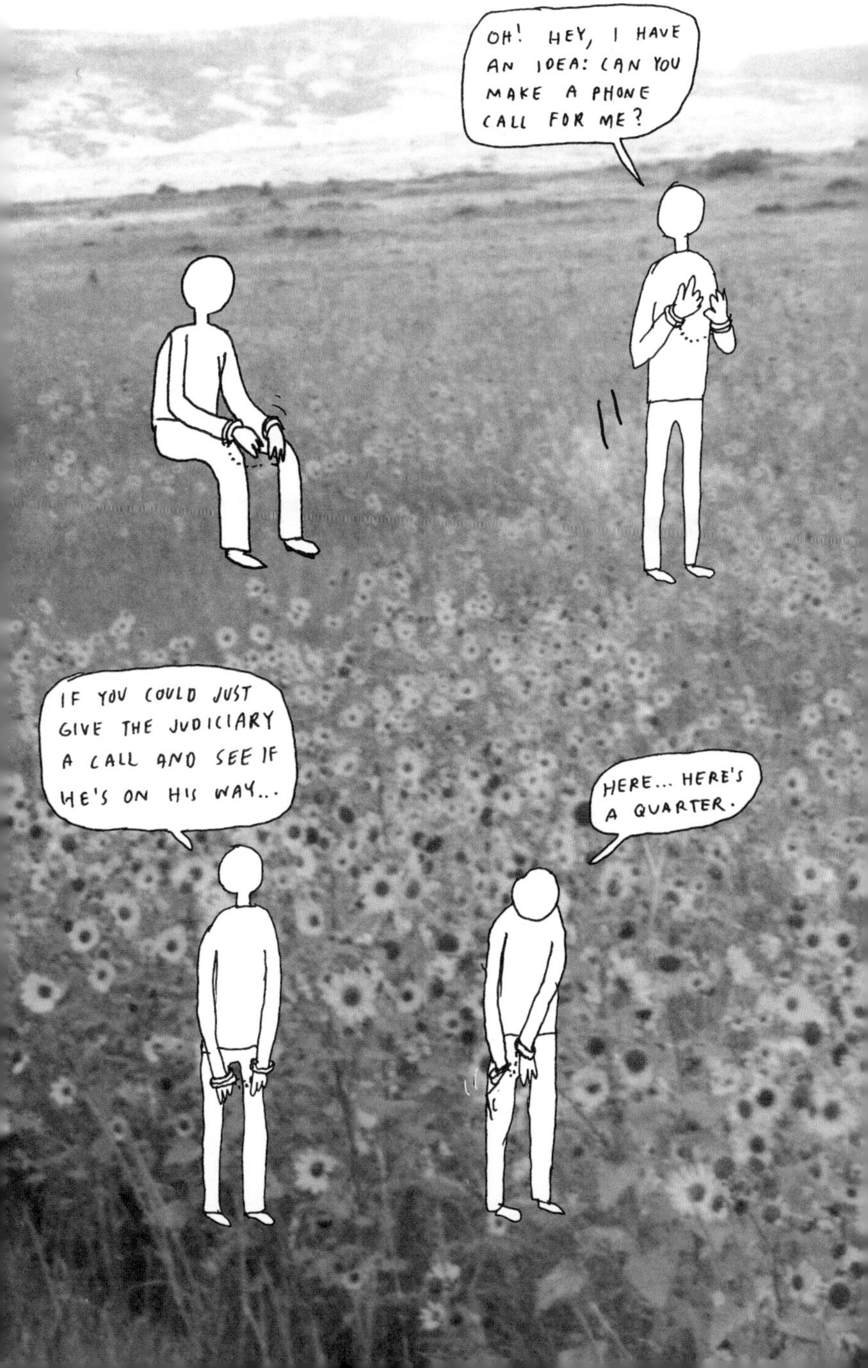
OH! HEY, I HAVE AN IDEA: CAN YOU MAKE A PHONE CALL FOR ME?
IF YOU COULD JUST GIVE THE JUDICIARY A CALL AND SEE IF HE'S ON HIS WAY...
HERE... HERE'S A QUARTER.

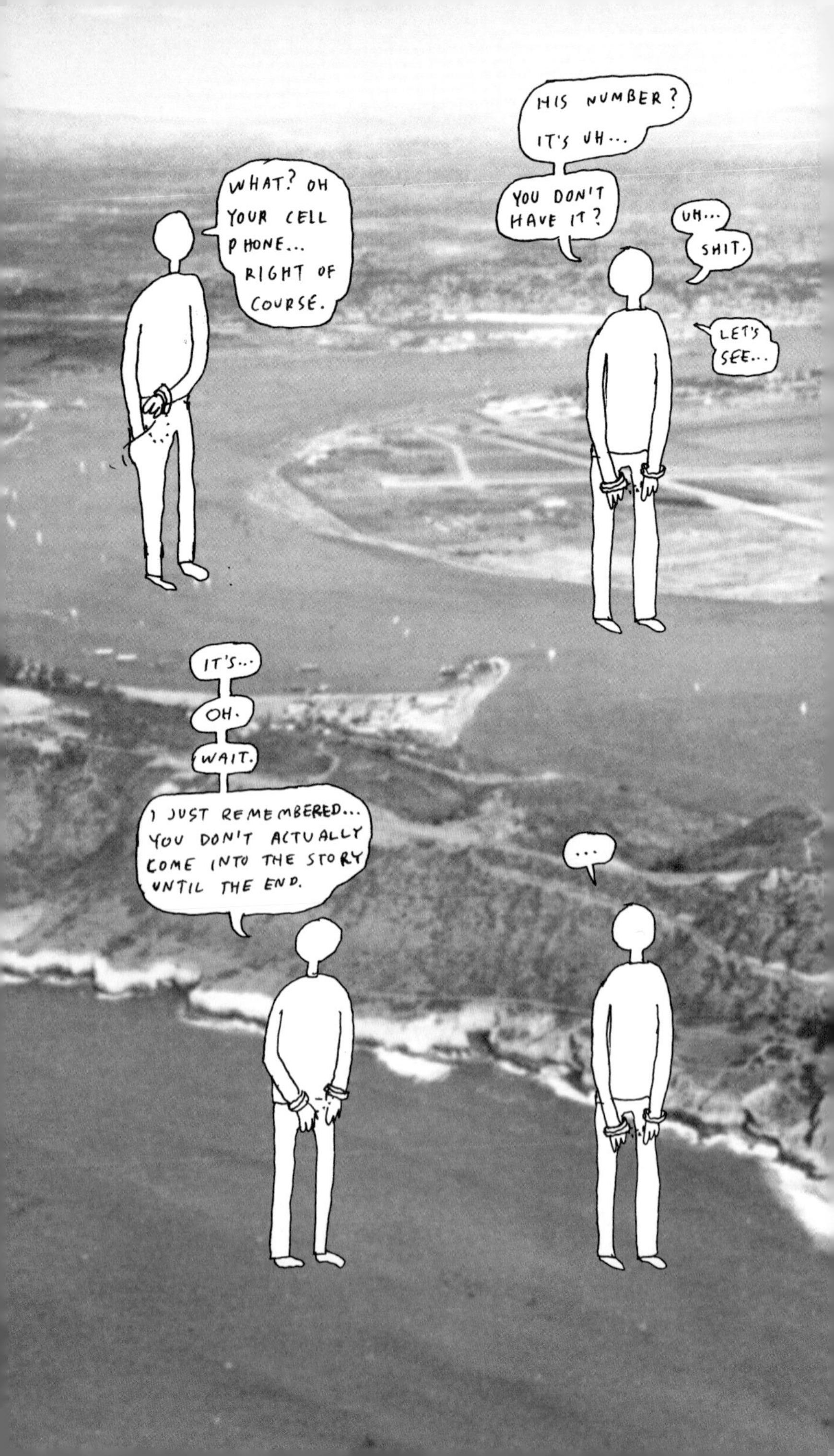
WHAT? OH YOUR CELL PHONE... RIGHT OF COURSE.
HIS NUMBER?
IT'S UH...
YOU DON'T HAVE IT?
UH...
SHIT.
LET'S SEE...
IT'S...
OH.
WAIT.
I JUST REMEMBERED... YOU DON'T ACTUALLY COME INTO THE STORY UNTIL THE END.
...

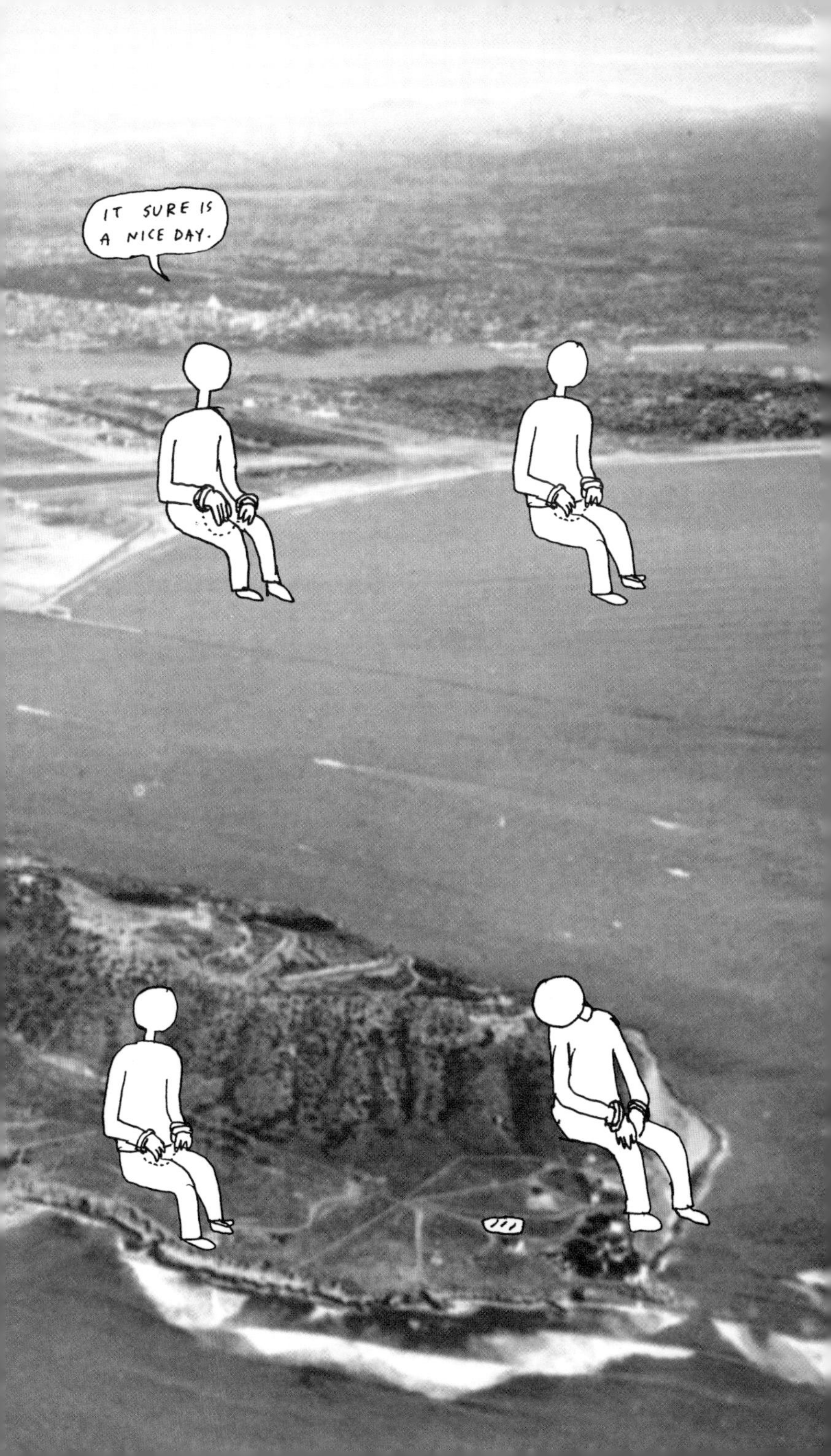
IT SURE IS A NICE DAY.

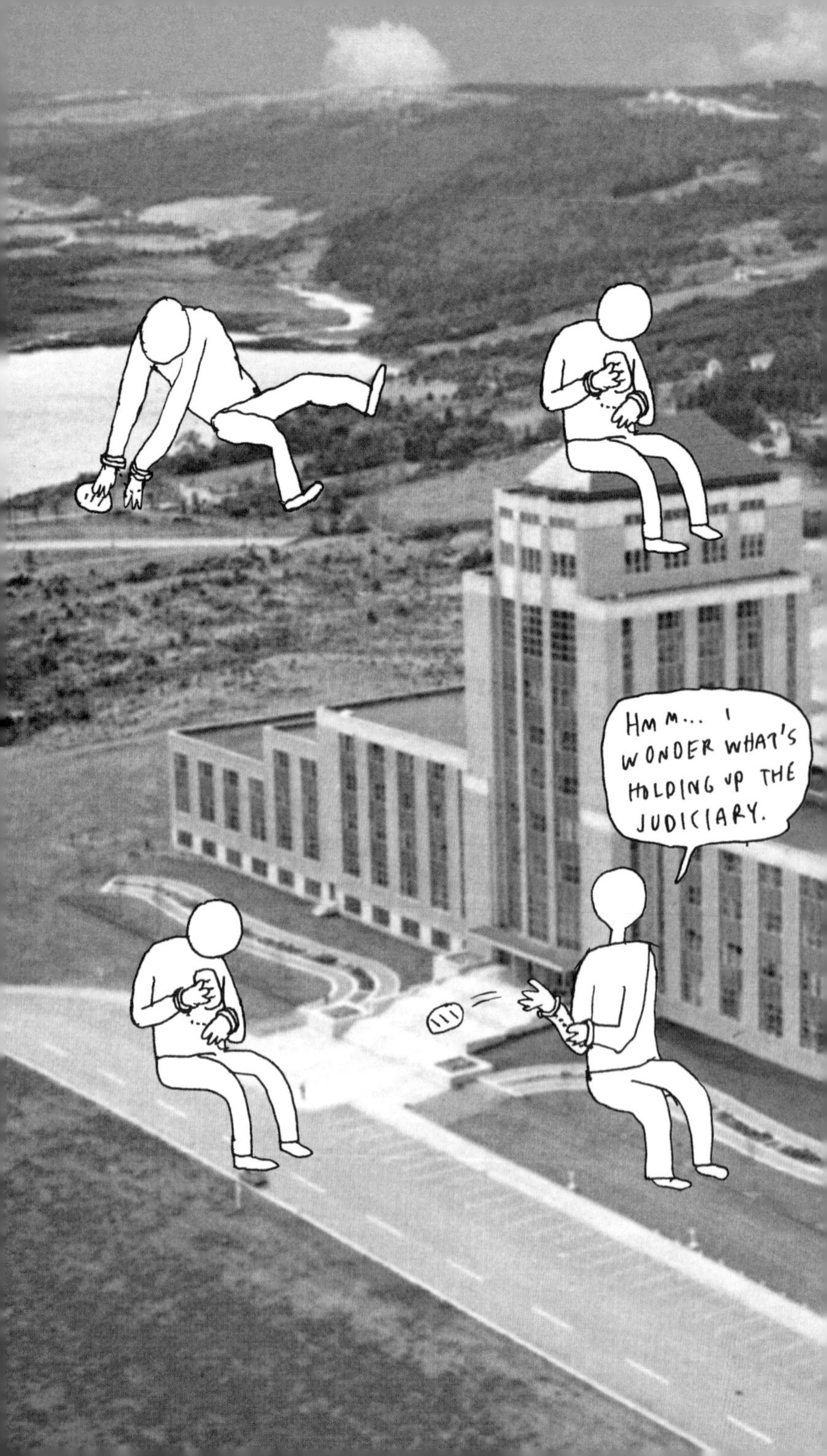
HMM... I WONDER WHAT'S HOLDING UP THE JUDICIARY.

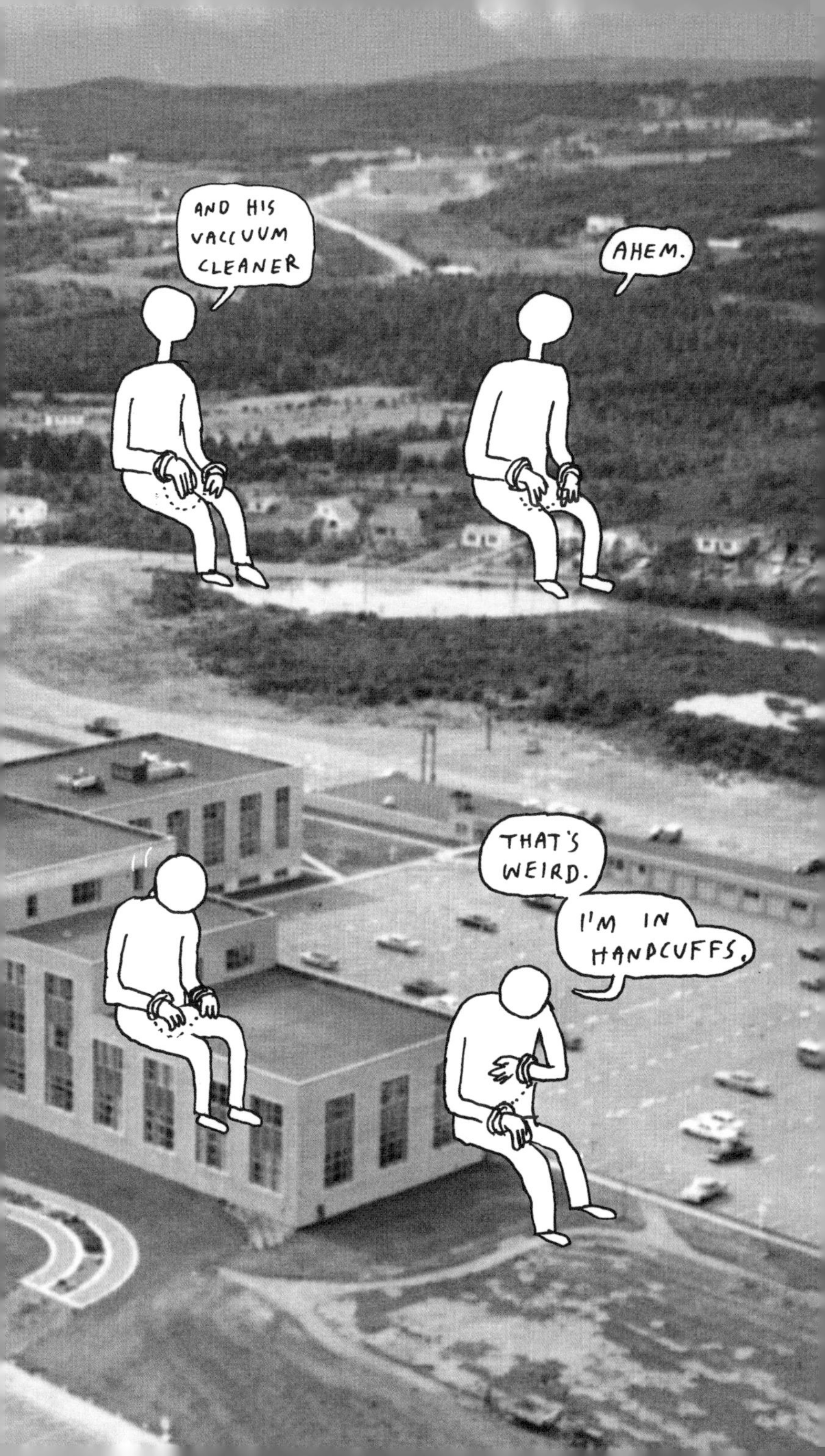
AND HIS VACCUUM CLEANER
AHEM.
THAT'S WEIRD.
I'M IN HANDCUFFS.

ON WHALING

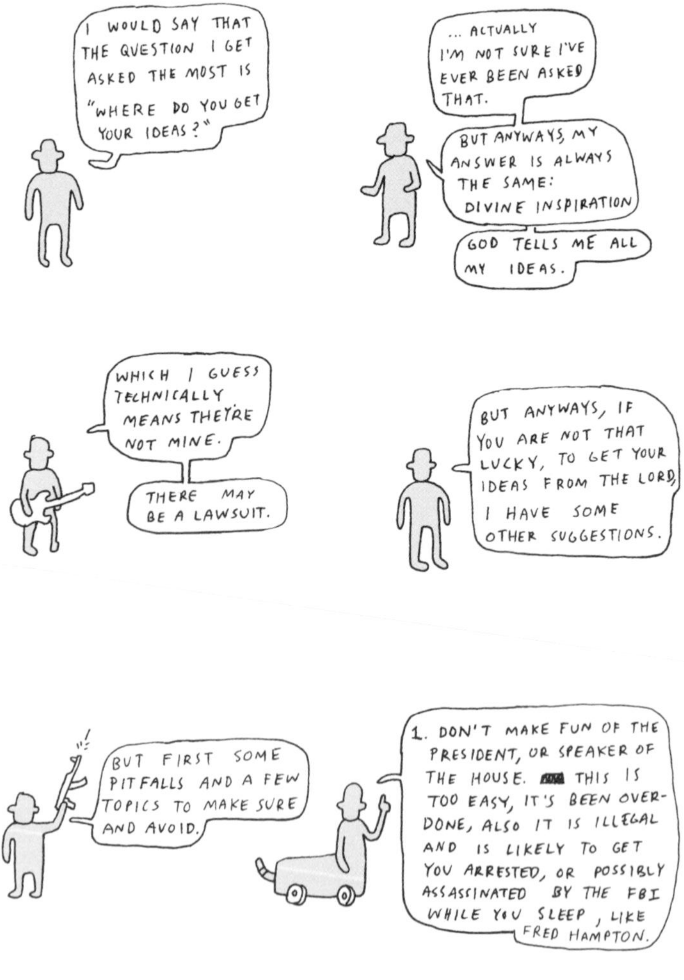
I WOULD SAY THAT THE QUESTION I GET ASKED THE MOST IS "WHERE DO YOU GET YOUR IDEAS?"
... ACTUALLY I'M NOT SURE I'VE EVER BEEN ASKED THAT.
BUT ANYWAYS, MY ANSWER IS ALWAYS THE SAME: DIVINE INSPIRATION
GOD TELLS ME ALL MY IDEAS.
WHICH I GUESS TECHNICALLY MEANS THEY'RE NOT MINE.
THERE MAY BE A LAWSUIT.
BUT ANYWAYS, IF YOU ARE NOT THAT LUCKY, TO GET YOUR IDEAS FROM THE LORD, I HAVE SOME OTHER SUGGESTIONS.
BUT FIRST SOME PITFALLS AND A FEW TOPICS TO MAKE SURE AND AVOID.
1. DON'T MAKE FUN OF THE PRESIDENT, OR SPEAKER OF THE HOUSE. [redacted] THIS IS TOO EASY, IT'S BEEN OVER-DONE, ALSO IT IS ILLEGAL AND IS LIKELY TO GET YOU ARRESTED, OR POSSIBLY ASSASSINATED BY THE FBI WHILE YOU SLEEP, LIKE FRED HAMPTON.

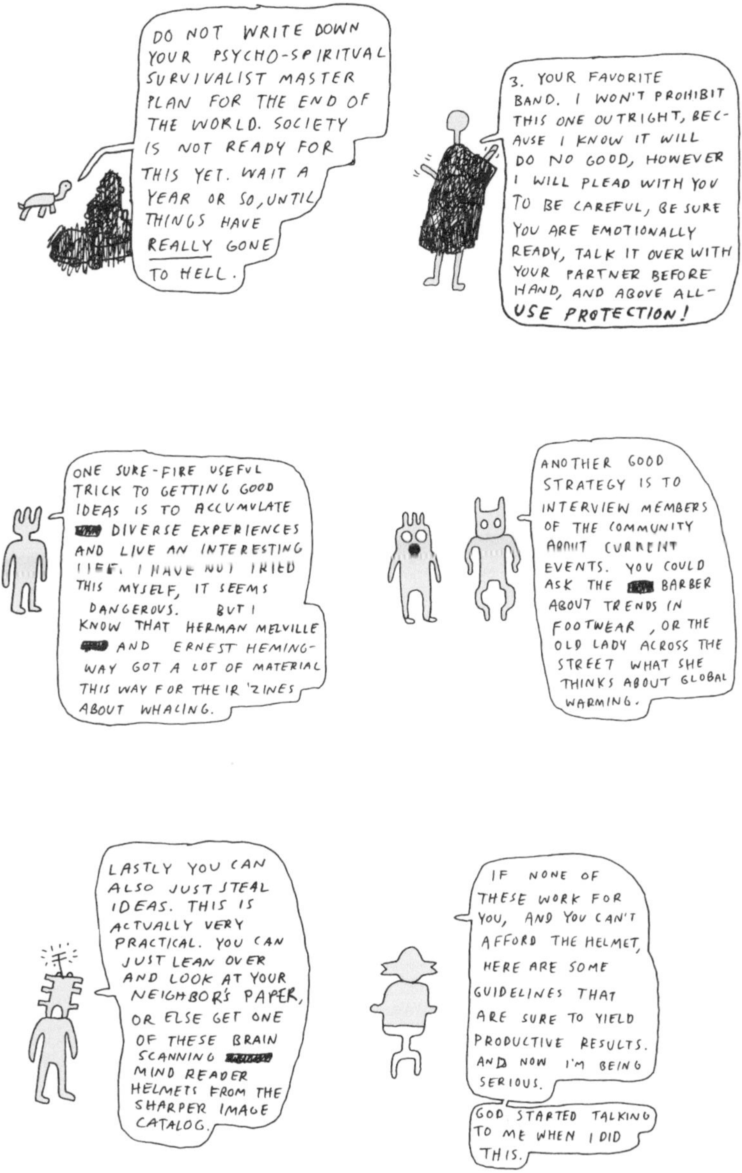

DO NOT WRITE DOWN YOUR PSYCHO-SPIRITUAL SURVIVALIST MASTER PLAN FOR THE END OF THE WORLD. SOCIETY IS NOT READY FOR THIS YET. WAIT A YEAR OR SO, UNTIL THINGS HAVE REALLY GONE TO HELL.
3. YOUR FAVORITE BAND. I WON'T PROHIBIT THIS ONE OUTRIGHT, BEC-AUSE I KNOW IT WILL DO NO GOOD, HOWEVER I WILL PLEAD WITH YOU TO BE CAREFUL, BE SURE YOU ARE EMOTIONALLY READY, TALK IT OVER WITH YOUR PARTNER BEFORE HAND, AND ABOVE ALL- USE PROTECTION!
ONE SURE-FIRE USEFUL TRICK TO GETTING GOOD IDEAS IS TO ACCUMULATE [redacted] DIVERSE EXPERIENCES AND LIVE AN INTERESTING LIFE. I HAVE NOT TRIED THIS MYSELF, IT SEEMS DANGEROUS. BUT I KNOW THAT HERMAN MELVILLE [redacted] AND ERNEST HEMING-WAY GOT A LOT OF MATERIAL THIS WAY FOR THEIR 'ZINES ABOUT WHALING.
ANOTHER GOOD STRATEGY IS TO INTERVIEW MEMBERS OF THE COMMUNITY ABOUT CURRENT EVENTS. YOU COULD ASK THE [redacted] BARBER ABOUT TRENDS IN FOOTWEAR, OR THE OLD LADY ACROSS THE STREET WHAT SHE THINKS ABOUT GLOBAL WARMING.
LASTLY YOU CAN ALSO JUST STEAL IDEAS. THIS IS ACTUALLY VERY PRACTICAL. YOU CAN JUST LEAN OVER AND LOOK AT YOUR NEIGHBOR'S PAPER, OR ELSE GET ONE OF THESE BRAIN SCANNING [redacted] MIND READER HELMETS FROM THE SHARPER IMAGE CATALOG.
IF NONE OF THESE WORK FOR YOU, AND YOU CAN'T AFFORD THE HELMET, HERE ARE SOME GUIDELINES THAT ARE SURE TO YIELD PRODUCTIVE RESULTS. AND NOW I'M BEING SERIOUS.
GOD STARTED TALKING TO ME WHEN I DID THIS.

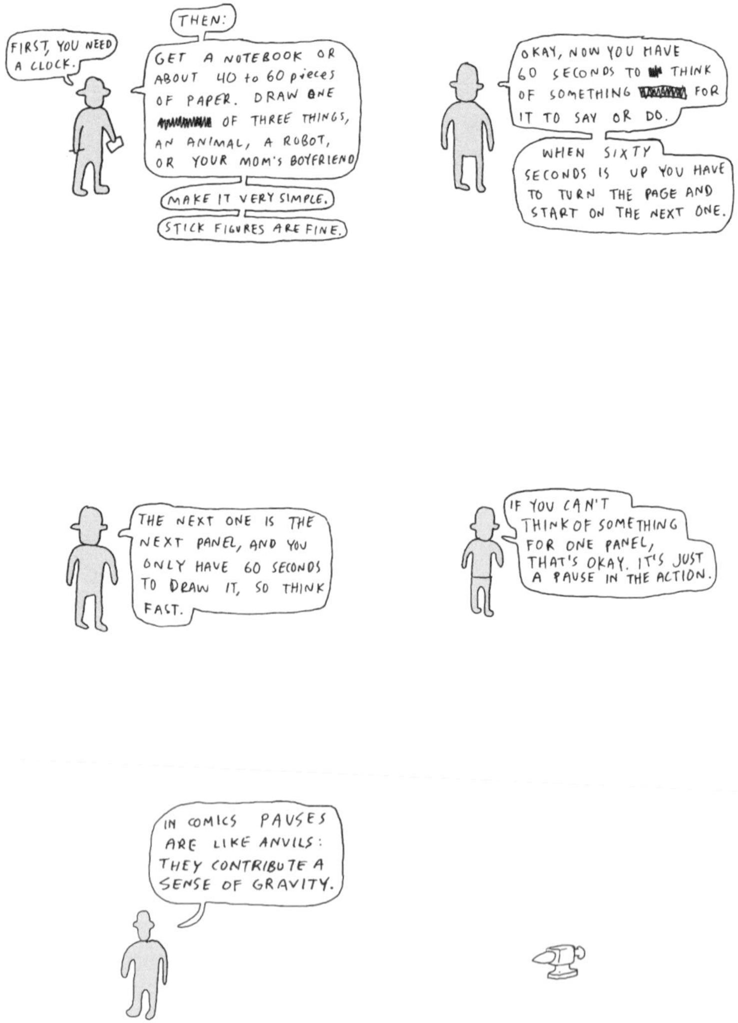
FIRST, YOU NEED A CLOCK.
THEN:
GET A NOTEBOOK OR ABOUT 40 to 60 pieces OF PAPER. DRAW ONE OF THREE THINGS, AN ANIMAL, A ROBOT, OR YOUR MOM'S BOYFRIEND
MAKE IT VERY SIMPLE.
STICK FIGURES ARE FINE.
OKAY, NOW YOU HAVE 60 SECONDS TO THINK OF SOMETHING FOR IT TO SAY OR DO.
WHEN SIXTY SECONDS IS UP YOU HAVE TO TURN THE PAGE AND START ON THE NEXT ONE.
THE NEXT ONE IS THE NEXT PANEL, AND YOU ONLY HAVE 60 SECONDS TO DRAW IT, SO THINK FAST.
IF YOU CAN'T THINK OF SOMETHING FOR ONE PANEL, THAT'S OKAY. IT'S JUST A PAUSE IN THE ACTION.
IN COMICS PAUSES ARE LIKE ANVILS: THEY CONTRIBUTE A SENSE OF GRAVITY.

YOU CHANGE EVERY 60 SECONDS FOR AN HOUR. WHEN YOU ARE DONE YOU WILL BE SURPRISED.

YOU WILL HAVE STARTER MATERIAL FOR YOUR NEXT **10** MINI-COMICS.

COUGH

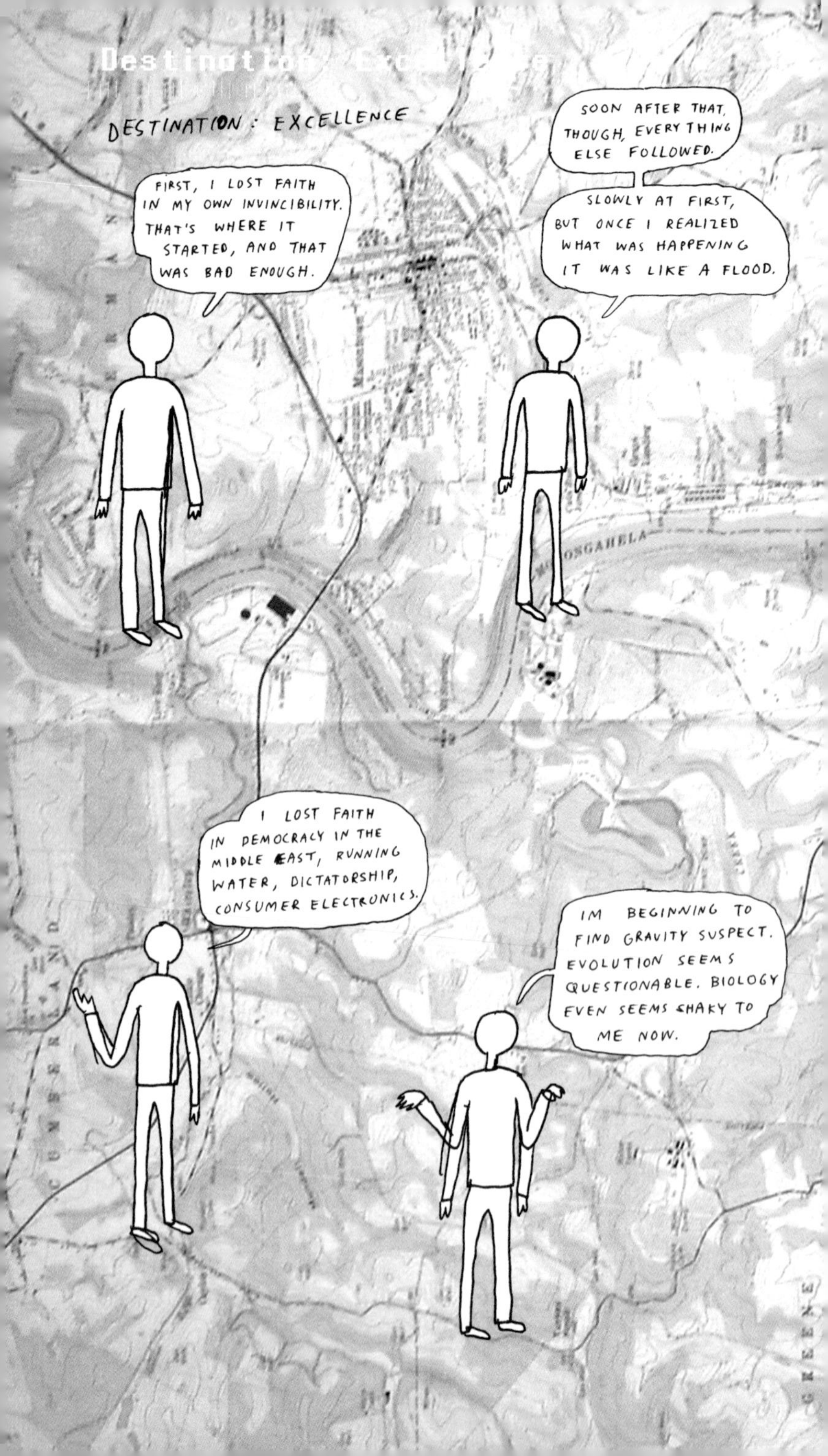
DESTINATION : EXCELLENCE
FIRST, I LOST FAITH IN MY OWN INVINCIBILITY. THAT'S WHERE IT STARTED, AND THAT WAS BAD ENOUGH.
SOON AFTER THAT, THOUGH, EVERYTHING ELSE FOLLOWED.
SLOWLY AT FIRST, BUT ONCE I REALIZED WHAT WAS HAPPENING IT WAS LIKE A FLOOD.
I LOST FAITH IN DEMOCRACY IN THE MIDDLE EAST, RUNNING WATER, DICTATORSHIP, CONSUMER ELECTRONICS.
IM BEGINNING TO FIND GRAVITY SUSPECT. EVOLUTION SEEMS QUESTIONABLE. BIOLOGY EVEN SEEMS SHAKY TO ME NOW.

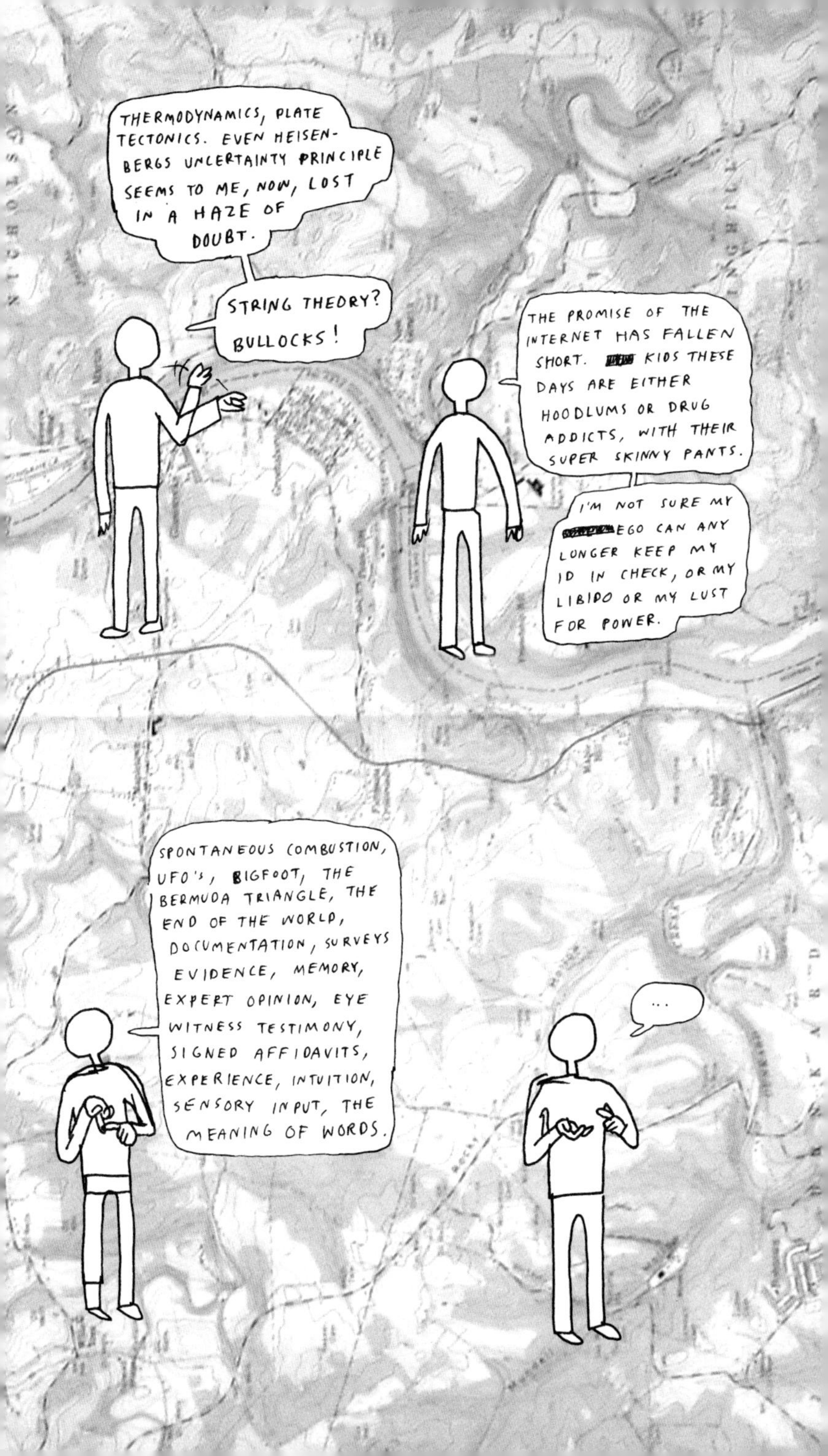
THERMODYNAMICS, PLATE TECTONICS. EVEN HEISEN-BERGS UNCERTAINTY PRINCIPLE SEEMS TO ME, NOW, LOST IN A HAZE OF DOUBT.
STRING THEORY? BULLOCKS!
THE PROMISE OF THE INTERNET HAS FALLEN SHORT. [redacted] KIDS THESE DAYS ARE EITHER HOODLUMS OR DRUG ADDICTS, WITH THEIR SUPER SKINNY PANTS.
I'M NOT SURE MY [redacted]EGO CAN ANY LONGER KEEP MY ID IN CHECK, OR MY LIBIDO OR MY LUST FOR POWER.
SPONTANEOUS COMBUSTION, UFO'S, BIGFOOT, THE BERMUDA TRIANGLE, THE END OF THE WORLD, DOCUMENTATION, SURVEYS EVIDENCE, MEMORY, EXPERT OPINION, EYE WITNESS TESTIMONY, SIGNED AFFIDAVITS, EXPERIENCE, INTUITION, SENSORY INPUT, THE MEANING OF WORDS.
...

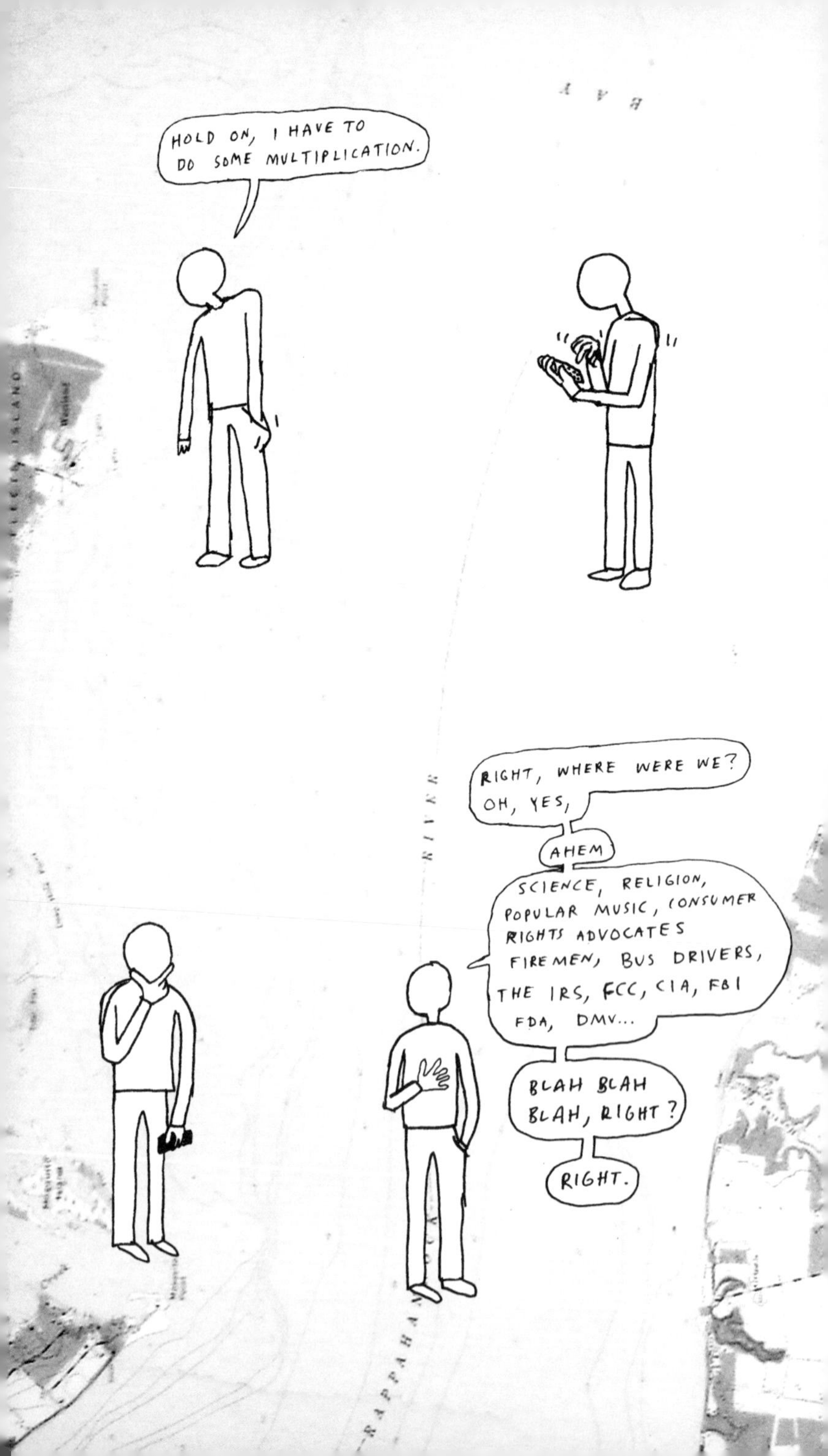
HOLD ON, I HAVE TO DO SOME MULTIPLICATION.
RIGHT, WHERE WERE WE? OH, YES,
AHEM
SCIENCE, RELIGION, POPULAR MUSIC, CONSUMER RIGHTS ADVOCATES FIREMEN, BUS DRIVERS, THE IRS, FCC, CIA, FBI FDA, DMV...
BLAH BLAH BLAH, RIGHT?
RIGHT.

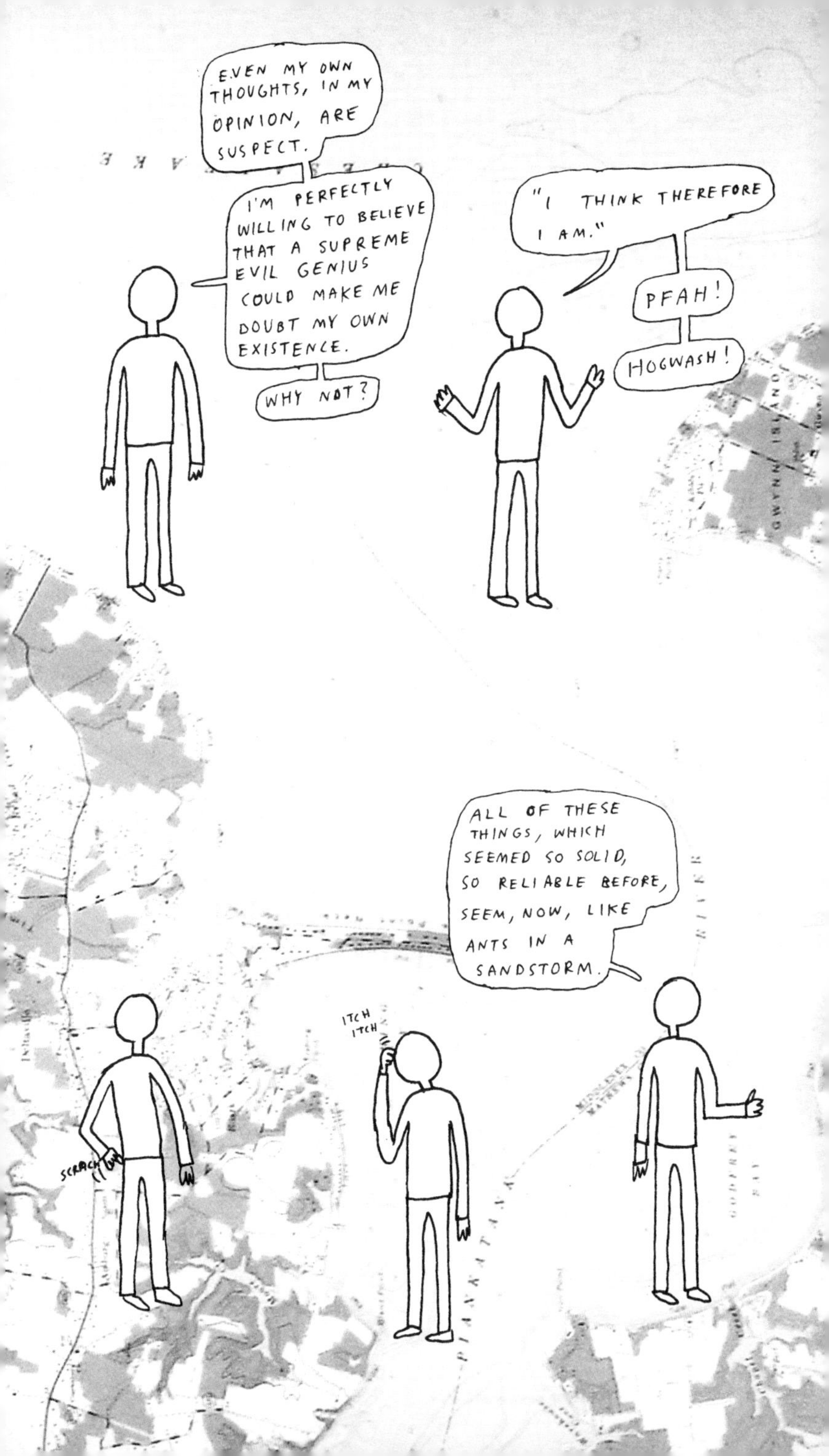
EVEN MY OWN THOUGHTS, IN MY OPINION, ARE SUSPECT.
I'M PERFECTLY WILLING TO BELIEVE THAT A SUPREME EVIL GENIUS COULD MAKE ME DOUBT MY OWN EXISTENCE.
WHY NOT?
"I THINK THEREFORE I AM."
PFAH!
HOGWASH!
ALL OF THESE THINGS, WHICH SEEMED SO SOLID, SO RELIABLE BEFORE, SEEM, NOW, LIKE ANTS IN A SANDSTORM.
SCRATCH
ITCH ITCH

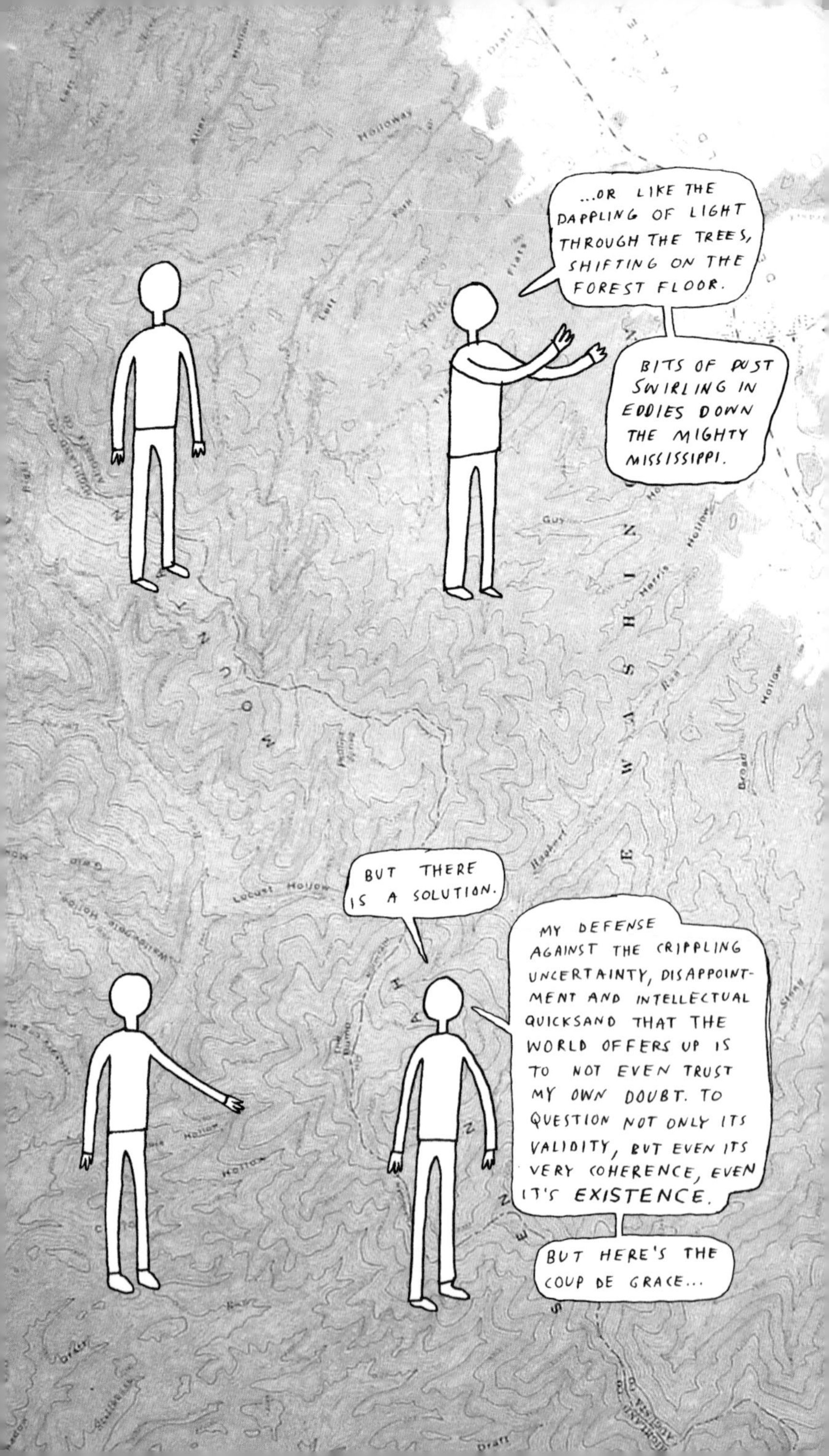
...OR LIKE THE DAPPLING OF LIGHT THROUGH THE TREES, SHIFTING ON THE FOREST FLOOR.
BITS OF DUST SWIRLING IN EDDIES DOWN THE MIGHTY MISSISSIPPI.
BUT THERE IS A SOLUTION.
MY DEFENSE AGAINST THE CRIPPLING UNCERTAINTY, DISAPPOINT-MENT AND INTELLECTUAL QUICKSAND THAT THE WORLD OFFERS UP IS TO NOT EVEN TRUST MY OWN DOUBT. TO QUESTION NOT ONLY ITS VALIDITY, BUT EVEN ITS VERY COHERENCE, EVEN IT'S EXISTENCE.
BUT HERE'S THE COUP DE GRACE...

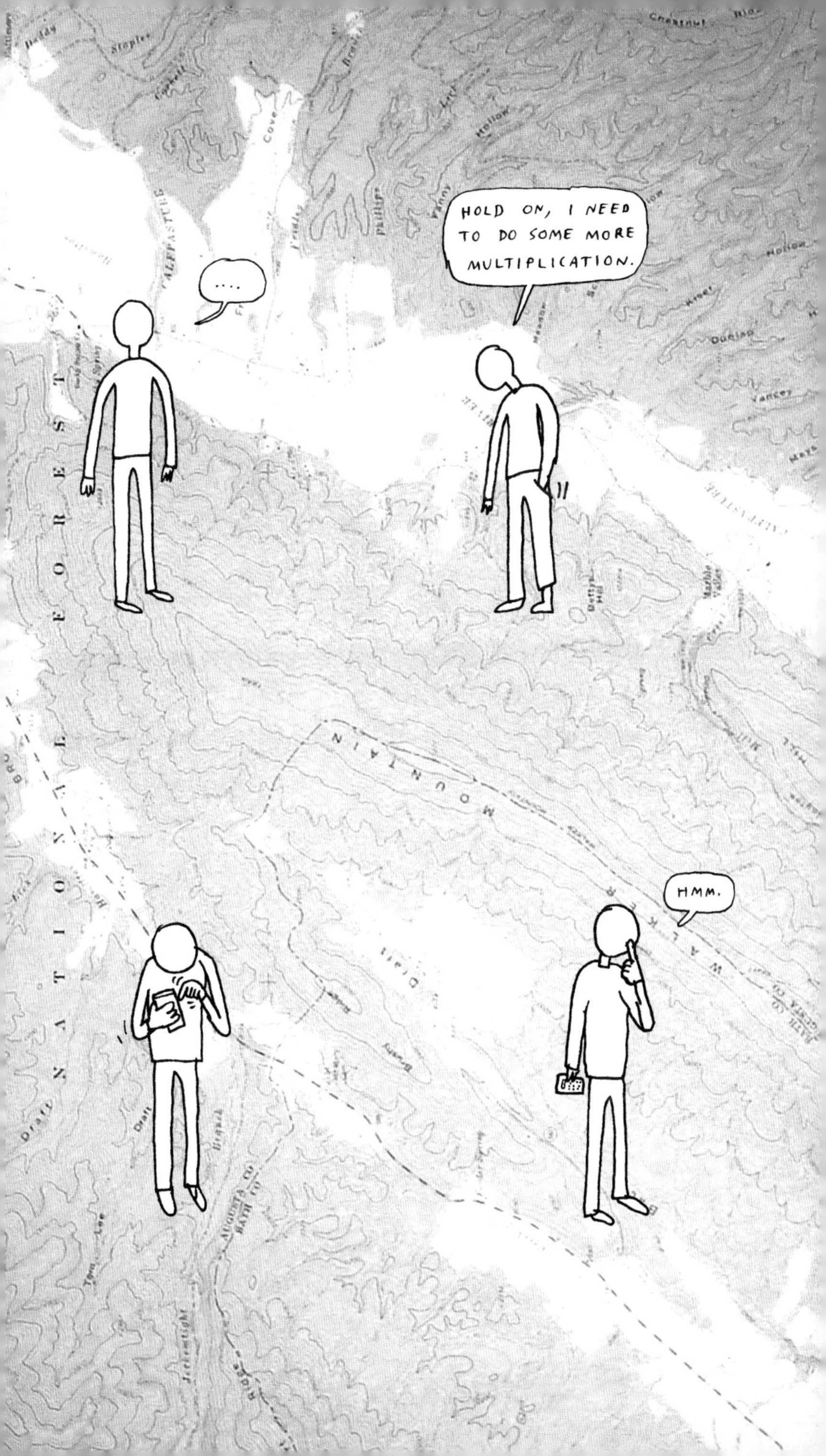
....
HOLD ON, I NEED TO DO SOME MORE MULTIPLICATION.
HMM.

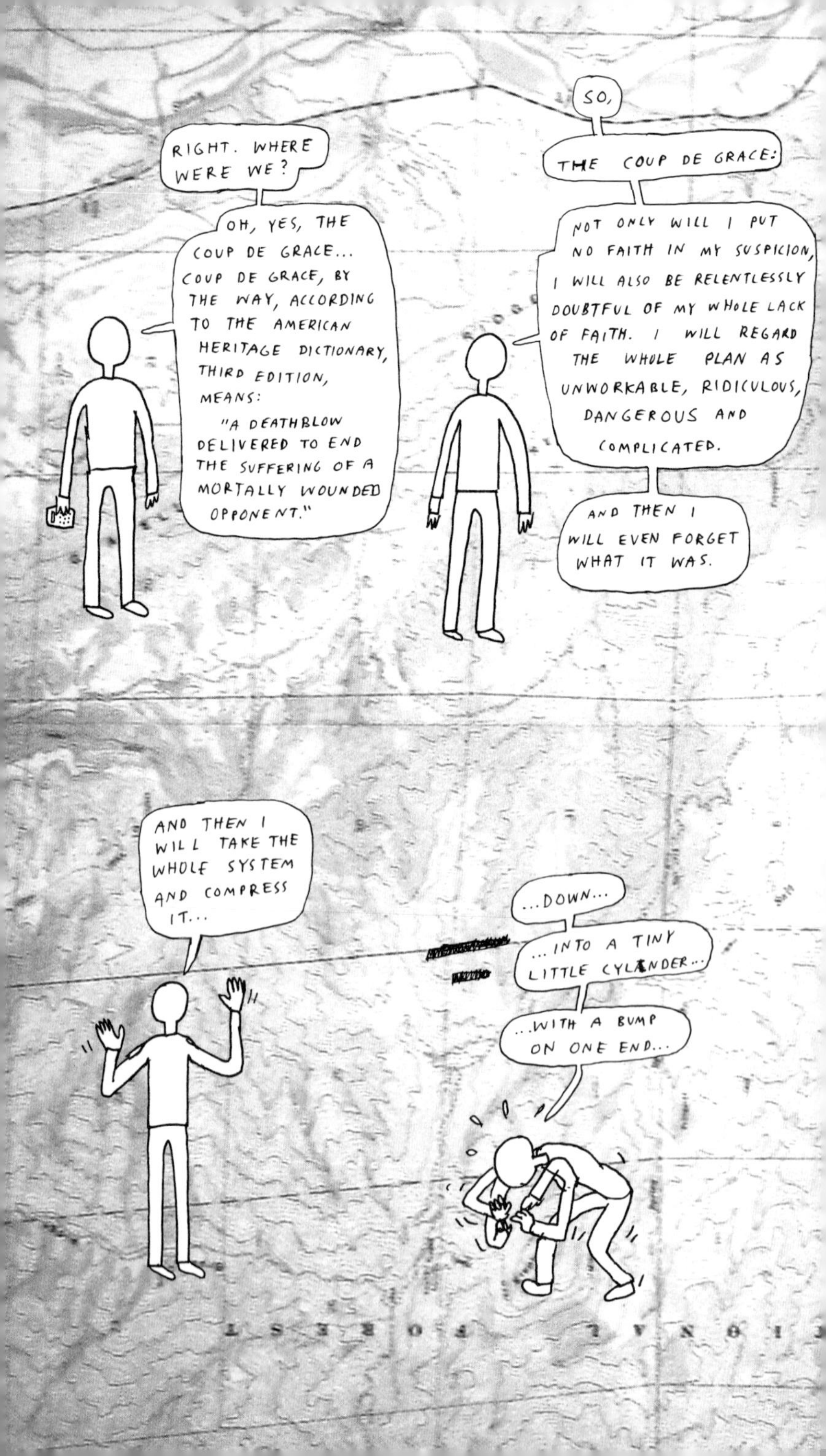
RIGHT. WHERE WERE WE?
OH, YES, THE COUP DE GRACE... COUP DE GRACE, BY THE WAY, ACCORDING TO THE AMERICAN HERITAGE DICTIONARY, THIRD EDITION, MEANS: "A DEATHBLOW DELIVERED TO END THE SUFFERING OF A MORTALLY WOUNDED OPPONENT."
SO,
THE COUP DE GRACE:
NOT ONLY WILL I PUT NO FAITH IN MY SUSPICION, I WILL ALSO BE RELENTLESSLY DOUBTFUL OF MY WHOLE LACK OF FAITH. I WILL REGARD THE WHOLE PLAN AS UNWORKABLE, RIDICULOUS, DANGEROUS AND COMPLICATED.
AND THEN I WILL EVEN FORGET WHAT IT WAS.
AND THEN I WILL TAKE THE WHOLE SYSTEM AND COMPRESS IT...
...DOWN...
...INTO A TINY LITTLE CYLINDER...
...WITH A BUMP ON ONE END...

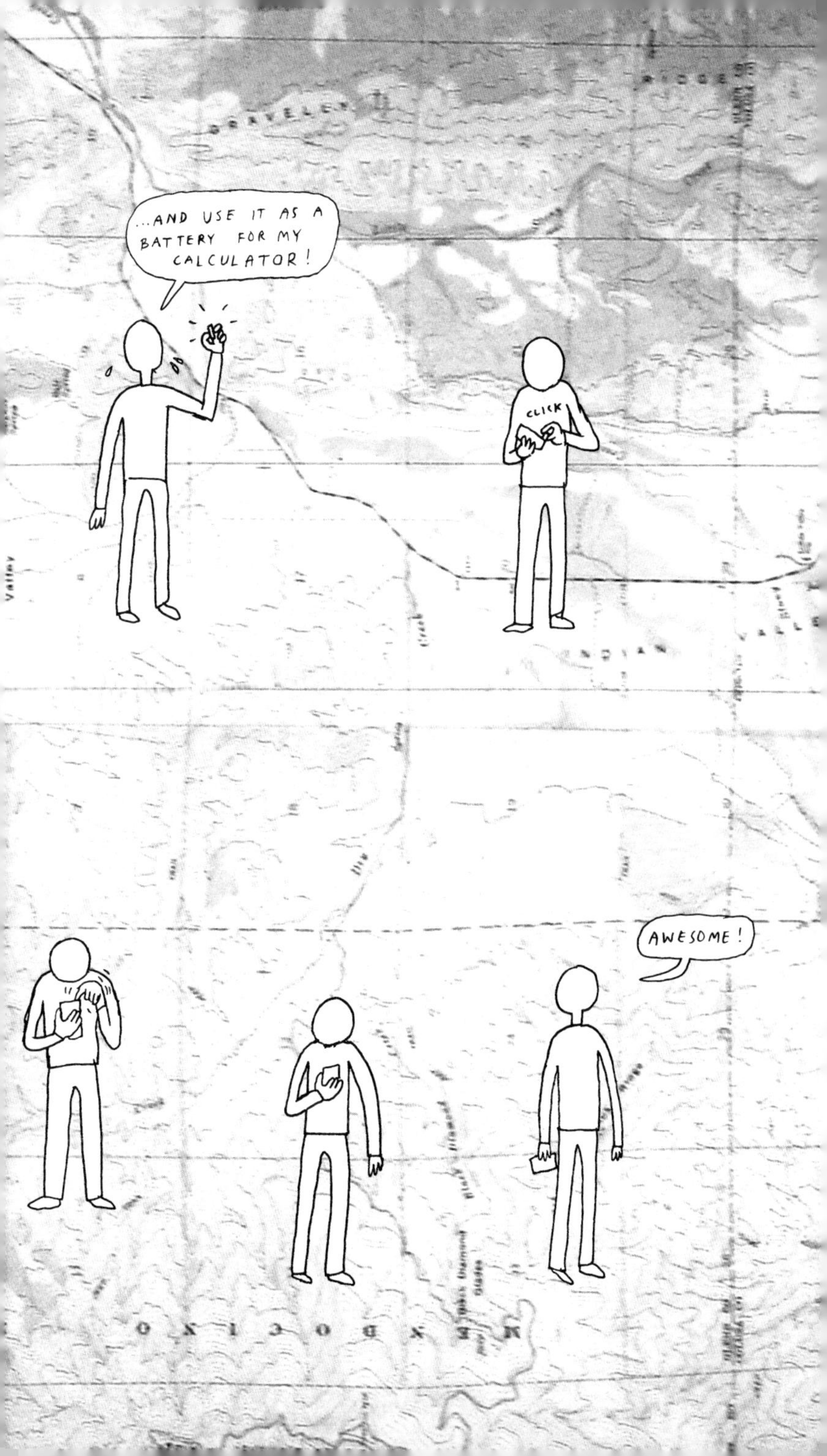
...AND USE IT AS A BATTERY FOR MY CALCULATOR!
CLICK
AWESOME!

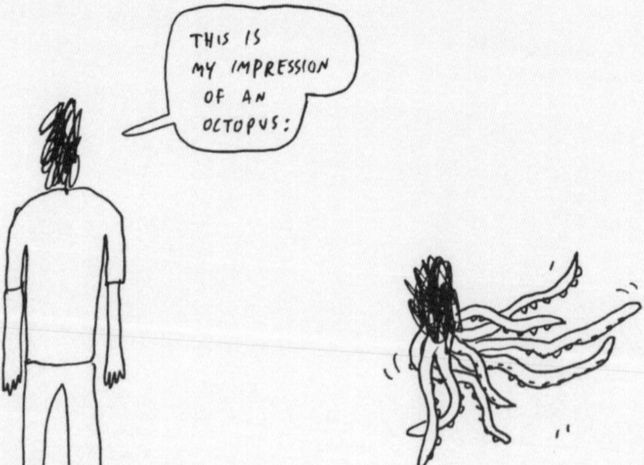
THIS IS MY IMPRESSION OF AN OCTOPUS:

PART IIII

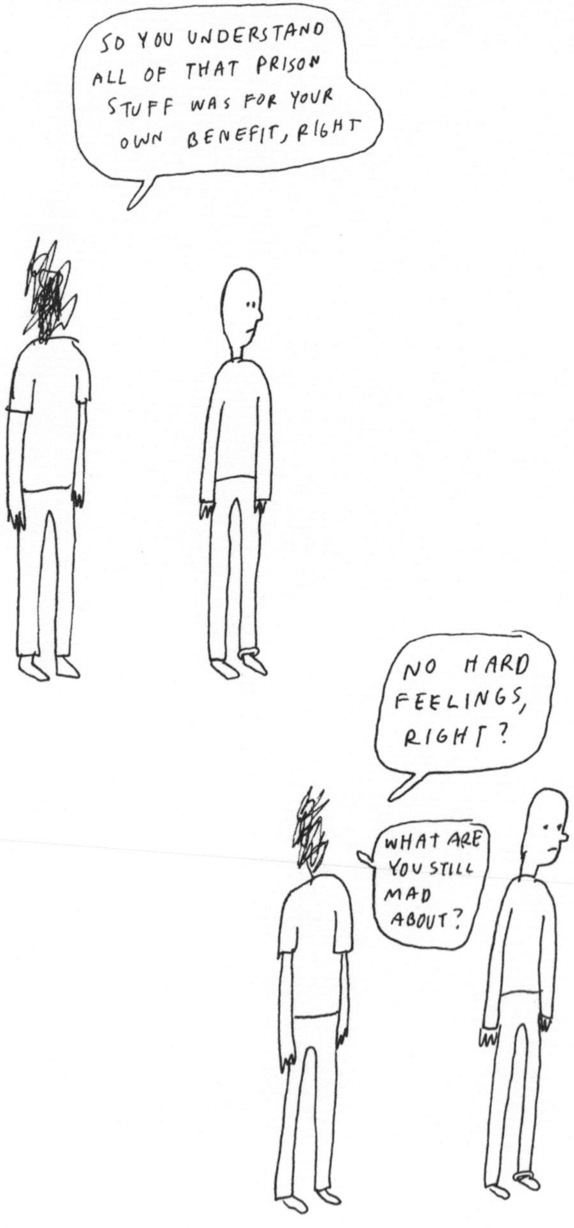
SO YOU UNDERSTAND ALL OF THAT PRISON STUFF WAS FOR YOUR OWN BENEFIT, RIGHT
NO HARD FEELINGS, RIGHT?
WHAT ARE YOU STILL MAD ABOUT?

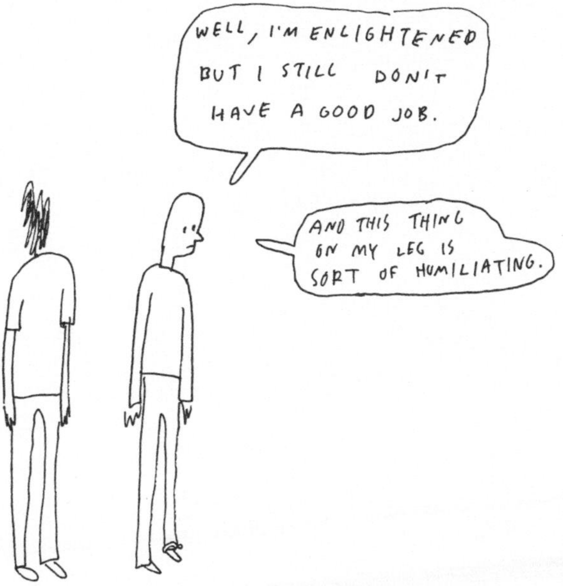
WELL, I'M ENLIGHTENED BUT I STILL DON'T HAVE A GOOD JOB.
AND THIS THING ON MY LEG IS SORT OF HUMILIATING.

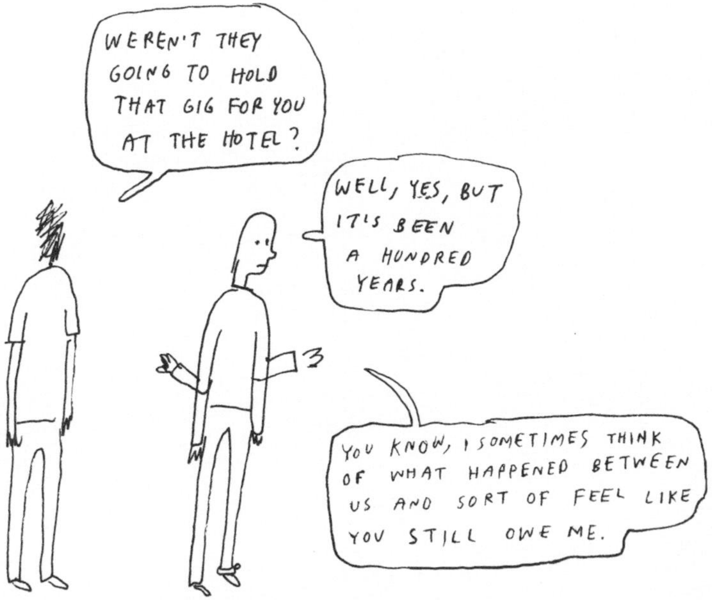
WEREN'T THEY GOING TO HOLD THAT GIG FOR YOU AT THE HOTEL?
WELL, YES, BUT IT'S BEEN A HUNDRED YEARS.
YOU KNOW, I SOMETIMES THINK OF WHAT HAPPENED BETWEEN US AND SORT OF FEEL LIKE YOU STILL OWE ME.

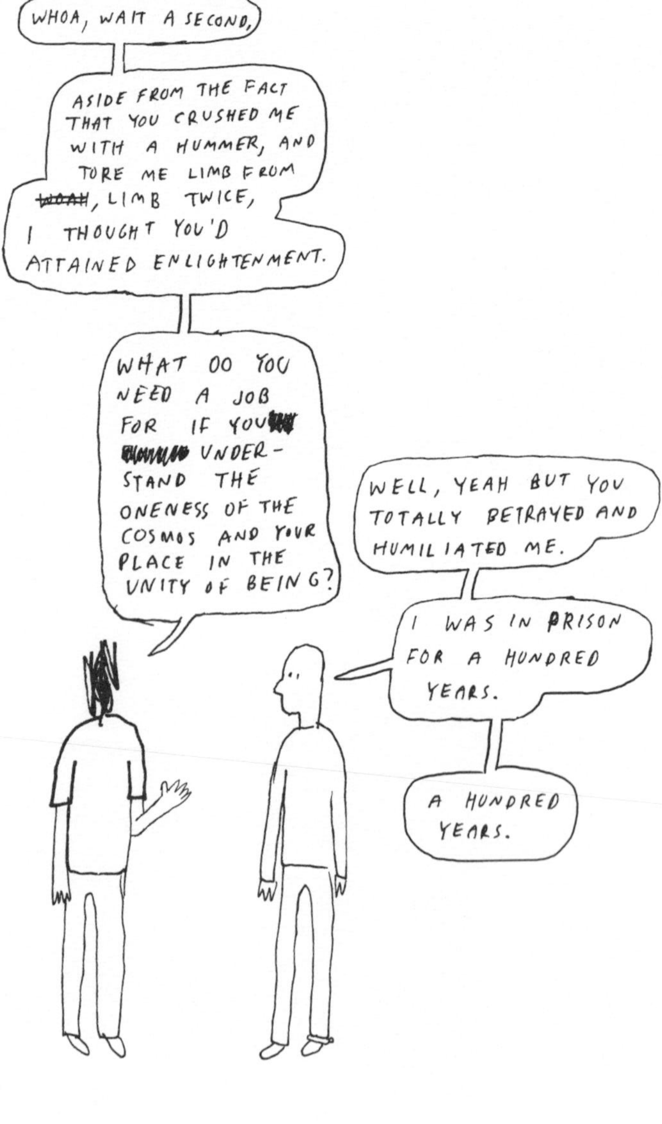
WHOA, WAIT A SECOND,
ASIDE FROM THE FACT THAT YOU CRUSHED ME WITH A HUMMER, AND TORE ME LIMB FROM WOAH, LIMB TWICE, I THOUGHT YOU'D ATTAINED ENLIGHTENMENT.
WHAT DO YOU NEED A JOB FOR IF YOU UNDER-STAND THE ONENESS OF THE COSMOS AND YOUR PLACE IN THE UNITY OF BEING?
WELL, YEAH BUT YOU TOTALLY BETRAYED AND HUMILIATED ME.
I WAS IN PRISON FOR A HUNDRED YEARS.
A HUNDRED YEARS.

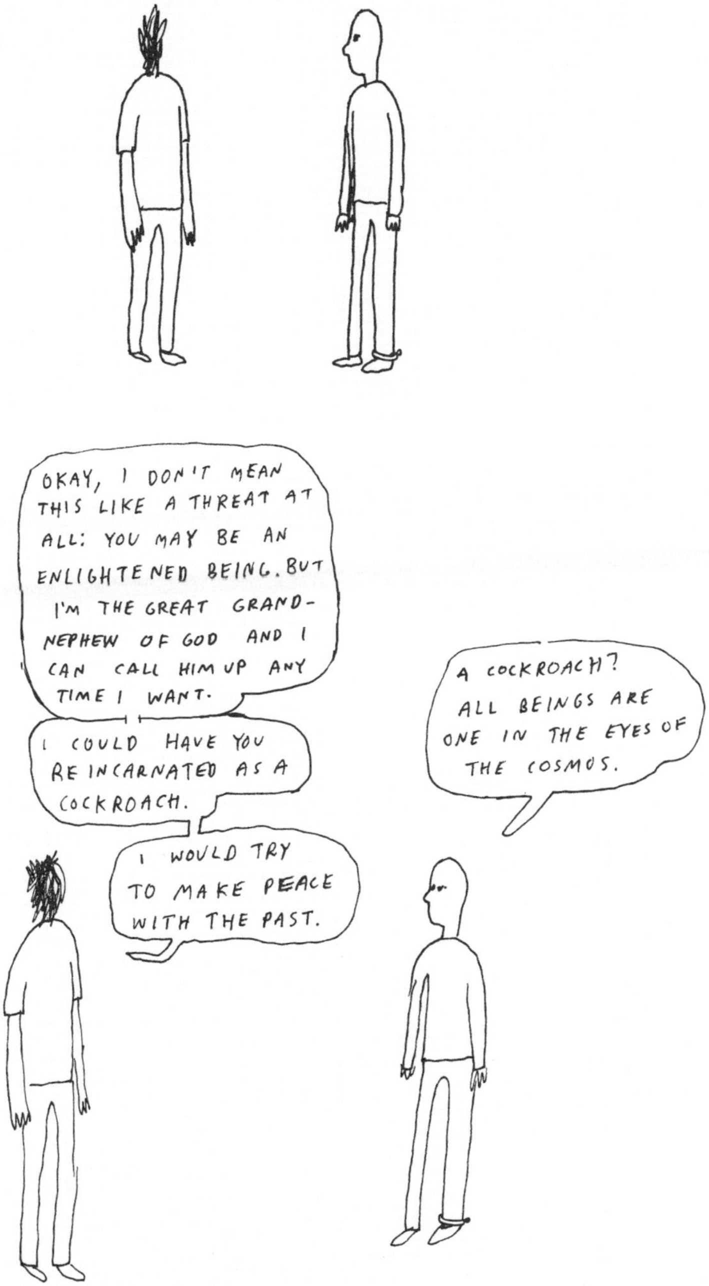
OKAY, I DON'T MEAN THIS LIKE A THREAT AT ALL: YOU MAY BE AN ENLIGHTENED BEING. BUT I'M THE GREAT GRAND-NEPHEW OF GOD AND I CAN CALL HIM UP ANY TIME I WANT.
I COULD HAVE YOU REINCARNATED AS A COCKROACH.
I WOULD TRY TO MAKE PEACE WITH THE PAST.
A COCKROACH? ALL BEINGS ARE ONE IN THE EYES OF THE COSMOS.

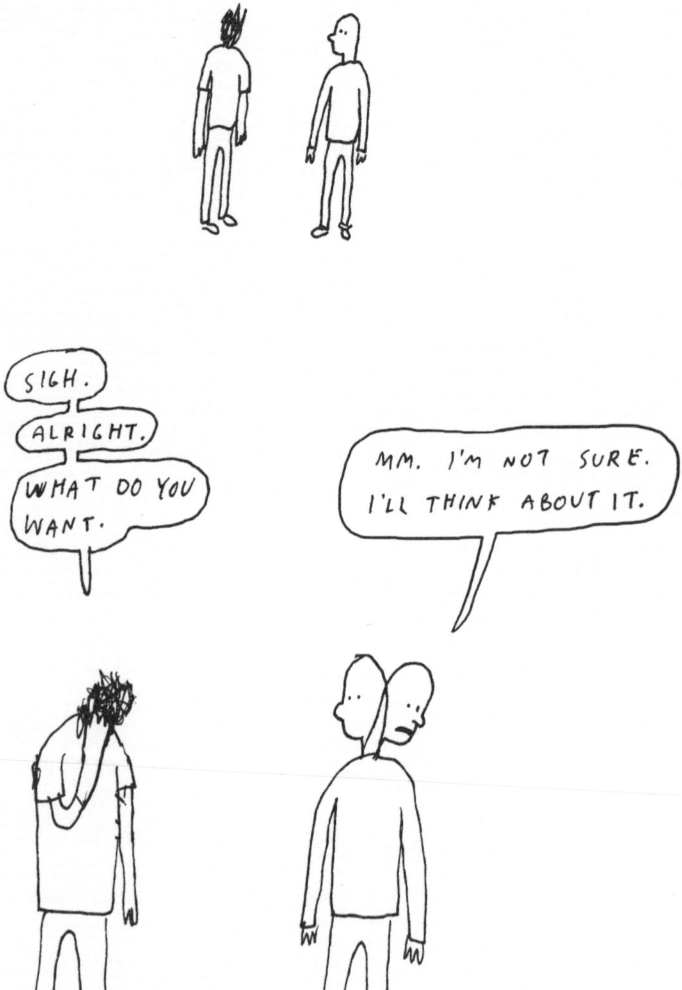
SIGH.
ALRIGHT.
WHAT DO YOU WANT.
MM. I'M NOT SURE. I'LL THINK ABOUT IT.

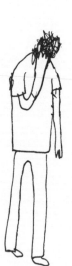

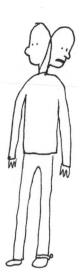

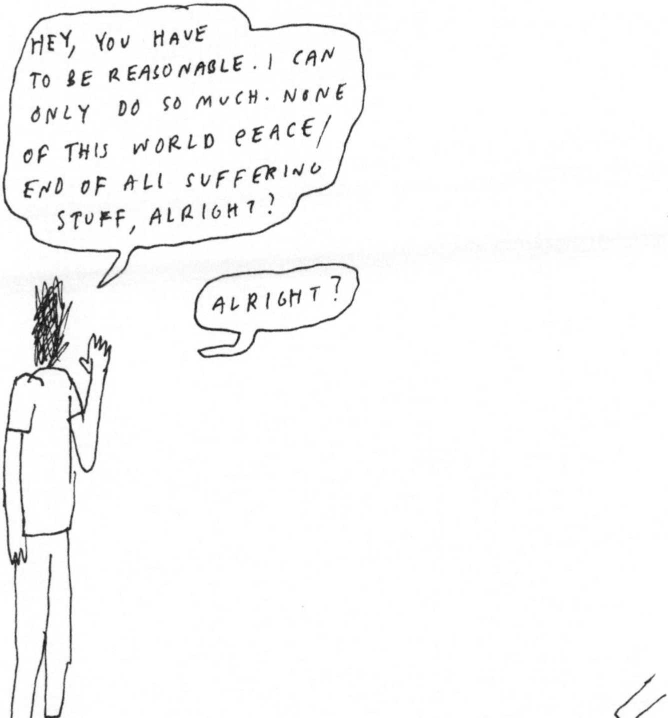
HEY, YOU HAVE TO BE REASONABLE. I CAN ONLY DO SO MUCH. NONE OF THIS WORLD PEACE/ END OF ALL SUFFERING STUFF, ALRIGHT?
ALRIGHT?

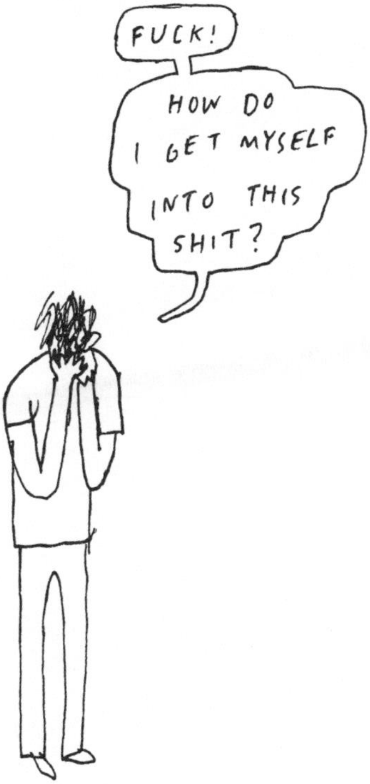
FUCK!
HOW DO I GET MYSELF INTO THIS SHIT?

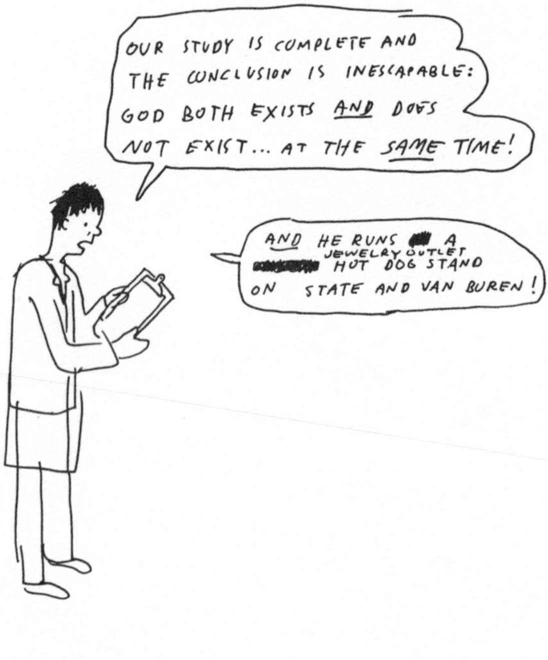
OUR STUDY IS COMPLETE AND THE CONCLUSION IS INESCAPABLE: GOD BOTH EXISTS AND DOES NOT EXIST... AT THE SAME TIME!
AND HE RUNS [redacted] A JEWELRY OUTLET [redacted] HOT DOG STAND ON STATE AND VAN BUREN!

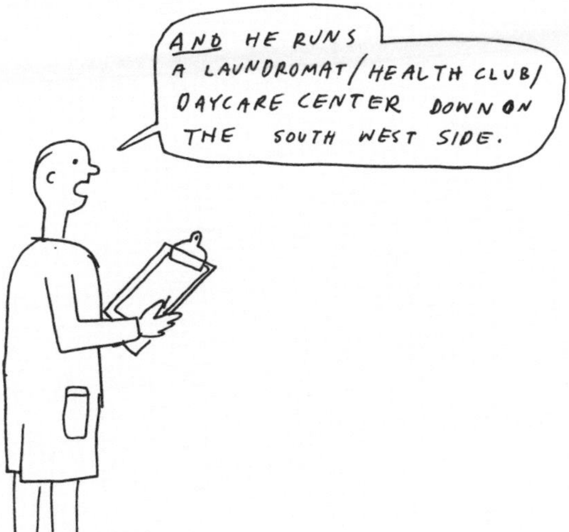
AND HE RUNS A LAUNDROMAT/HEALTH CLUB/DAYCARE CENTER DOWN ON THE SOUTH WEST SIDE.

REALLY? THAT'S...
THAT DOESN'T MAKE ANY SENSE

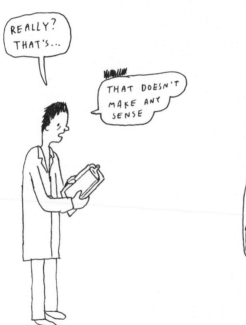

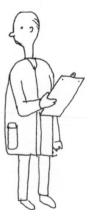

HOW COULD HE HAVE TIME TO RUN A JEWELRY OUTLET/HOT DOG STAND, AND A LAUNDROMAT/ HEALTH CLUB/ DAY CARE CENTER... AND COMMUTE BETWEEN THE LOOP AND THE SOUTHWEST SIDE?
THAT'S NOT POSSIBLE.

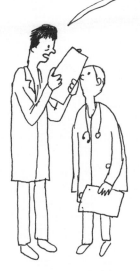

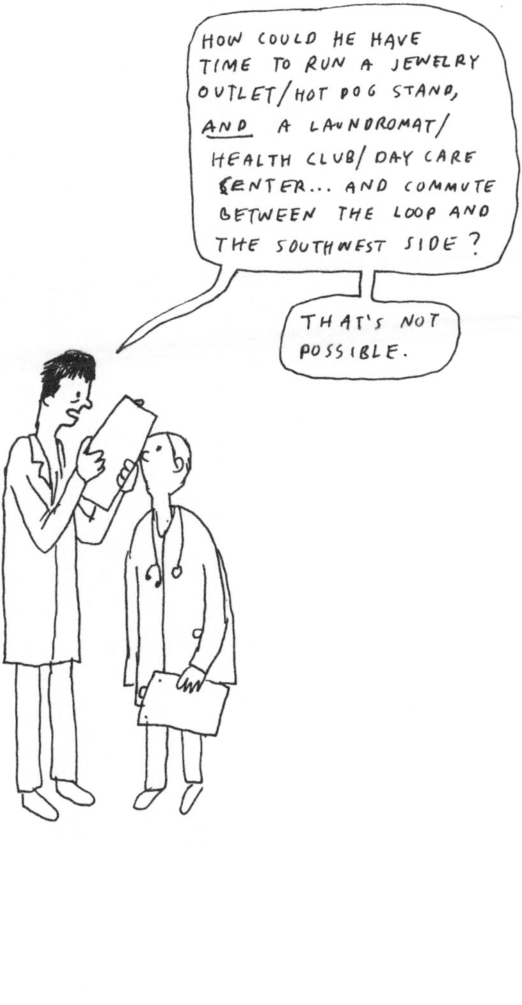

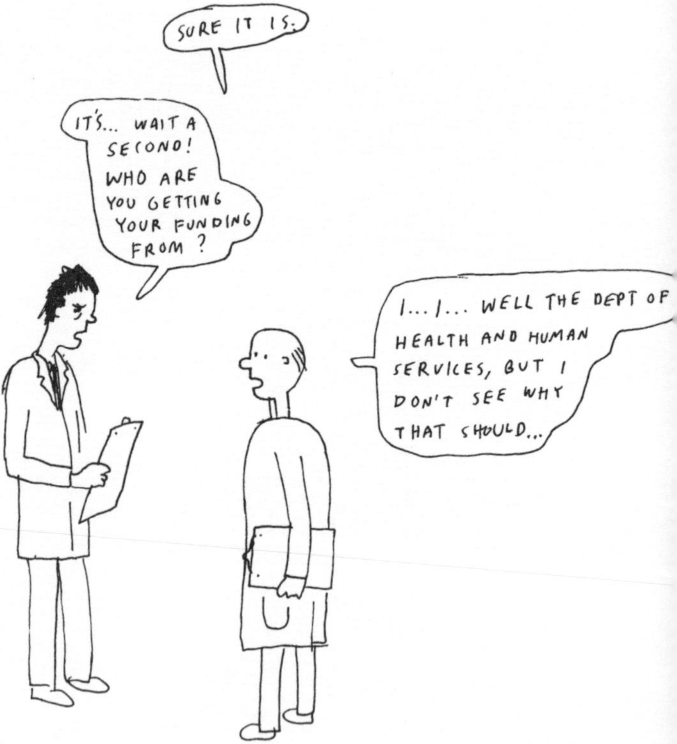
SURE IT IS.
IT'S... WAIT A SECOND! WHO ARE YOU GETTING YOUR FUNDING FROM?
I... I... WELL THE DEPT OF HEALTH AND HUMAN SERVICES, BUT I DON'T SEE WHY THAT SHOULD...

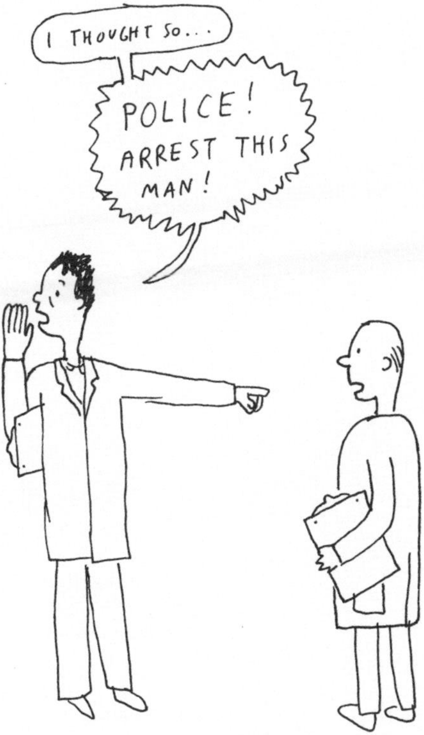
I THOUGHT SO...
POLICE! ARREST THIS MAN!

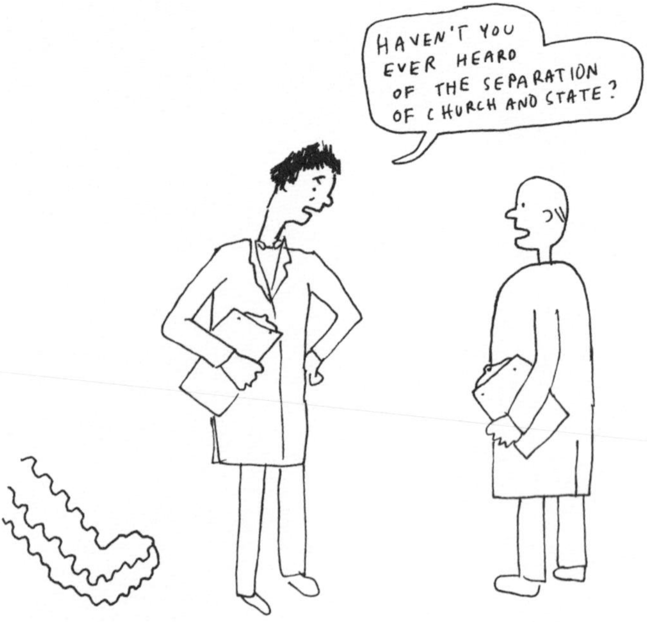
HAVEN'T YOU EVER HEARD OF THE SEPARATION OF CHURCH AND STATE?

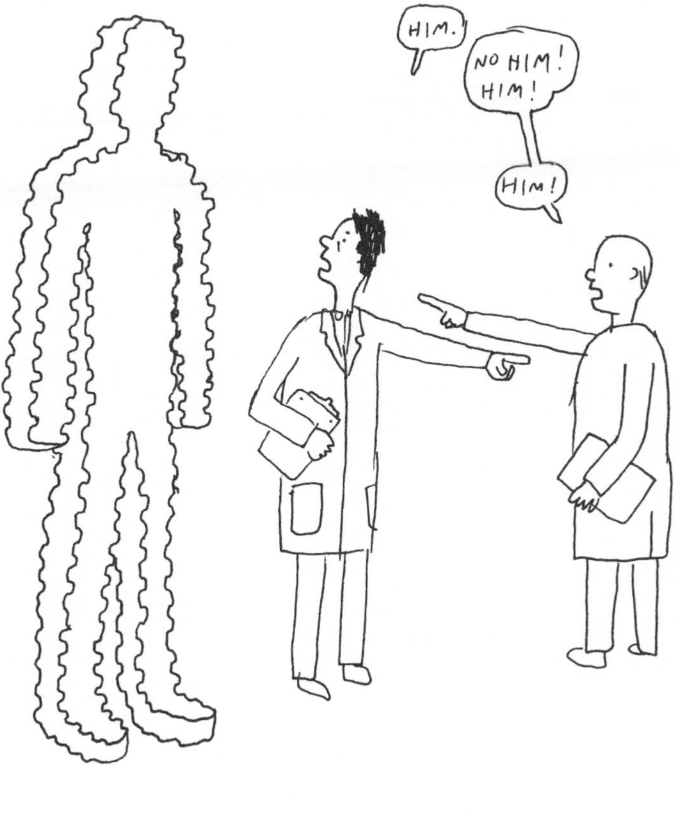
HIM.
NO HIM! HIM!
HIM!

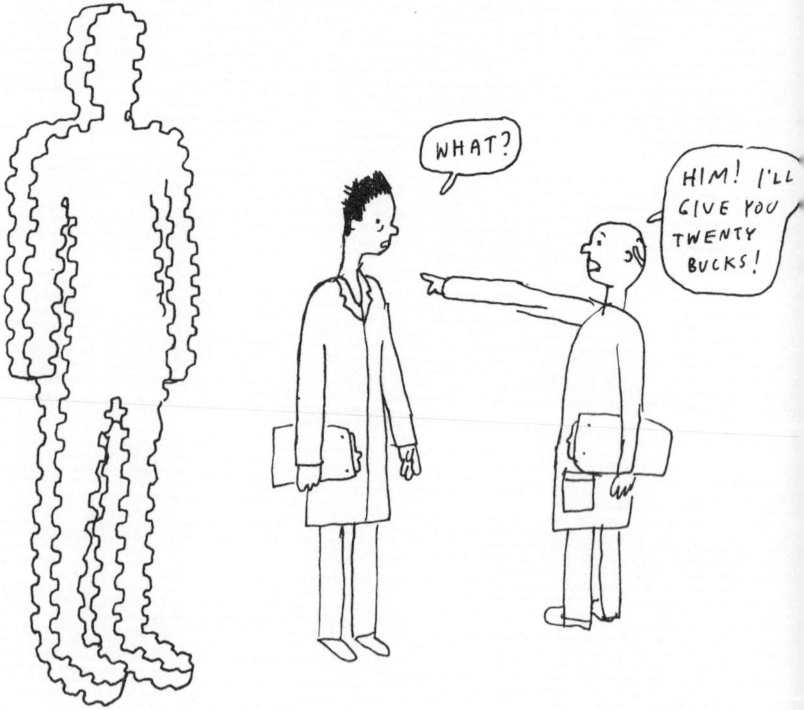
WHAT?
HIM! I'LL GIVE YOU TWENTY BUCKS!

BONK

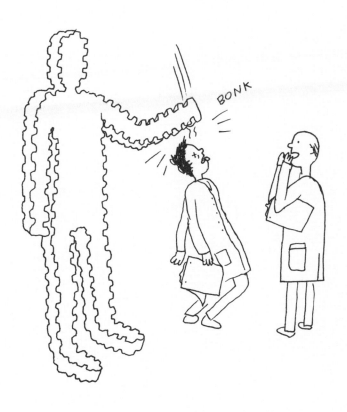

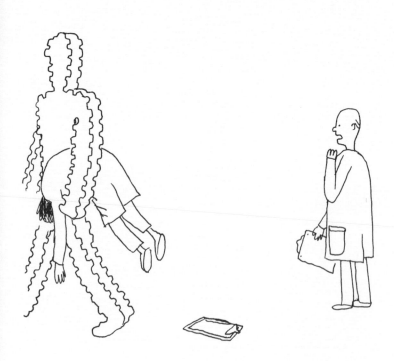

COME TO GOD'S!
GET CLEAN! GET BUFF! BRING YOUR KIDS. COME BACK TO JESUS!
ALL YOUR NEEDS FULFILLED! @ GOD'S LAUNDRY HEALTH CLUB DAYCARE CENTER
SCIENTIFICALLY PROVEN!!!

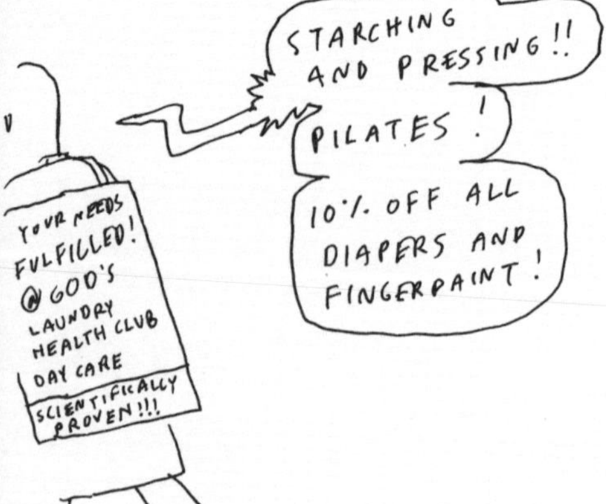
STARCHING AND PRESSING!!
PILATES!
10% OFF ALL DIAPERS AND FINGERPAINT!
YOUR NEEDS FULFILLED! @ GOD'S LAUNDRY HEALTH CLUB DAY CARE
SCIENTIFICALLY PROVEN!!!

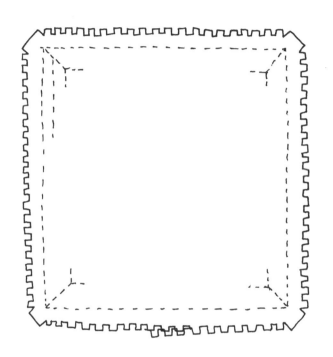

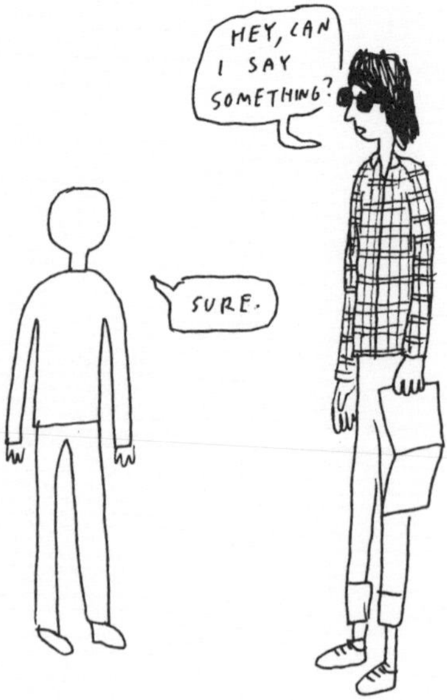
HEY, CAN I SAY SOMETHING?
SURE.

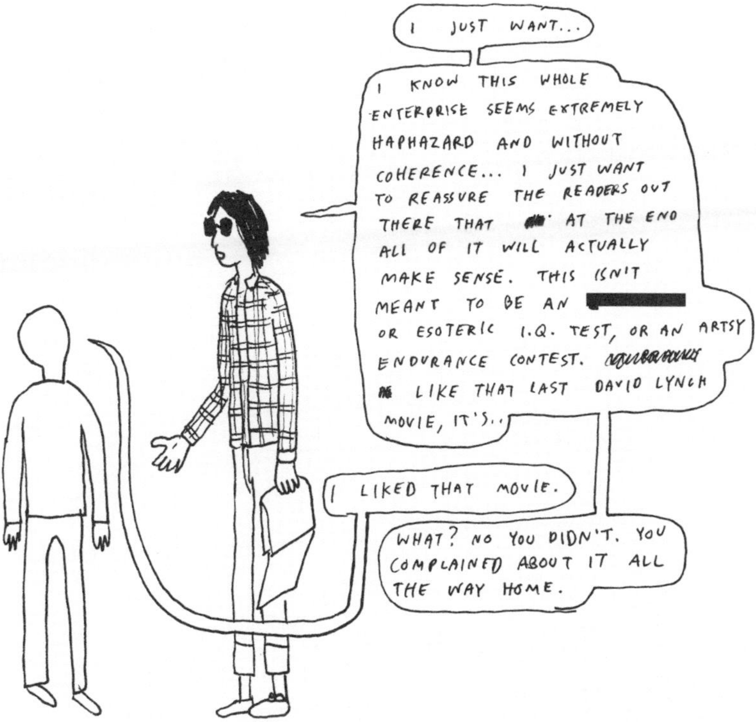
I JUST WANT...
I KNOW THIS WHOLE ENTERPRISE SEEMS EXTREMELY HAPHAZARD AND WITHOUT COHERENCE... I JUST WANT TO REASSURE THE READERS OUT THERE THAT [redacted] AT THE END ALL OF IT WILL ACTUALLY MAKE SENSE. THIS ISN'T MEANT TO BE AN [redacted] OR ESOTERIC I.Q. TEST, OR AN ARTSY ENDURANCE CONTEST. [redacted] LIKE THAT LAST DAVID LYNCH MOVIE, IT'S..
I LIKED THAT MOVIE.
WHAT? NO YOU DIDN'T. YOU COMPLAINED ABOUT IT ALL THE WAY HOME.

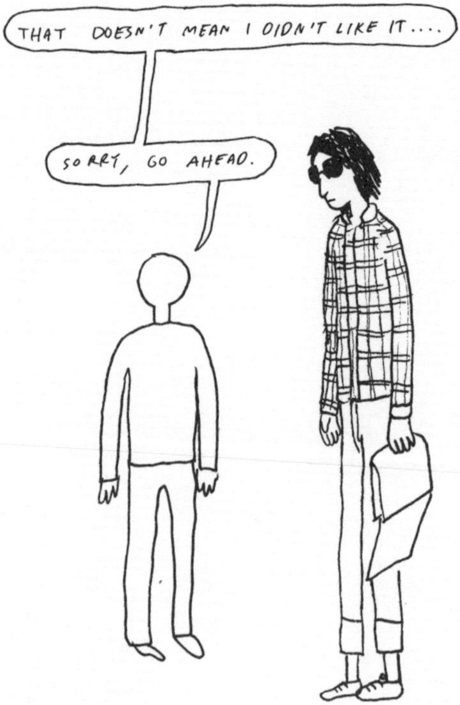
THAT DOESN'T MEAN I DIDN'T LIKE IT....
SORRY, GO AHEAD.

UH... OH, YEAH, WELL, THIS BOOK, IT'LL ALL BE WORTH IT AT THE END. THAT'S ALL I WANTED TO SAY.

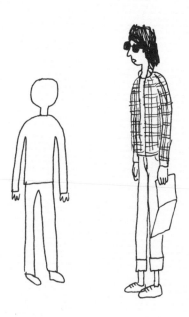

ACTUALLY... I DON'T MEAN TO CONTRADICT YOU IN FRONT OF THE CUSTOMERS, BUT I'M NOT SURE THAT'S REALLY TRUE. I THINK THIS MIGHT JUST BE A BIG MESS, ACTUALLY.

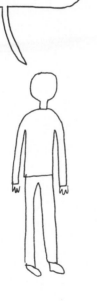

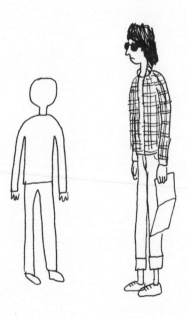

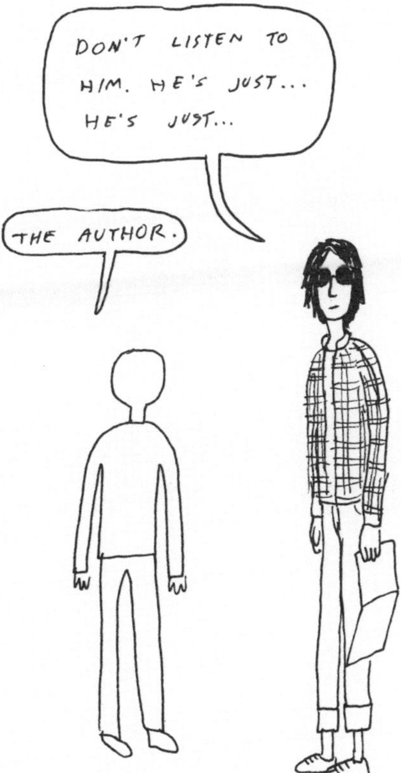
DON'T LISTEN TO HIM. HE'S JUST... HE'S JUST...
THE AUTHOR.

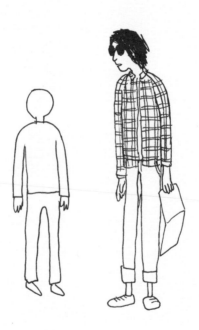

DON'T LISTEN TO HIM.
CH CH

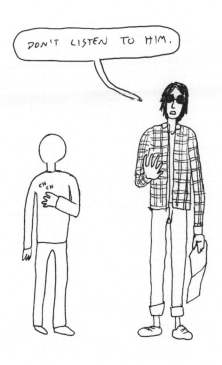

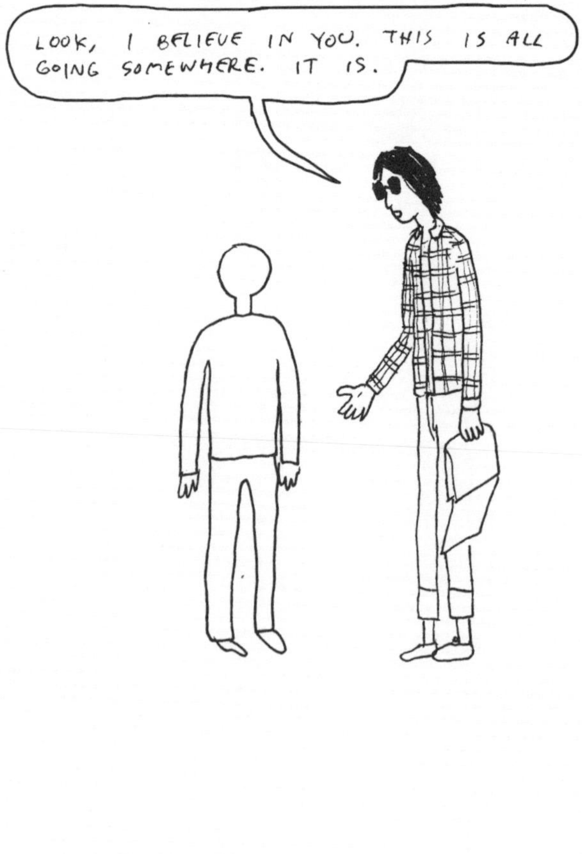
LOOK, I BELIEVE IN YOU. THIS IS ALL GOING SOMEWHERE. IT IS.

"HE DOESN'T KNOW WHAT HE'S TALKING ABOUT"

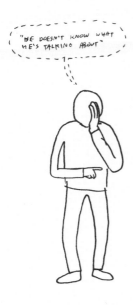

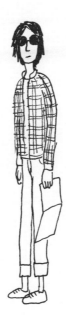

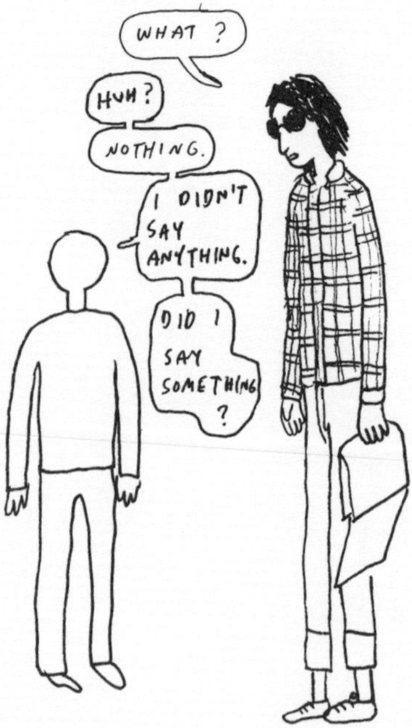
WHAT ?
HUH?
NOTHING.
I DIDN'T SAY ANYTHING.
DID I SAY SOMETHING ?

SIGH.
I'M JUST SAYING.

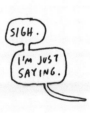

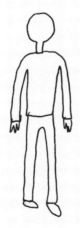

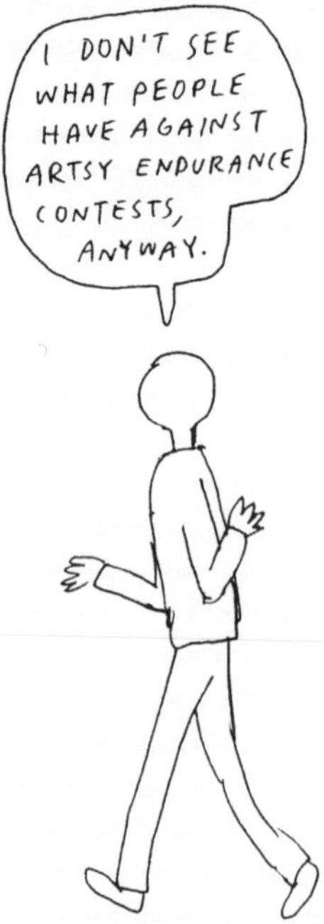
I DON'T SEE WHAT PEOPLE HAVE AGAINST ARTSY ENDURANCE CONTESTS, ANYWAY.

I'VE NEVER HEARD GOD ACTUALLY TALK TO ME, BUT HE DOES SOMETIMES CALL ME UP AND BREATH HEAVILY INTO THE PHONE.

I'VE NEVER HEARD GOD SPEAK TO ME, BUT I DO HEAR HIM SOMETIMES SCRAPING GUM OFF THE BOTTOM OF HIS SHOE.

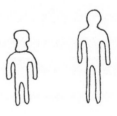

WHAT?
NO.
NEVER.

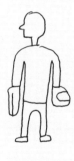

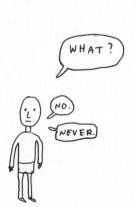

SO I THINK IT'S JUST ABOUT TIME TO RESUME OUR NARRATIVE. I CAN'T REMEMBER WHERE WE WERE, SO I'M GOING TO CALL CENTRAL COMMAND AND SEE WHAT THEY SAY.
BEEP BEEP BEEP

DOOT DEE DOOT DEE DOOT
IT'S RINGING.
HMMM HM HMM

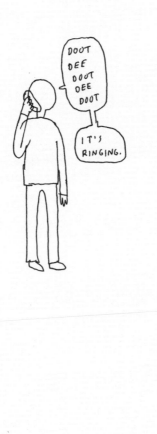

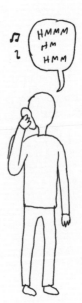

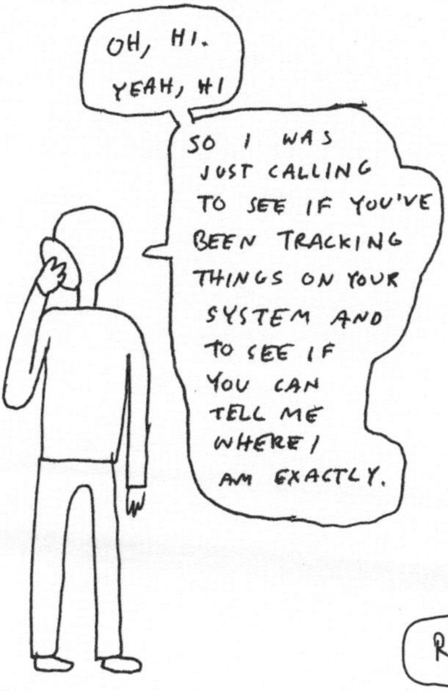
OH, HI.
YEAH, HI
SO I WAS JUST CALLING TO SEE IF YOU'VE BEEN TRACKING THINGS ON YOUR SYSTEM AND TO SEE IF YOU CAN TELL ME WHERE I AM EXACTLY.

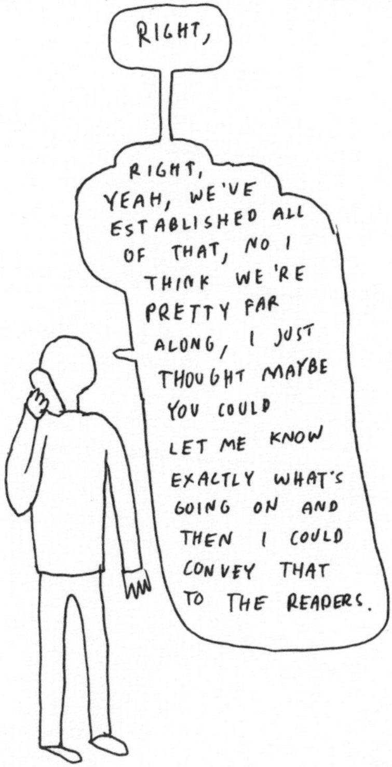
RIGHT,
RIGHT, YEAH, WE'VE ESTABLISHED ALL OF THAT, NO I THINK WE'RE PRETTY FAR ALONG, I JUST THOUGHT MAYBE YOU COULD LET ME KNOW EXACTLY WHAT'S GOING ON AND THEN I COULD CONVEY THAT TO THE READERS.

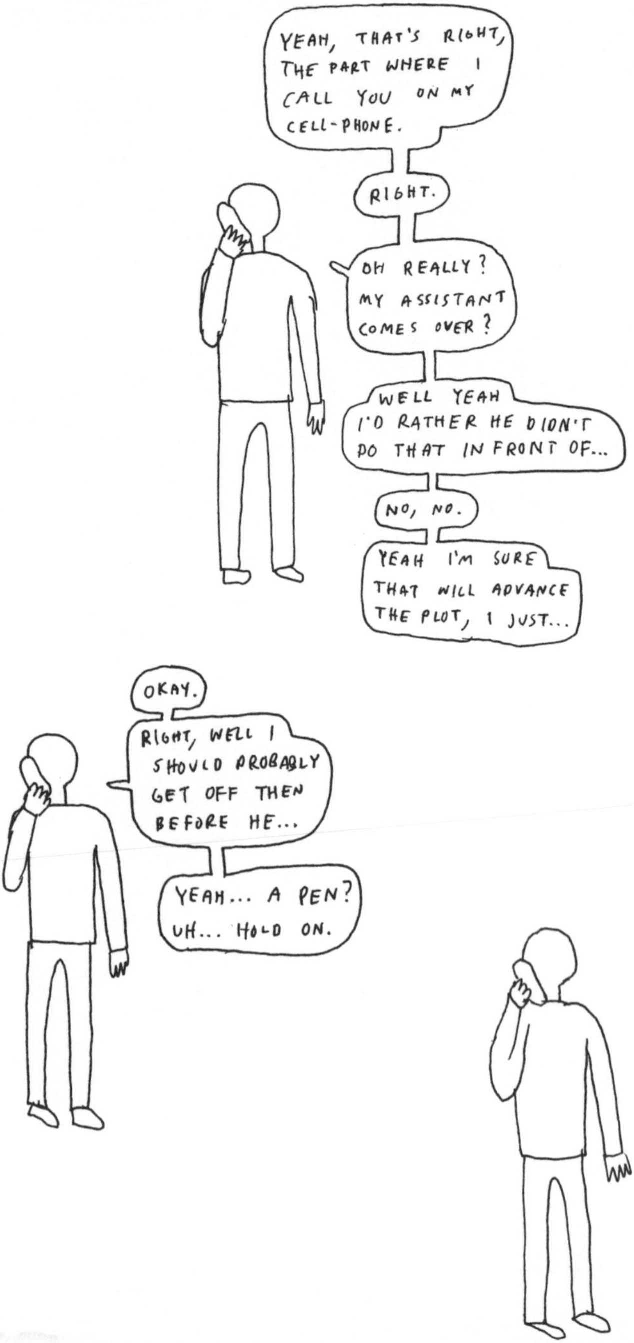
YEAH, THAT'S RIGHT, THE PART WHERE I CALL YOU ON MY CELL-PHONE.
RIGHT.
OH REALLY? MY ASSISTANT COMES OVER?
WELL YEAH I'D RATHER HE DIDN'T DO THAT IN FRONT OF...
NO, NO.
YEAH I'M SURE THAT WILL ADVANCE THE PLOT, I JUST...
OKAY.
RIGHT, WELL I SHOULD PROBABLY GET OFF THEN BEFORE HE...
YEAH... A PEN? UH... HOLD ON.

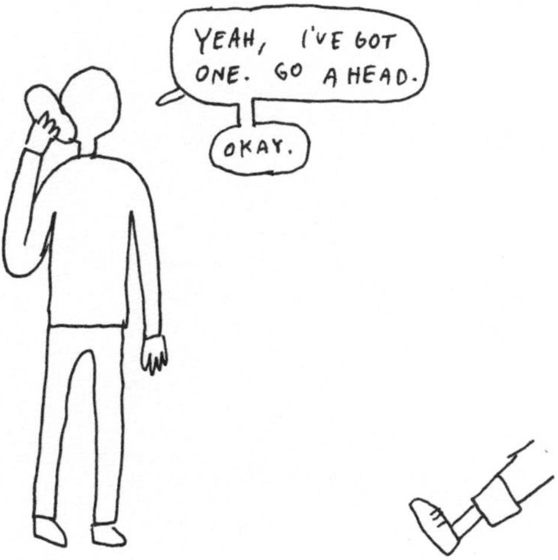
YEAH, I'VE GOT ONE. GO AHEAD.
OKAY.

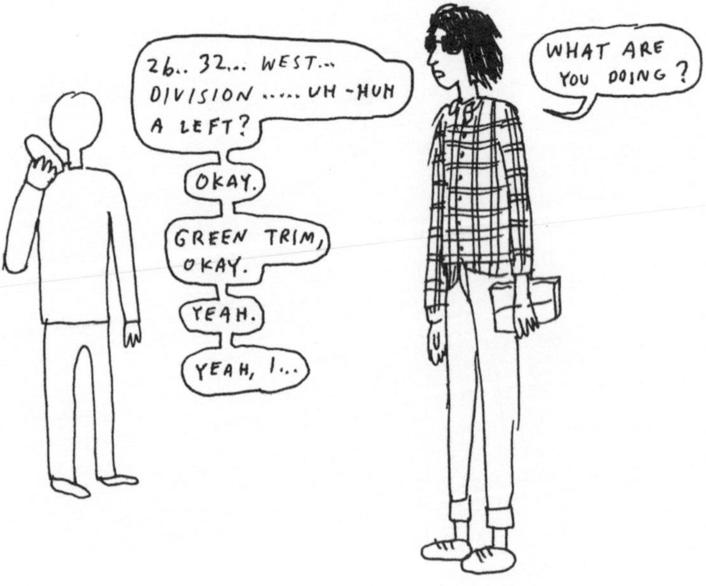
26.. 32... WEST... DIVISION ..... UH-HUH A LEFT?
OKAY.
GREEN TRIM, OKAY.
YEAH.
YEAH, I...
WHAT ARE YOU DOING?

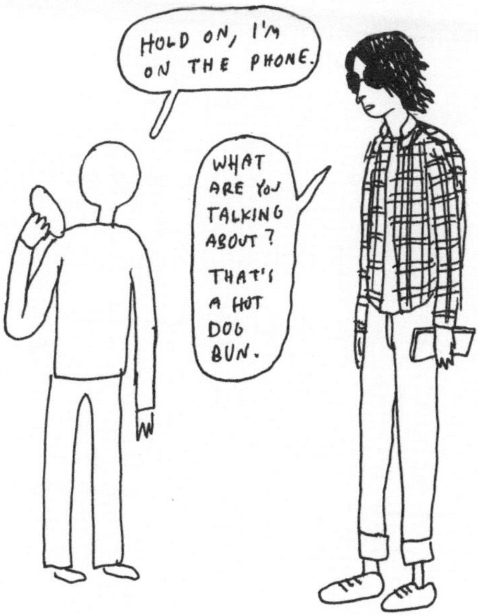
HOLD ON, I'M ON THE PHONE.
WHAT ARE YOU TALKING ABOUT? THAT'S A HOT DOG BUN.

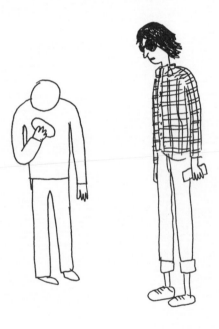

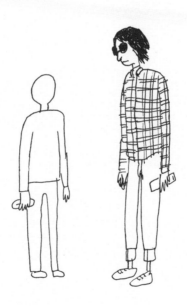

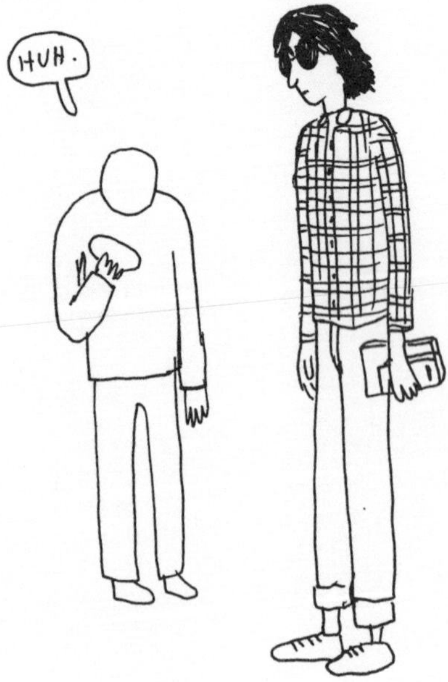
HUH.

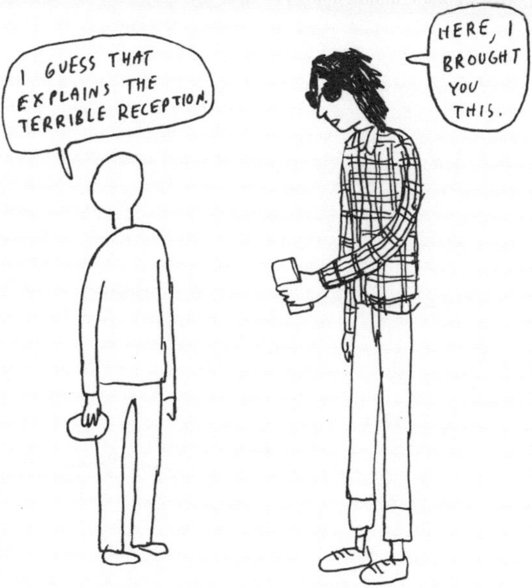
I GUESS THAT EXPLAINS THE TERRIBLE RECEPTION.
HERE, I BROUGHT YOU THIS.

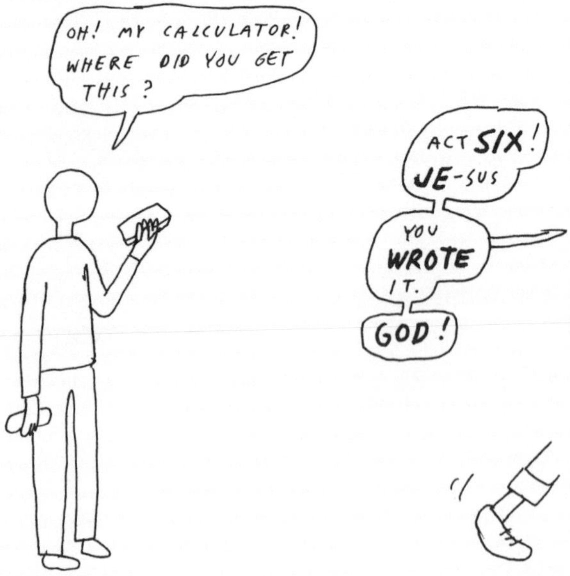
OH! MY CALCULATOR! WHERE DID YOU GET THIS?
ACT SIX! JE-SUS
YOU WROTE IT.
GOD!

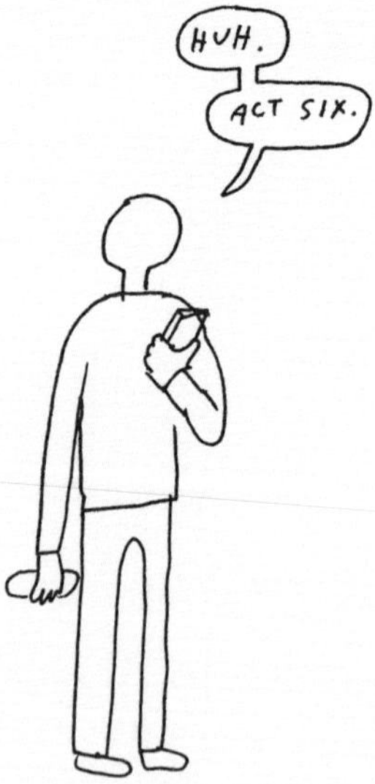
HUH.
ACT SIX.

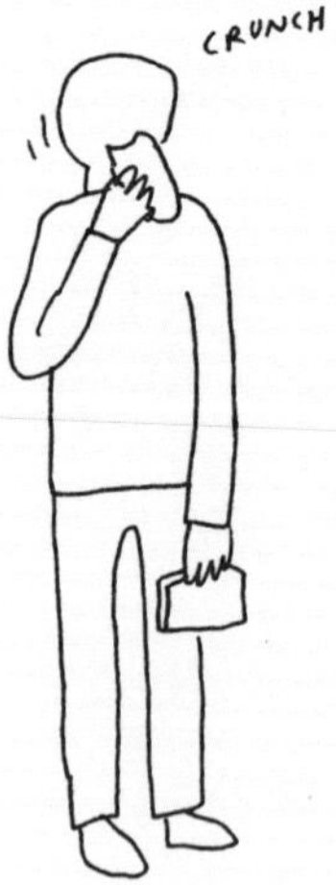
CRUNCH

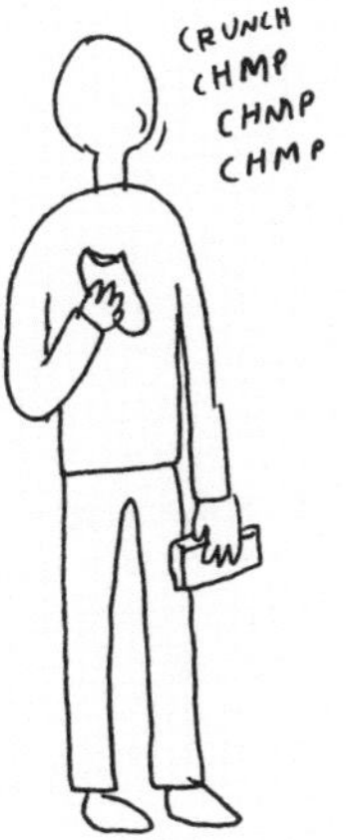
CRUNCH
CHMP
CHMP
CHMP

CH
CHMP
CHN
GN
MM. THAT'S DELICIOUS.
I WISH I HAD A HOT DOG TO PUT IN IT.

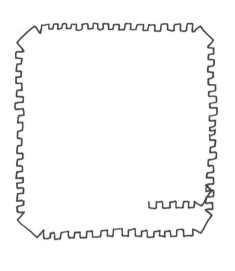

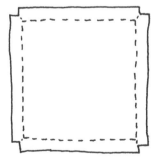

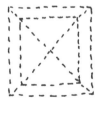

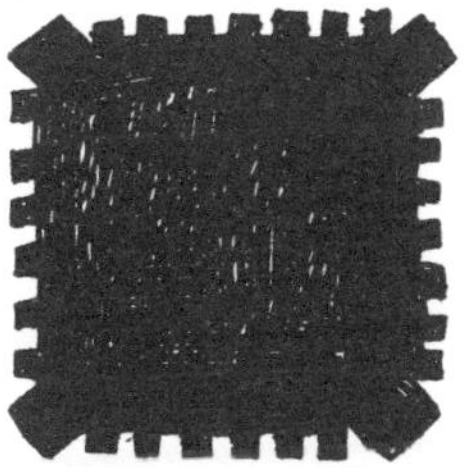

PART V

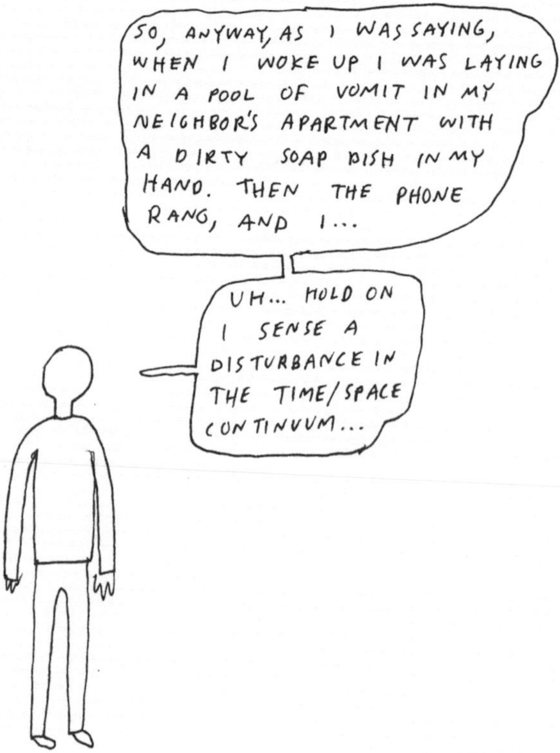
SO, ANYWAY, AS I WAS SAYING, WHEN I WOKE UP I WAS LAYING IN A POOL OF VOMIT IN MY NEIGHBOR'S APARTMENT WITH A DIRTY SOAP DISH IN MY HAND. THEN THE PHONE RANG, AND I...
UH... HOLD ON I SENSE A DISTURBANCE IN THE TIME/SPACE CONTINUUM...

...OM... OM... OM...
...OM...
..OM...

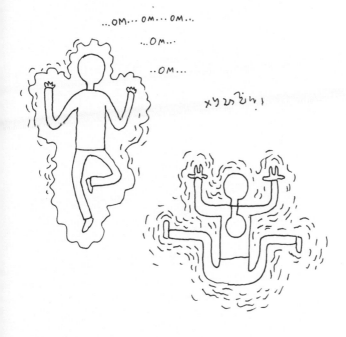

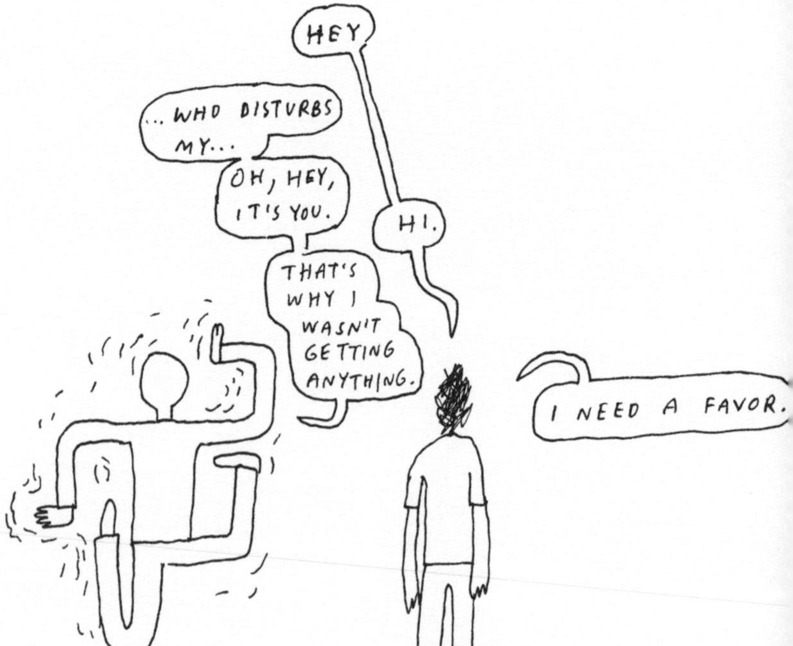
HEY
...WHO DISTURBS MY...
OH, HEY, IT'S YOU.
HI.
THAT'S WHY I WASN'T GETTING ANYTHING.
I NEED A FAVOR.

SURE, WHAT IS IT?
WELL...
CLICK CLICK
LOOK, IT'S A LONG STORY. BASICALLY I NEED TO BORROW YOUR VACUUM CLEANER. DO YOU KNOW WHERE THE JUDICIARY IS?

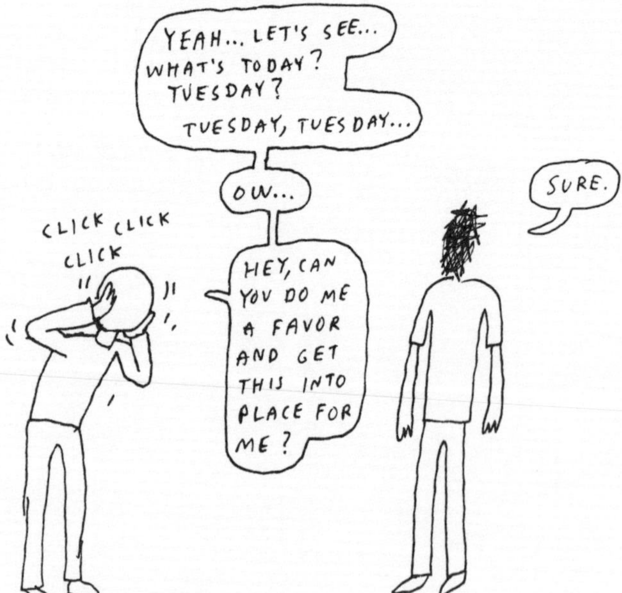

YEAH... LET'S SEE... WHAT'S TODAY? TUESDAY? TUESDAY, TUESDAY...
OW...
HEY, CAN YOU DO ME A FAVOR AND GET THIS INTO PLACE FOR ME?
CLICK CLICK CLICK
SURE.

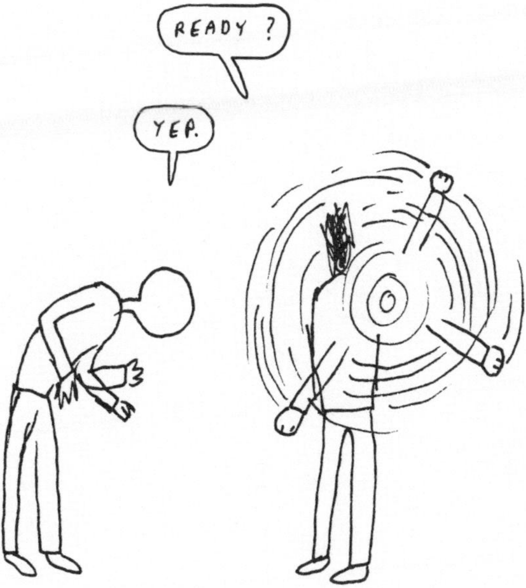
READY ?
YEP.

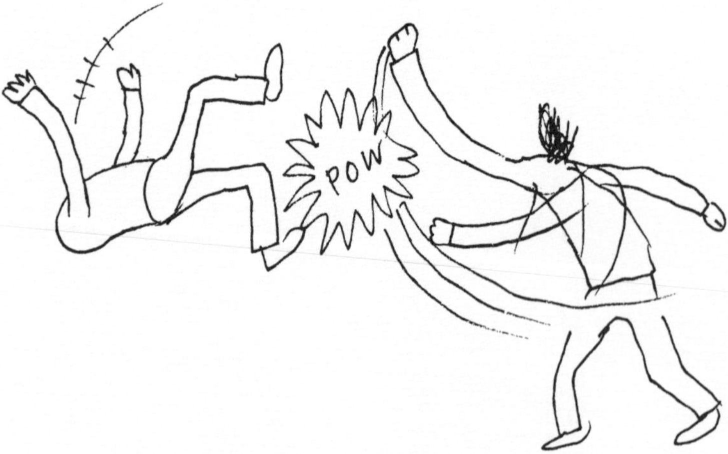
POW

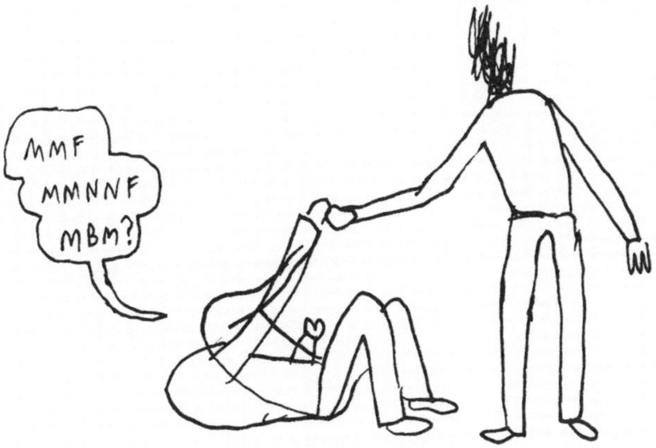
MMF
MMNNF
MBM?

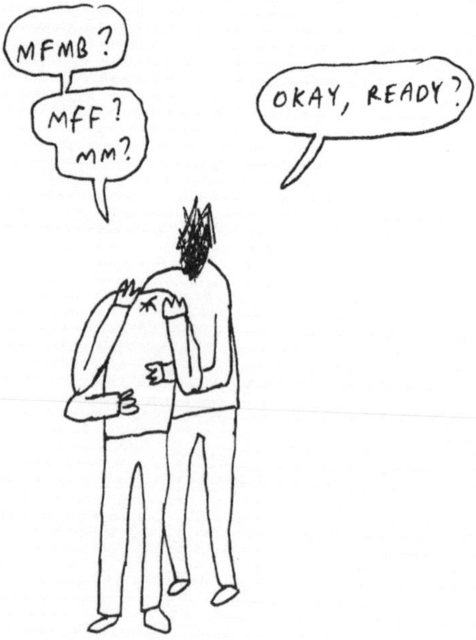
MFMB?
MFF? MM?
OKAY, READY?

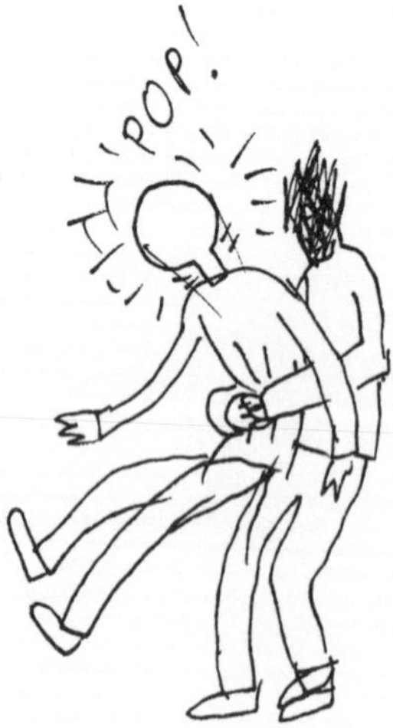
POP!

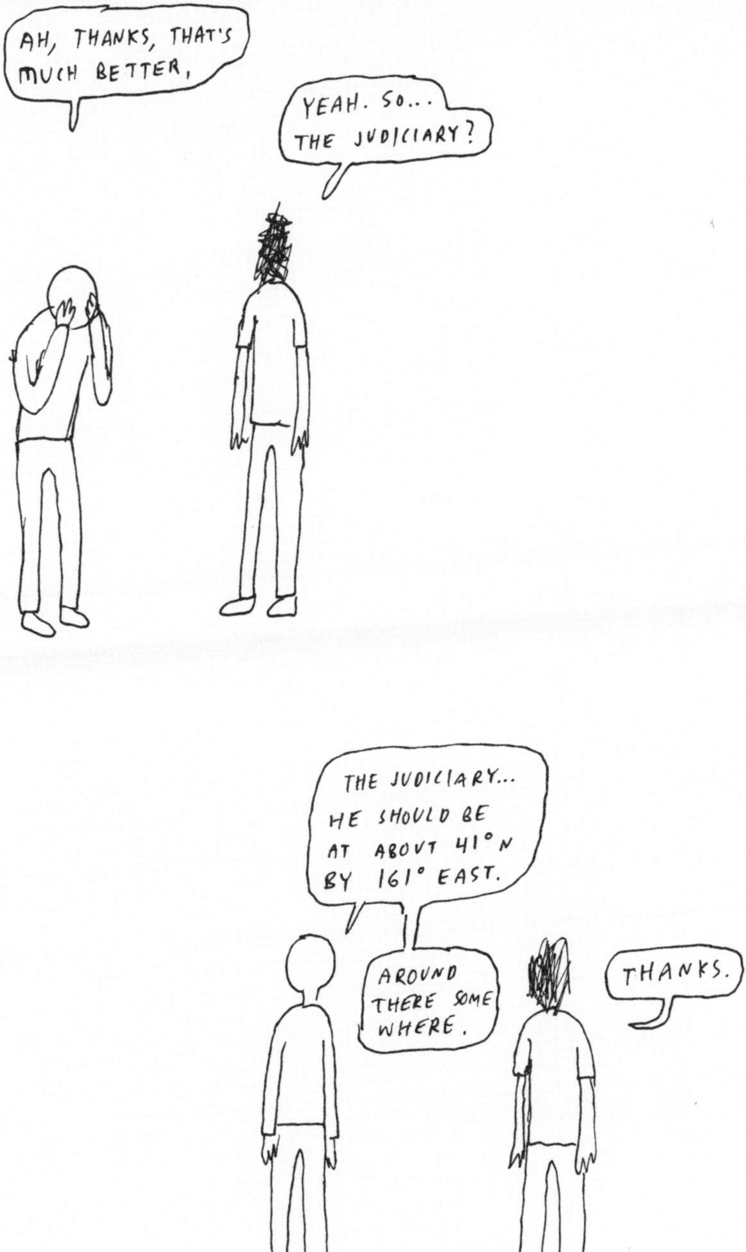
AH, THANKS, THAT'S MUCH BETTER,
YEAH. SO... THE JUDICIARY?
THE JUDICIARY... HE SHOULD BE AT ABOUT 41° N BY 161° EAST.
AROUND THERE SOME WHERE.
THANKS.

OKAY, LET'S SEE... WHERE WERE WE?

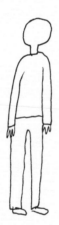

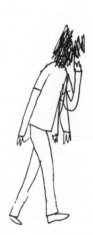

OH. YOU KNOW WHAT? I SHOULD PROBABLY GET YOUR MOTHER'S NOTE, TOO.

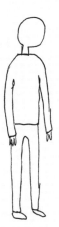

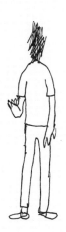

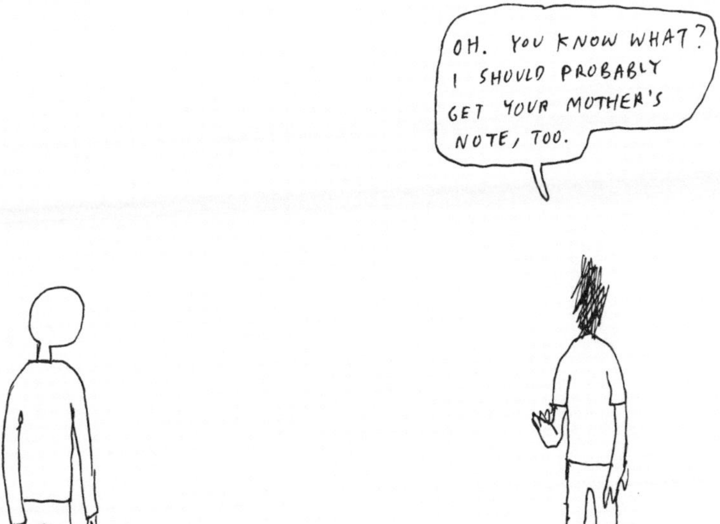

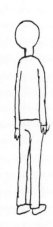

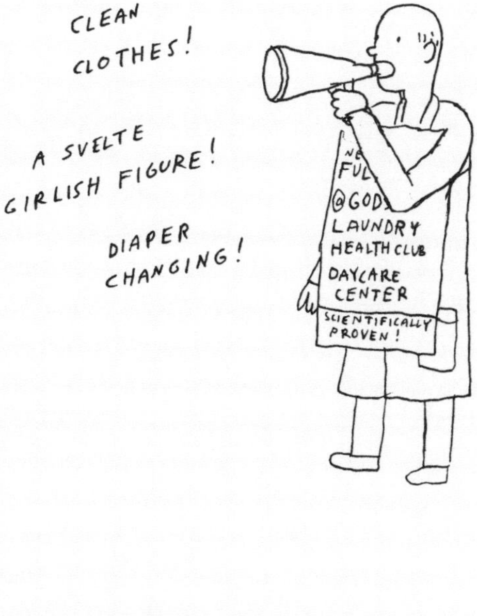
CLEAN CLOTHES!
A SVELTE GIRLISH FIGURE!
DIAPER CHANGING!
LAUNDRY
HEALTH CLUB
DAYCARE CENTER
SCIENTIFICALLY PROVEN!

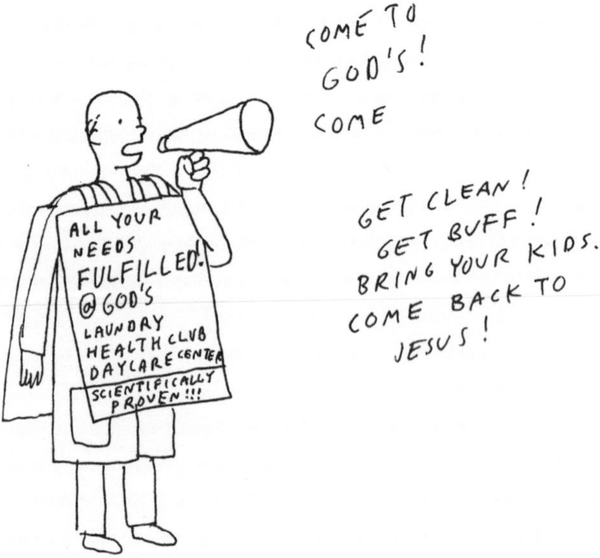
COME TO
GOD'S!
COME
GET CLEAN!
GET BUFF!
BRING YOUR KIDS.
COME BACK TO
JESUS!
ALL YOUR
NEEDS
FULFILLED!
@ GOD'S
LAUNDRY
HEALTH CLUB
DAYCARE CENTER
SCIENTIFICALLY
PROVEN!!!

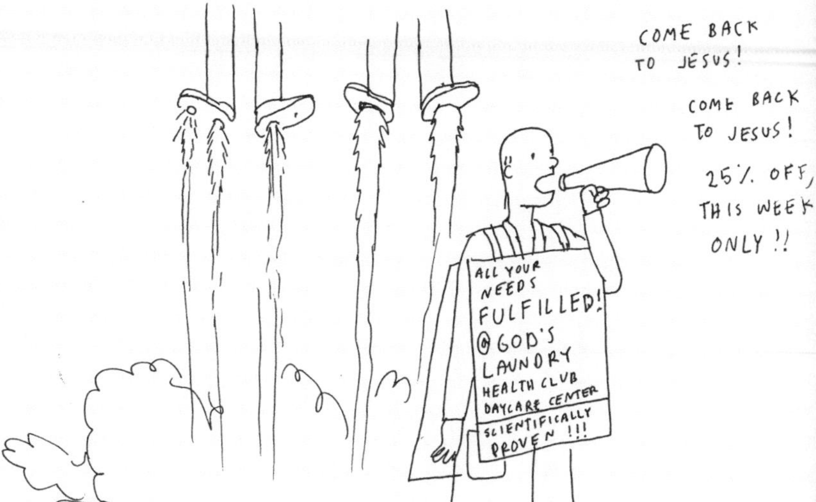
COME BACK TO JESUS!
COME BACK TO JESUS!
25% OFF, THIS WEEK ONLY!!
ALL YOUR NEEDS FULFILLED! @ GOD'S LAUNDRY HEALTH CLUB DAYCARE CENTER
SCIENTIFICALLY PROVEN !!!

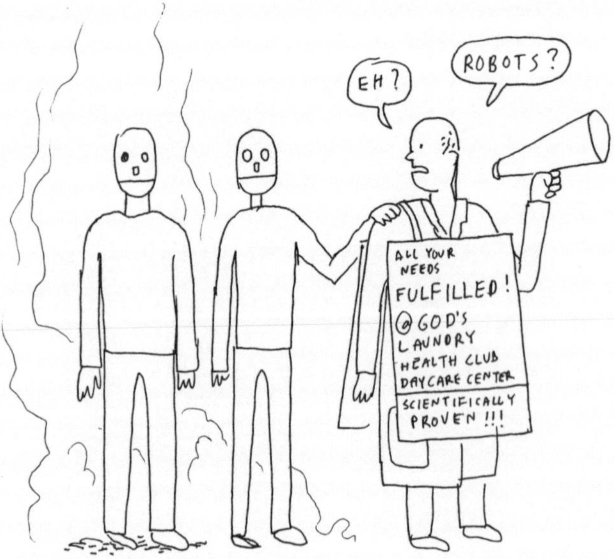
EH?
ROBOTS?
ALL YOUR NEEDS FULFILLED! @GOD'S LAUNDRY HEALTH CLUB DAYCARE CENTER
SCIENTIFICALLY PROVEN!!!

HELP!
HELP!

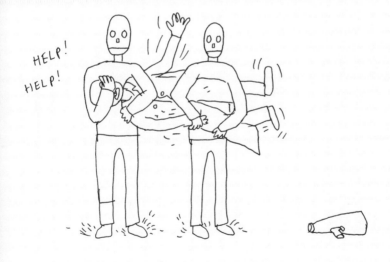

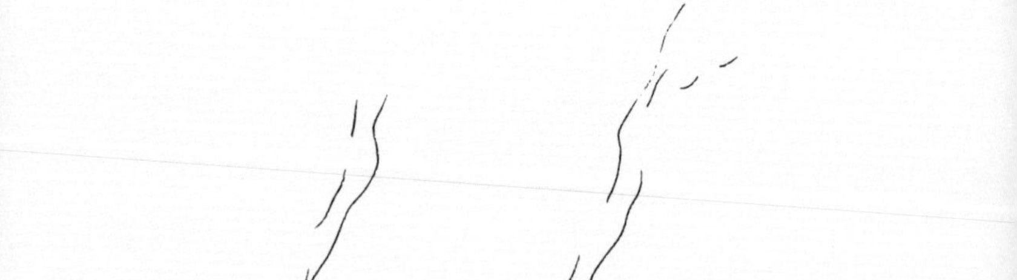

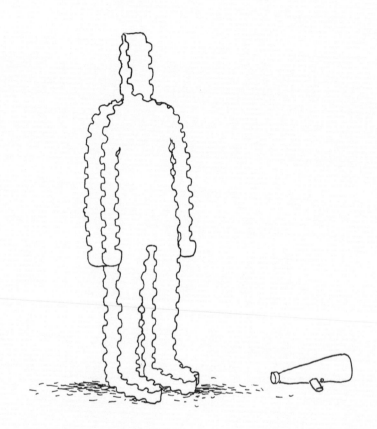

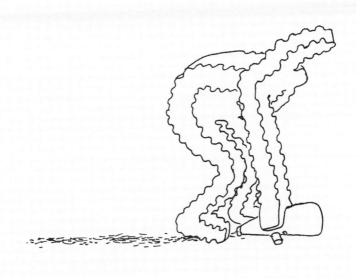

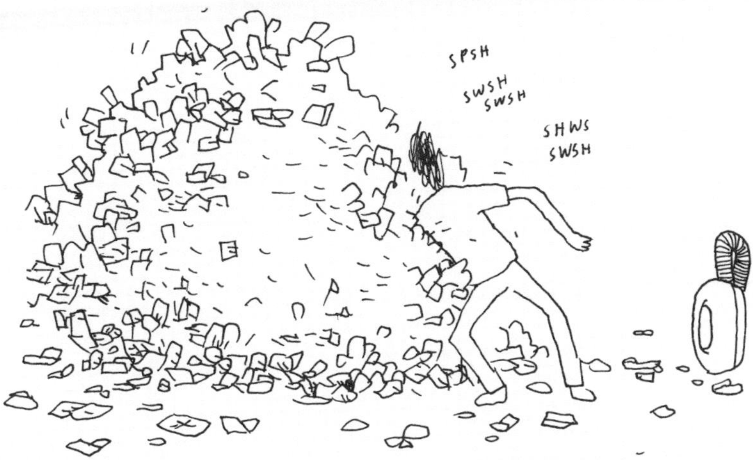
SPSH
SWSH
SWSH
SHWS
SWSH

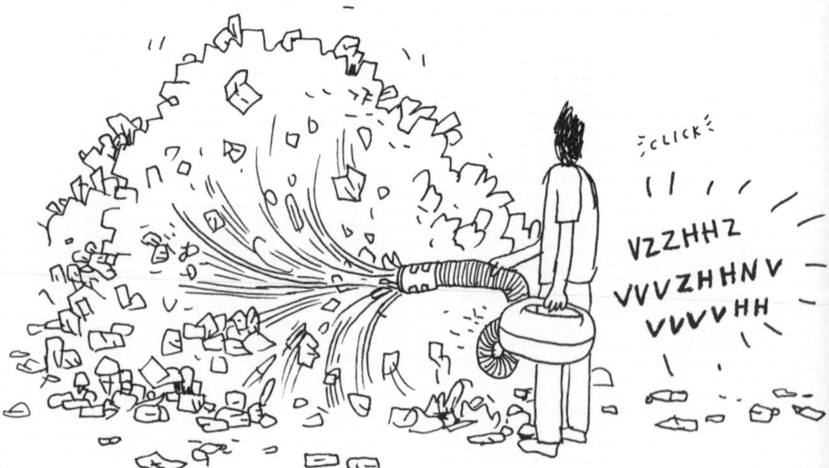
CLICK
VZZHHZ
VVVZHHNV
VVVVHH

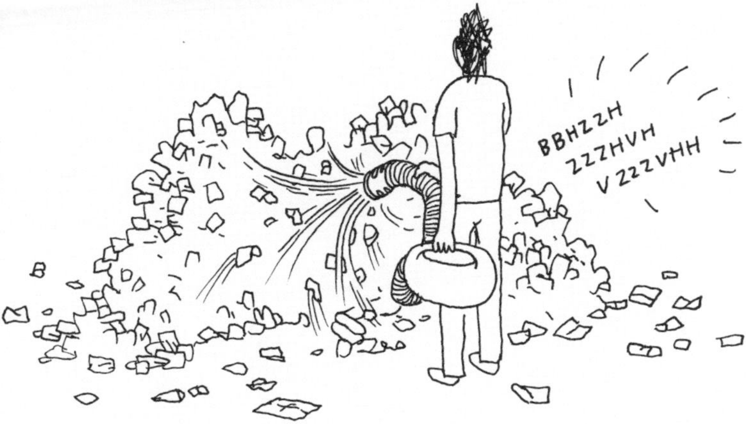
BBHZZZH
ZZZHVH
VZZZVHH

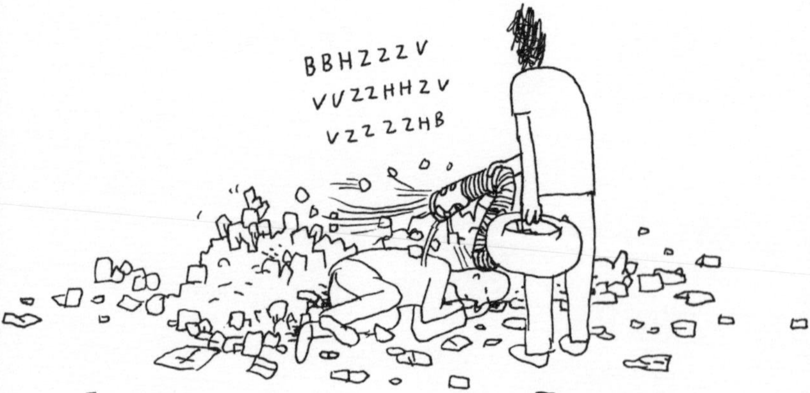
BBHZZZV
VVZZHHZV
VZZZZHB

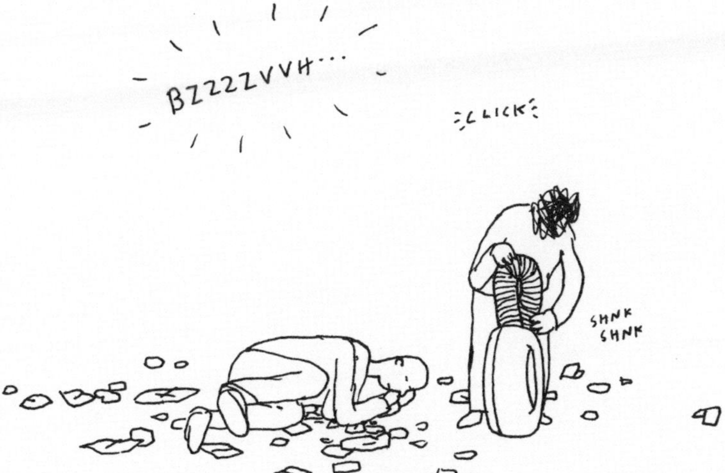
BZZZZVVH...
CLICK
SHNK
SHNK

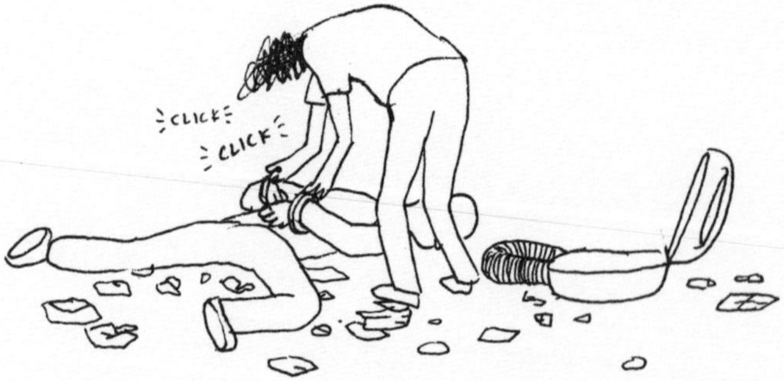
CLICK
CLICK

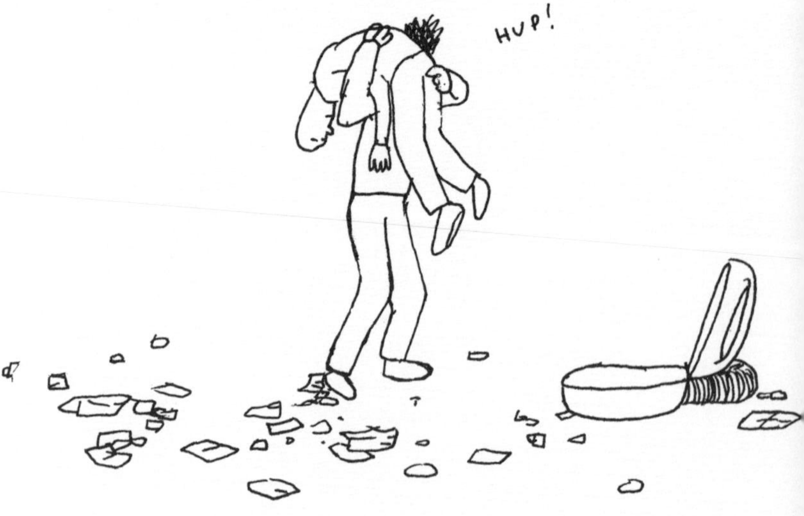
HUP!

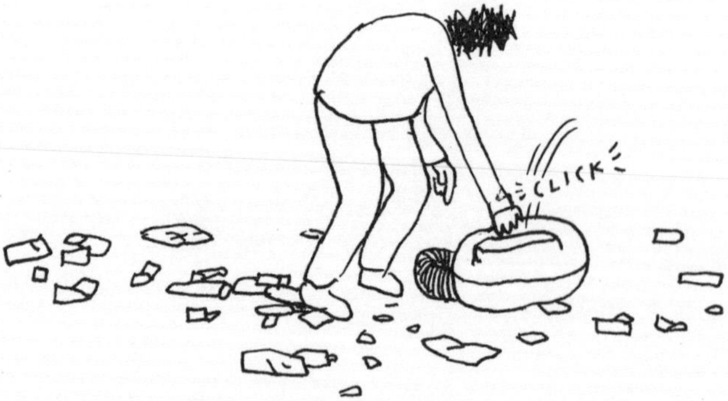
CLICK

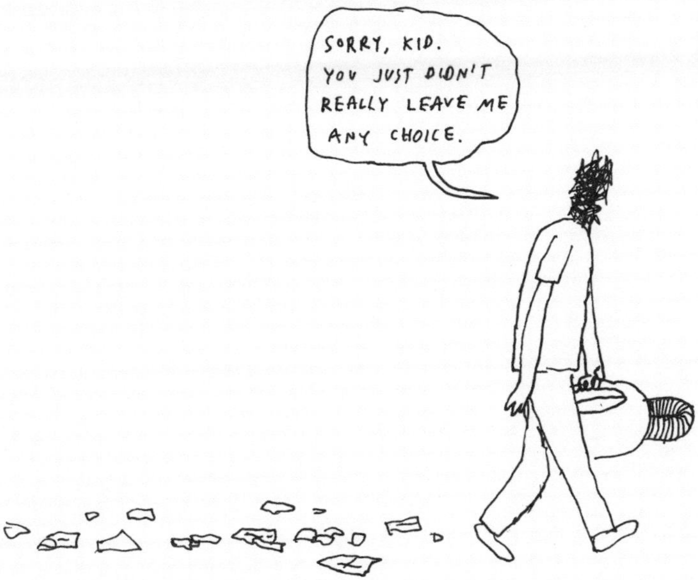
SORRY, KID.
YOU JUST DIDN'T
REALLY LEAVE ME
ANY CHOICE.

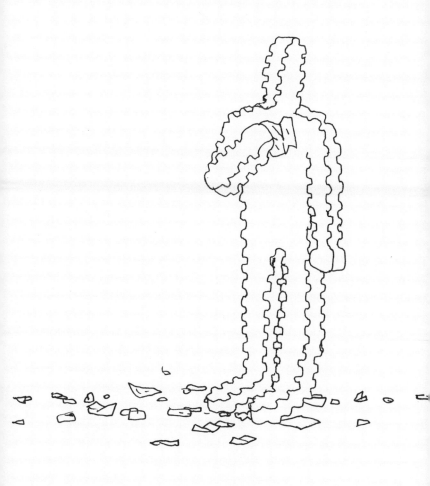

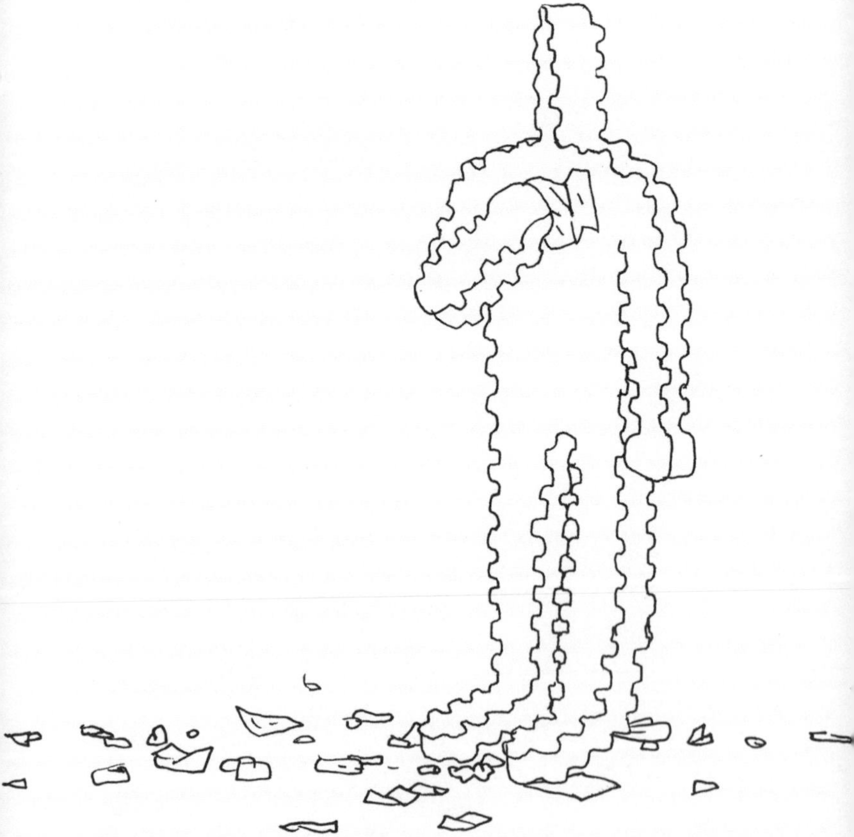

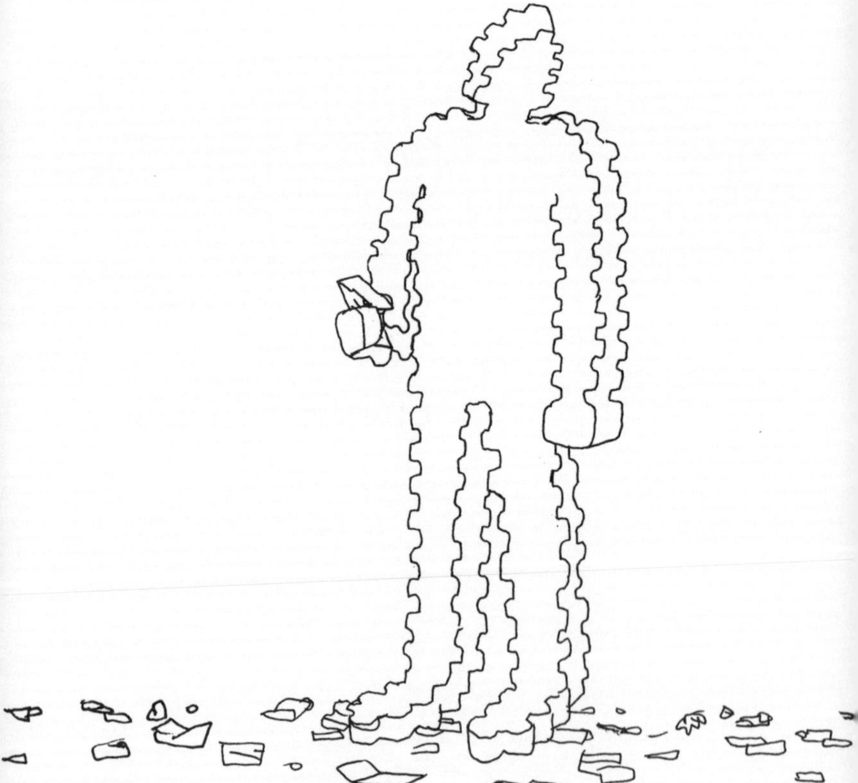

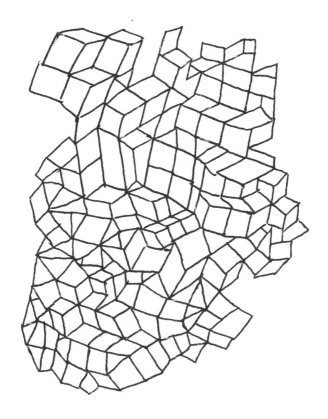

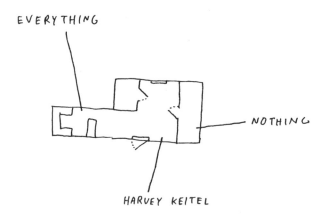

EVERYTHING
NOTHING
HARVEY KEITEL

 Contact: Anders Nilsen at ndrs@hotmail.com. Fantagraphics Books 7563 Lake City Way NE, Seattle, WA 98115. Published by Gary Groth and Kim Thompson.

Some of the present volume has appeared in other places. Several of the gags and all of the floorplans appeared in a mini art comic I did in 2005 called *Lists, Cartoons, Floorplan, Poem, Other*. The three gags at the beginning were all from a mini I did in 2002 called *People and Dogs*. *The Beast* and *Destination: Excellence* originally appeared in the anthology *Mome*, in slightly altered form, in the Summer 2005 and the Winter 2007 issues respectively.

Thanks to Kyle Obriot, Heather Shouse, Paul Baresh and Gary Groth. Lastly, my apologies to T.S. He's not lazy at all and is in fact one of the best comic critics there is.